Issues in Historiography

The Debate on Black Civil Rights in America

MANCHESTER
1824

Manchester University Press

Issues in Historiography
General editor
R. C. RICHARDSON
University of Winchester

Issues in Historiography

The Debate
on Black Civil Rights in America

KEVERN VERNEY

MANCHESTER
UNIVERSITY PRESS
MANCHESTER AND NEW YORK

distributed exclusively in the USA by Palgrave

Published by Manchester University Press
Oxford Road, Manchester M13 9NR, UK
and Room 400, 175 Fifth Avenue, New York, NY 10010, USA
www.manchesteruniversitypress.co.uk

Distributed exclusively in the USA by
Palgrave, 175 Fifth Avenue, New York,
NY 10010, USA

Distributed exclusively in Canada by
UBC Press, University of British Columbia, 2029 West Mall,
Vancouver, BC, Canada V6T 1Z2

British Library Cataloguing-in-Publication Data
A catalogue record for this book is available from the British Library

Library of Congress Cataloging-in-Publication Data applied for

ISBN 0 7190 6760 X *hardback*
EAN 978 0 7190 6760 0

ISBN 0 7190 6761 8 *paperback*
EAN 978 0 7190 6761 7

First published 2006

15 14 13 12 11 10 09 08 07 06   10 9 8 7 6 5 4 3 2 1

Typeset by Action Publishing Technology Ltd, Gloucester
Printed in Great Britain by
Bell & Bain Ltd, Glasgow

CONTENTS

GENERAL EDITOR'S FOREWORD

History without historiography is a contradiction in terms. No historian writes in isolation from the work of his or her predecessors, nor can the historian stand aloof from the insistent pressures, priorities and demands of the ever-changing present. Though historians address the past as their subject they always do so in ways that are shaped – consciously or unconsciously as the case may be – by the society and systems of their own day, and they communicate their findings in ways that are specifically intelligible and relevant to a reading public consisting of their own contemporaries. For these reasons the study of history is concerned not with dead facts and sterile, permanent verdicts but with highly charged dialogues, disagreements and controversies among its presenters, and with the changing methodologies and discourse of the subject over time. *Issues in Historiography* is a series designed to address such matters by means of case studies.

Black civil rights, sidelined for so long despite the emancipation of slaves after the Civil War, became in due course a burning issue in American society and politics, with figures such as Martin Luther King and Malcolm X occupying centre stage in the nation's affairs. Not surprisingly the politics of the present from the 1950s have redirected attention to a neglected and shameful dimension of the national past and led to bold and insistent claims for integrating what had been a largely separate compartment of study, pursued by a minority of historians, into the mainstream picture of America's past. Feminism also played its part in the same process. Dr Verney's book on the historiography of Black civil rights in America, though not the first in the field, is distinctively different from its predecessors and offers a telling overview of the anger, turmoils and crusades associated with it. He charts a clear course through the different stages of debate from the 1890s to the present day, placing individual historians such as W. E. B. Du Bois, John Hope Franklin, August Meier and Howard Zinn within the changing context of the times in which they lived and within the changing contours of historical methodology and interpretation. Thus we see displayed here the varied impact of the Ku Klux Klan, the Cold War, McCarthyism and the Vietnam War on this field of study and the different questions and approaches – social, political, cultural, and gendered – to the history of Black civil rights which have been advanced and argued over. This book offers a classic case study in 'history from below' and, more generally, in national redefinition. Generations of activist historians – white as well as black – dedicated to a cause form the subject matter of this volume.

R. C. Richardson
March 2005

PREFACE

For many years students looking for an analytical narrative history of black life in the United States were largely restricted in choice to John Hope Franklin's 1947 account *From Slavery to Freedom: A History of Negro Americans*. A seminal study by a leading African American scholar, the outstanding merit of this work is attested to by the fact that at the end of the twentieth century it had passed through seven editions and still remained in print.[1] Less encouragingly, Franklin dominated the field for so long not just by virtue of his considerable scholarly ability but also, in part, because of a near total lack of serious competition.

Fortunately, times have changed. Readers in search of a one-volume history of the African American experience in the twentieth century are now able to choose from a variety of clear, concise and authoritative studies.[2] This notwithstanding, gaps in the academic literature still remain. In particular, despite an extensive, exponentially expanding, number of specialist studies and scholarly monographs, there is no one work that provides teachers, students and general readers with a succinct historiographical introduction to the subject, explaining how, why, and in what ways, the thoughts and ideas of successive generations of historians of black civil rights have changed over time. It is this need that this volume in the *Issues in Historiography* series seeks to address, examining the study of the principal developments and events in African American history from the 1890s through to the first years of the twenty-first century.[3] It should, however, be noted that the substantial body of academic literature on the earlier slavery, Civil War and Reconstruction eras is beyond the scope of this work. A succinct and scholarly analysis of the rich, complex and diverse historiography on these periods can instead be found in Hugh Tulloch's excellent study *The Debate on the American Civil War Era*.[4]

At the same time the still broad scope of the period under consideration has also required some difficult editorial decisions. The scholarly contributions of many well-researched studies are mentioned only briefly and, in some instances, not at all. This is both intentional and unavoidable. Intentional, because the objective of this study is to assess in broad terms the changing ways that scholars have interpreted issues in African American history, not to provide an individual review of every serious publication on black life in twentieth-century America. Unavoidable, because the sheer volume of works in this category makes any such task impossible. Similarly, the never-ending proliferation of fresh, seminal and insightful studies creates an insuperable problem of topicality in respect to keeping up with the latest developments. Readers should thus be aware that, with occasional exceptions, this book does not include works published after the end of January 2005.

On-line materials, e-publications, and the rapidly growing number of internet websites on African American history are also beyond the scope of this work. However, for readers seeking information on such sources a good recent guide is Abdul Alkalimat and Elaine Westbrooks, *African American History and Culture on the Web* (2003). [5]

Notes

1 John Hope Franklin, *From Slavery to Freedom: A History of Negro Americans* (New York, 1947).
2 For example, John White, *Black Leadership in America, 1895–1968* (London, 1991); William T. Martin Riches, *The Civil Rights Movement: Struggle and Resistance* (Houndmills, Basingstoke, Hampshire, 1997); Robert Cook, *Sweet Land of Liberty? The African American Struggle for Civil Rights in the Twentieth Century* (London, 1998); Vivian Saunders, *Race Relations in the USA since 1900* (London, 2000); Kevern Verney, *Black Civil Rights in America* (London, 2000); Adam Fairclough, *Better Day Coming: Blacks and Equality, 1890–2000* (New York, 2001).
3 The best book-length studies from a historiographical perspective are Darlene Clark Hine (ed.), *The State of Afro-American History: Past, Present and Future* (Baton Rouge, Louisiana, 1986) and August Meier and Elliott Rudwick, *Black History and the Historical Profession, 1915–1980* (Urbana, Illinois, 1986). However, neither of these works seeks to provide a sustained, systematic, discussion of all the major topics and subject areas in twentieth-century African American history. Hine's study, which grew out of a 1983 conference on 'The Study and Teaching of Afro-American History' sponsored by the American Historical Association, takes the form of a collection of essays by different scholars on selected themes, such as 'slavery studies', 'emancipation studies', 'urban studies' and 'black history and the community'. Meier and Rudwick engage in a general philosophical overview of the changing attitudes of the American historical profession in the twentieth

century towards the study of black history.

4 Hugh Tulloch, *The Debate on the American Civil War Era* (Manchester, 1999).

5 Abdul Alkalimat and Elaine Westbrooks, *African American History and Culture on the Web* (Wilmington, Delaware, 2003).

ACKNOWLEDGEMENTS

The image of the historian writing in scholarly isolation, preferably in a lofty garret with a wet towel wrapped around the forehead for inspiration, has a certain romantic appeal. It is also misleading. Although requiring sustained individual endeavour, the successful completion of any book is a team effort. I would therefore like to take this opportunity to thank everyone at Manchester University Press involved in the production process for their contribution in making the task as easy and as painless as possible. In particular Professor Roger Richardson, the Issues in Historiography series editor, provided invaluable advice and encouragement in equal measure throughout, and when both were needed most. I am also grateful to John Kirk for his many comments and suggestions on the draft manuscript, and which helped to improve it immeasurably. Last, but by no means least, I would like to thank my partner Juliet Hadley for patiently enduring the many hours I spent at home in writing and revising this work. Without her constant love and support it could never been completed.

INTRODUCTION

The study of black American history can, as the distinguished African American scholar John Hope Franklin has noted, be divided into four broad chronological periods.[1] In 1882 the publication of a two-volume *History of the Negro Race in America* by the African American author George Washington Williams is generally credited with the distinction of being 'the first scholarly account of the history of black Americans'.[2] A minister of religion and self-trained historian, Williams also typified the first era of scholarship in African American history that lasted from 1882 down to 1909. The leading writers on black history in this period, such as the internationally renowned Tuskegee educator and race leader Booker T. Washington, were almost invariably African Americans. They were also, with the notable exception of the formidable Harvard trained W. E. B. Du Bois, amateur scholars rather than trained historians. In other respects it is hard to generalize about the writers of this first generation other than to broadly note that their 'primary concern' was 'to explain the process of adjustment African Americans made to conditions in the United States' and to cite historical experience to support their own views on race relations.[3]

The second era of scholarship, which lasted from 1909 through to the mid 1930s, was marked by a growing professionalization in the study of African American history. This reflected wider changes taking place at this time in American colleges and universities, principally an expansion in the number of salaried full-time scholars and increasing emphasis on new 'scientific' methodologies to study the past.[4] Inevitably, the multi-talented Du Bois was one of the leading figures of this period. A colossus in the development of African American studies, he published a series of influential literary texts as well as scholarly essays and monographs in history and sociology. In 1909 he was one of the principal founders of the civil rights organization the National Association for the Advancement of Colored People (NAACP) and rapidly became established as the Association's best-known and most influential African American spokesperson. Between

1

1911 and 1934 he both served on the NAACP's governing board and held the position of the Association's Director of Research, and in this latter capacity edited its journal *The Crisis*. Publishing race-related news stories alongside essays on black history and culture, he turned the organ into the best-selling national monthly periodical for African Americans.

Born in 1868, Du Bois had spent his childhood years in Great Barrington, a small, predominantly middle-class township in Massachusetts. In contrast, the other dominant individual in the development of black American history at this time, Carter G. Woodson, born in 1875, was the son of ex-slaves and raised in poverty. In terms of personal output Woodson was unable to consistently match either Du Bois's Olympian academic rigour or his prolific rate of publication. In other respects, however, it was Woodson who was arguably the more significant figure, for whereas Du Bois penned 'influential monographs in scholarly isolation', it was Woodson's organizational skills that 'created the black history movement'.[5]

This accomplishment was the more remarkable in that it was achieved during a period of overwhelming adversity. The early decades of the twentieth century constituted a nadir in US race relations, reflected in the wholesale denial of black voting rights in the southern states and the spread of racial segregation throughout the nation. Members of the mainstream historical profession shared the racial values of the society that shaped their intellectual development. White scholars thus showed an almost complete lack of interest in the experiences of African Americans, even when the subject matter of their research appeared to make it a fundamental requirement. In his influential 1918 study *American Negro Slavery*, Ulrich Bonnell Phillips, himself descended from a slave-owning family, examined the institution of slavery almost exclusively from the perspective of whites. 'In just the same way as a writer of the history of New England in describing the fisheries of that section would have little to say about the species figuring conspicuously in that industry', Woodson noted in a wry review of Phillips's publication, 'so the author treated the Negro in his work.'[6]

Similarly, from 1886 to 1920 the racially conservative William Dunning and the Reconstruction school of historians he established at Columbia University published a series of detailed accounts of life in the southern states after the Civil War, but all from a white point of view. The four million newly emancipated black slaves in the region were, at best, portrayed as benign racial inferiors, at worst, as dangerously deluded malcontents seeking revenge on their former masters and intoxicated by 'fanciful' notions of achieving social equality with their Anglo-Saxon superiors.

In his concerted efforts to redress such caricatured imagery and neglect, Woodson established himself as one of the father figures of the study of African American history. During 1915 he became the principal founder of the Association for the Study of Negro Life and History (ASNLH) and in 1916 launched and edited the *Journal of Negro History* (*JNH*), establishing it as the leading national academic periodical in the field.

Many of the articles published in *JNH* were penned by rising young African American scholars, such as Alrutheus Ambush Taylor, Luther Porter Jackson, Rayford W. Logan and Charles H. Wesley, whose work Woodson encouraged and directed. The extent of Woodson's influence is reflected in the fact that eight of the fourteen African Americans awarded PhD degrees by American colleges and universities before 1940 were members of his ASNLH group. Collectively, 'it was this first generation of professionally trained black doctorates associated with Woodson', as historians August Meier and Elliott Rudwick have observed, 'who were chiefly responsible for laying the foundation for the study of Afro-American history as a genuine scholarly speciality'.[7]

One of the principal motivations for Woodson in his work, as he himself noted, was 'to save and publish the records of the Negro, that the race may not become a negligible factor in the thought of the world'. One consequence of this objective was that Woodson placed considerable emphasis on 'Builders and Heroes', notable black achievers in history, in the hope that drawing attention to their exploits would 'both raise self-esteem among blacks and reduce prejudice among whites'. Committed to 'a petit-bourgeois philosophy of individual and business striving', Woodson was a lifelong admirer of the Crown Prince of black self-help, Booker T. Washington.[8]

Although understandable, and in many respects worthy, Woodson's philosophy made him a target of criticism for later generations of scholars. Over time Washington, and the conservative values that he espoused, became increasingly unfashionable. Moreover, by focusing on heroic achievers Woodson could be seen as encouraging a distorted and inaccurate image of the African American past. The first indications of a reaction against Woodson's teachings came during the third era of African American scholarship, which lasted from the mid-1930s through to the end of the 1960s. In the late 1930s and early 1940s a new generation of black historians such as Benjamin Quarles and, most notably, John Hope Franklin, began to take over academic leadership in African American history from the Woodson school. Born in 1915, the son of a poor Oklahoma lawyer, Franklin was a graduate of Fisk and Harvard Universities. In common with other young black academics of his generation, he was less interested in black achievers than the collective experience of the race and interactions between blacks and whites.[9]

In another significant development, a small but growing number of white scholars also started to show an interest in African American history. The reasons for this change were varied. Some researchers came from a family background that encouraged them to take a personal interest in black history. Herbert Aptheker, Philip Foner and August Meier were thus perhaps especially sensitive to the experiences of an oppressed minority because of their own Jewish ancestry at a time of rising anti-Semitism in Nazi Germany. Aptheker's and Foner's communist leanings also made them untypical in their radical political beliefs.[10]

In common with other young white scholars, such as northerners Francis Broderick and Elliott Rudwick and the rising southern historian C. Vann Woodward, Meier was influenced by the liberalism of Franklin Roosevelt's New Deal programmes, 1933–41. Both of Meier's parents were radical New Dealers, and from them 'he absorbed a concern for social justice that, colored by his sense of ethnic marginality, intensified with the increasing salience of the racial issue that marked the World War II period'.[11]

In the same vein a number of young white historians had

their outlook on race relations broadened at a key stage in their intellectual development as a result of military service during the Second World War. Booker T. Washington's future biographers Louis Harlan and Samuel R. Spencer were both influenced by their wartime contact with black servicemen and struck by the institutionalized racial discrimination and segregation in the armed forces, as was Rudwick, a later chronicler of the life of Du Bois. Fittingly, Richard Dalfiume, who in the 1960s was to author a seminal text on the desegregation of the armed forces, was himself moved by his positive experiences with black comrades in arms. Joel Williamson's naval service did not come until the 1950s, but still 'provided a vital broadening experience in which he overcame his South Carolina parochialism'.[12]

In the early post-war years the political prominence of civil rights issues, reflected most notably in President Truman's desegregation of the armed forces in 1948, provided further impetus for the growing interest by white scholars in African American history. This desire for a better understanding of the black past increased dramatically during the 1950s and 1960s with the rise of Martin Luther King and the Civil Rights Movement. Some historians, such as Leon Litwack, August Meier, Allan Spear and Howard Zinn, combined academic research into black history with active participation in the civil rights struggle. In a major departure from the Ulrich B. Phillips tradition, liberal white historians Kenneth Stampp and Stanley Elkins provided seminal new studies on slavery that examined the Peculiar Institution from the perspective of its black victims rather than their white masters. Although many of the conclusions reached by Stampp and Elkins were later challenged, their works constituted the beginning of a historiographical revolution. Thereafter twentieth-century studies on slavery focused predominantly on the experience of black slaves and the subtle means by which they sought to resist the debilitating oppression of their condition, most notably through the development of a vibrant, life-affirming slave culture. By the end of the 1960s articles on African American history, by scholars black and white, were being published not just in the *Journal of Negro History* but also in more traditional mainstream academic periodicals such as the *American Historical Review*, the *Journal of American History* and the *Journal of Southern History*.

5

White historians regularly attended the annual meetings of the ASNLH.[13]

The fourth era of scholarship in African American history, dating from around 1970, thus began with a paradox. The importance of black history was now fully recognized by the American historical profession. Indeed, during the last three decades of the twentieth century it is possible that more academic monographs and scholarly articles were published in the United States on African American history than any other single aspect of the nation's past. Moreover, the new scholars of black history in these years were, when viewed collectively, better trained than any of the preceding generations and came from leading colleges and universities across the nation.[14] At the same time, after the assassination of Martin Luther King in 1968, the Civil Rights Movement itself went into a period of rapid decline in the early 1970s, and the 1980s and 1990s saw growing problems in American race relations.

The gradual passage of time meant that the emerging scholars increasingly had little direct experience of the civil rights struggle of the 1950s and 1960s. Indeed, by the early years of the twenty-first century it is probable that any historian under the age of forty-five would have had little, if any, personal recollection of Martin Luther King or the confrontations of his era. Admittedly, it is probable that the large majority of new scholars writing about African American history held liberal views on race relations but, in comparison with earlier historians, such idealism was less likely to be the principal motivating factor in their research. Black history, as a rich and fertile area of scholarly debate, had a natural attraction for young historians in its own right.

At the same time the post-war Civil Rights Movement continued to have a profound influence on the development of African American historiography. During the 1980s and 1990s there were more scholarly publications on the civil rights struggles of the 1950s and 1960s than any other period of African American history. Similarly, although over time historians began to devote increasing attention to the black experience in earlier decades of the twentieth century, this was often the result of the desire to obtain a better understanding of the long-term causes of the post-war Civil Rights Movement. Equally, there was a tendency in early studies of the black experience since 1970 to analyse this period in terms of what it revealed about the long-term achievements and failures of the 1950s and 1960s, rather than as a distinct era in its own right. A large stone cast into the centre of a pond will send forth ripples that extend outwards in diminishing intensity to the peripheries of the watery expanse. In the same way the shock-waves created by the post-war Civil Rights Movement continue to impact on the study of African American history some thirty to forty years later. 'The past', as the great southern novelist William Faulkner once observed, 'is never dead. It's not even past.'[15]

Notes

1 John Hope Franklin, 'On the Evolution of Scholarship in Afro-American History', in Darlene Clark Hine (ed.), *The State of Afro-American History: Past, Present, and Future* (Baton Rouge, Louisiana, 1986), p. 13.

2 August Meier and Elliott Rudwick, *Black History and the Historical Profession, 1915–1980* (Urbana, Illinois, 1986), p. 3.

3 Franklin, 'On the Evolution of Scholarship', p. 13.

4 Meier and Rudwick, *Black History and the Historical Profession*, p. 3

5 Meier and Rudwick, *Black History and the Historical Profession*, p. 7.

6 Quoted in Meier and Rudwick, *Black History and the Historical Profession*, p. 4.

7 Meier and Rudwick, *Black History*, p. 95; Franklin, 'On the Evolution of Scholarship', pp. 4–5.

8 Meier and Rudwick, *Black History and the Historical Profession*, pp. 9–11; Franklin, 'On the Evolution of Scholarship', p. 15.

9 Franklin, 'On the Evolution of Scholarship', pp. 16–17; Meier and Rudwick, *Black History and the Historical Profession*, pp. 116, 119, 121; William Palmer, *Engagement with the Past: The Lives and Works of the World War II Generation of Historians* (Lexington, Kentucky, 2001), pp. 16–17, 27.

10 Franklin, 'On the Evolution of Scholarship', p. 17; Meier and Rudwick, *Black History and the Historical Profession*, pp. 101, 109; August Meier, *A White Scholar and the Black Community, 1945–1965: Essays and Reflections* (Amherst, Massachusetts, 1992), p. 3.

11 Meier and Rudwick, *Black History and the Historical Profession*, pp. 112, 144–5; Meier, *A White Scholar and the Black Community*, p. 3.

12 Meier and Rudwick, *Black History and the Historical Profession*, pp. 146, 148–9, 167.

13 Meier and Rudwick, *Black History and the Historical Profession*, pp. 143–5, 164–6; Meier, *A White Scholar and the Black Community*, pp. 22–5; Franklin, 'On the Evolution of Scholarship', p. 17; Kenneth Stampp, *The Peculiar Institution* (New York, 1956); Stanley Elkins, *Slavery: A Problem in American Institutional and Intellectual Life* (Chicago, 1959). The most

important of the subsequent key works on slavery include Ann Lane (ed.), *The Debate Over Slavery* (Urbana, Illinois, 1971); John Blassingame, *The Slave Community: Plantation Life in the Antebellum South* (New York, 1972); George Rawick, *From Sundown to Sunup: The Making of the Black Community* (Westport, Connecticut, 1972); Robert Fogel and Stanley Engerman, *Time on the Cross*, 2 vols (London, 1974); Paul David, Herbert Gutman, Richard Sutch, Peter Temin and Gavin Wright (eds), *Reckoning With Slavery* (Oxford, 1976); Eugene Genovese, *Roll, Jordan, Roll: The World the Slaves Made* (New York, 1974); Herbert Gutman, *The Black Family in Slavery and Freedom, 1750–1925* (Oxford, 1976); Lawrence Levine, *Black Culture and Black Consciousness* (New York, 1977); Albert Raboteau, *Slave Religion: The 'Invisible Institution' in the Antebellum South* (New York, 1978). The cumulative impact of these studies provided a convincing rebuttal to the earlier gloomy assessment of Elkins, who had argued that the psychological damage inflicted by the institution of slavery was so severe that it had resulted in the effective infantilization of its unfortunate black victims. A detailed discussion of the historiographical debate on slavery can be found in Hugh Tulloch, *The Debate on the American Civil War Era* (Manchester, 1999), pp. 33–70.

14 Franklin, 'On the Evolution of Scholarship', p. 18.

15 William Faulkner, *Requiem for a Nun* (1951), cited in Elizabeth Knowles (ed.), *The Oxford Dictionary of Quotations*, 5th edn (Oxford, 1999), p. 307.

1

Segregation and accommodation, 1895–1915

Like the police sergeant in Gilbert and Sullivan's *The Pirates of Penzance*, the historian researching the lives of African Americans in the 1890s might justly claim that his or her lot was not a happy one. During this period many of the gains achieved by black Americans after their emancipation from slavery at the end of the Civil War in 1865, and during the Reconstruction era, 1865–77, were lost. In the South, where some 90 per cent of black Americans still lived, state governments dominated by conservative white Democrats systematically stripped black populations of their basic rights of citizenship. African Americans in the region were effectively denied the right to vote and forced to accept legal segregation in almost every aspect of their daily lives. Economically, black farm workers laboured in conditions of neo-serfdom that, in many respects, were only a marginal improvement on slavery.

The result of these developments was that the 1890s and the first decades of the twentieth century constituted a nadir in African American history that has been unsurpassed since the abolition of slavery. This fact perhaps, in part, helps to explain why, until comparatively recently, the era has been less well researched by scholars than some other periods of African American history. The blossoming of interest in black history since the 1950s was, as has already been noted, directly linked to the rise of Martin Luther King and the post-Second World War Civil Rights Movement. In the first instance it was understandable that many scholars from the mid-1950s through to the 1980s should be more interested in analysing the dramatic changes that had taken place since the

Second World War rather than more remote, and seemingly less relevant, events at the start of the century.

Moreover, the inspirational rhetoric of Dr King and the dramatic confrontations of the 1950s and 1960s encouraged historians to view the black freedom struggle in heroic, even romantic, terms. Any narrative history of black civil rights since the 1940s would inevitably include many instances of shocking violence and injustice but, in the racial climate of the late 1960s and early 1970s, it did appear to be a story that had a more or less happy ending. Although Martin Luther King had been martyred in 1968, he had at least claimed to have a vision of a future promised land. The advances achieved in desegregation and black voting rights since the 1950s suggested that this was a destination that King's children, and African Americans as a whole, would ultimately reach.

In contrast, research into the unrelenting misery, degradation and despair that seemingly characterized African American life at the start of the twentieth century was a less obvious source of inspiration. The daily struggles against racial injustice by black Americans at this time may have been no less courageous than those of their descendants but such victories that were achieved were few in number and less dramatic in scale. Most important of all, in comparison with the civil rights campaigners of the 1950s and the 1960s, they had clearly not overcome. Simply put, any chronicler of race relations in the 1890s, as historian Glenda Gilmore has noted, was committed to 'writing a tragedy'.[1]

For scholars writing before the 1950s such considerations clearly did not apply. However, the racial conservatism of American society in the first half of the twentieth century meant that few mainstream historians of the period were interested in the lives of African Americans at all. Such accounts as did appear in these years were written either by one of the small number of trained black scholars or by white authors who for some personal reason had a particular interest in their subject. In this vein the first studies of Booker T. Washington, the dominant black spokesperson in the United States from the mid-1890s through to his death in 1915, were initiated by Washington himself.

In 1900 *The Story of My Life and Work* chronicled Washington's life from his birth as a slave in West Virginia in

1856 through to his rise as an internationally renowned educator and Principal of the all-black Tuskegee Institute in Alabama in the 1880s and 1890s. Aimed primarily at black purchasers, the book was ostensibly penned by Washington's own hand, but in reality ghost-written by Edgar Webber, a young African American scholar selected by the Tuskegeean for the task. The following year a more polished and carefully edited account of Washington's life, *Up From Slavery*, was published for the benefit of white readers. On this occasion the 'ghost' employed was the northern white journalist and Tuskegee sympathizer Max Bennett Thrasher, reflecting the greater importance attached by Washington to the project.[2]

The effort paid off. *Up From Slavery* rapidly became an international best-seller and in the more than one hundred years since its initial publication has never been out of print. This success can be attributed to the fact that, with Thrasher's assistance, Washington carefully contrived to project an image of himself that was designed to appeal to the conservative racial and social values of his day. If committed to racial uplift, he was crucially non-threatening in tone. Rather than resenting his slave child-hood, he was grateful to the institution of slavery for instilling in him Christian values and a puritan commitment to hard work and self-discipline.

In particular the Tuskegeean was a leading advocate of the then fashionable philosophy of industrial education. This emphasized the virtues of teaching practical skills like carpentry, bricklaying and cooking, rather than schooling in more traditional academic subjects like algebra, literature and history. The principal drawbacks of such a programme were outlined in a 1903 essay, 'Of Mr Booker T. Washington and Others', by the civil rights campaigner and African American scholar, W. E. B. Du Bois. In what is now widely recognized as the classic critique of Washington's philosophy, the Harvard-trained historian argued that overemphasis on manual skills condemned black children to a lifetime of menial service, as servants and labourers, instead of encouraging their entry into professions like teaching, law and medicine. Equally, stress on economic advancement abandoned the defence of civil and political rights, leaving blacks without a voice in the democratic process.[3]

Although Du Bois's views were vindicated in the longer term, it was precisely these considerations that led most white Americans of the day to look to Washington rather than Du Bois as the leading spokesperson of his race. The Tusgekeean sought advancement for African Americans, but this would be within clearly defined limits that did not threaten white supremacy. Moreover, the primary responsibility for achieving such uplift lay with blacks themselves through economic self-help. Indeed, the intrinsic truth of this message was most powerfully demonstrated by Washington's own life which so spectacularly transcends his humble beginnings. By implication, the depressing and disadvantaged living conditions endured by the vast majority of blacks could be blamed on their own inadequacies rather than the unfair and unequal treatment afforded them by white America.

Washington's autobiographies had a fascination for his fellow citizens of all races, in that American social values at the turn of the century tended to lay undue emphasis on individual achievement at the expense of group experience. In the closing years of the nineteenth century the American economy was increasingly dominated by a small number of powerful business leaders. These industrial magnates, like Washington's benefactor Andrew Carnegie, had often overcome modest beginnings to achieve great wealth and influence. This fostered the belief that the major developments in human history could be attributed to the actions of a few dynamic visionary individuals rather than the more impersonal and abstract forces of socio-economic change.

It was this view that encouraged historians like the African American Carter Woodson to venerate Washington as one of the builders and achievers of his race. In keeping with such sentiments, scholarly admirers of Washington from both races perpetuated the mythic status of the Tuskegeean in a series of laudatory accounts of his work intended to inspire the next generation of African Americans, from whom future Washingtonian figures would emerge to lead black communities in the struggle for racial uplift. In 1901 Max Bennett Thrasher published *Tuskegee: Its Story and Its Work*, while in 1916 Washington's long-time personal secretary, Emmett J. Scott, co-authored *Booker T. Washington: Builder of a Civilization*. This remained the dominant trend in studies on Washington down to the 1940s, perpetuating his heroic status rather than engaging in balanced critical analysis of his human strengths and weaknesses.[4]

At the same time in the inter-war years there were indications that some scholars were willing to examine the more depressing realities of black life at the turn of the century, most notably in a series of academic studies on lynching. The unlawful killing of individuals by vigilante mobs, lynching was associated for much of the nineteenth century with the kind of rough justice meted out to cattle rustlers and other wrongdoers on the western frontier in the absence of any established legal system. Whatever its origins, by the late 1880s the crime had taken on an entirely different meaning and character. During the 1890s more than 80 per cent of lynchings took place in the South and the overwhelming majority of victims were black. Over the decade more than a hundred black southerners were killed every year in this manner, reaching a peak of 161 in 1892.[5]

There was, of course, widespread public awareness of such incidents at the time. In *Southern Horrors* (1892) and *A Red Record* (1895) the black anti-lynching campaigner Ida B. Wells provided two of the first notable accounts of the offence.[6] A radical black journalist from the South, Wells had suffered the loss of friends and colleagues at the hands of lynch mobs and herself had been forced to flee the region to avoid the risk of sharing a similar fate. She thus had deep-seated personal motives for embarking on what became a life-long crusade against lynching.[7] The leading scholars of her day did not share this dedication. In common with most white Americans, they were inclined to keep to themselves any feelings of disapproval they might have had at reports of the crime. Lynching was seen as a problem best left to southerners to resolve themselves. Moreover, the typical public defence advanced in mitigation of lynch mobs was that the black victim was guilty of the actual or attempted rape of a white woman and fully deserved his brutal end. Although such allegations were rarely substantiated, this meant that any author critical of the crime was open to the charge of taking the side of depraved black sexual offenders against lynching parties supposedly acting in defence of white womanhood.

By the end of the First World War this situation had changed. The incidence of lynching had sharply declined, and during the

1920s and 1930s American public opinion became less tolerant of such vigilante action. The leading black civil rights organization of the day, the National Association for the Advancement of Colored People (NAACP) launched a campaign to secure the passage of a federal anti-lynching law. This objective became a principal objective for the NAACP in the inter-war period and, although ultimately unsuccessful, the Association's efforts did much to highlight the evils of lynching in the public mind.

In 1929 Walter White's *Rope and Faggot: A Biography of Judge Lynch* constituted arguably the first serious full-length academic study of lynching.[8] White was both Assistant Secretary of the NAACP and an experienced African American author. His study was obviously intended to assist the Association's wider campaign and drew on the extensive records of the NAACP on lynching. It was, however, much more than just a propaganda text. Reflecting the growing popularity of the science of psychiatry, White became one of the first commentators to seek a psychological explanation for the actions of lynch mobs. In keeping with Freudian teachings, he looked to suppressed sexual anxieties to account for their crimes. In the most controversial chapter of the book, 'Sex and Lynching', he argued that the fact that so many lynch victims were accused of rape highlighted 'the Southern white woman's proneness to hysteria where Negroes are concerned'.

Thoroughly modern in his views, White also shared the growing distrust of many educated urban Americans of the 1920s towards traditional, conservative, religious values and Christian fundamentalism. He thus drew attention to the 'intense religiosity of the lynching states and the primitiveness of their religion'. He concluded that the puritanical teachings of southern evangelical churches forced worshippers to suppress their natural sexual thoughts and desires. Vigilante mobs achieved cathartic release from this unhealthy repression by the act of lynching. The frequent allegations of rape, acts of sadistic torture and castration associated with lynchings supported this conclusion.[9]

The Tragedy of Lynching (1933), by sociologist Arthur Raper, has generally been afforded greater scholarly recognition as a pioneering work in the field than White's earlier study.[10] It is a moot point as to whether or not such a perception is justified.

Other than highlighting illiteracy, poverty and cultural stagnation as root causes of lynching, Raper added little to White's findings. Moreover, in contrast to the extensive documentary evidence cited by White, Raper adopted a 'fundamentally ahistorical' approach, examining the causes of contemporary mob violence and projecting these back in time to explain past lynchings.[11]

This notwithstanding, Raper's work was notable in marking both the rising stature of sociology as an academic discipline and growing scholarly interest in the causes of lynching. These two developments were also highlighted in the late 1930s writings of sociologist John Dollard, who found other reasons for lynching. Unsurprisingly, Dollard concluded that mob violence was a means of reaffirming white supremacy, for blacks and whites alike. Like White, he also detected a psychological motive. Lynching was a result of 'frustration-aggression'. Whites in the South acquired pent up frustrations in their daily lives which they periodically released in violence against blacks, who symbolized the repressed fears and desires of the dominant racial group. Economic factors also played a part. Dollard found that when cotton prices were high the number of lynchings fell. When cotton prices fell the incidence of lynching increased. The level of lynching was thus a measure of the economic frustration of white southerners.[12]

Some fifty years after it was first published, C. Vann Woodward's *The Strange Career of Jim Crow* (1955) continues to be a seminal study in the modern historiography on the African American experience in the late nineteenth century. It is also the starting point for any discussion on the origins of racial segregation, or 'Jim Crow-ism' as it is also known. Moreover, in a long and distinguished career as a historian, *The Strange Career* is arguably the work for which Vann Woodward (1908-99) will be best remembered.[13]

Some of the themes in the book developed ideas outlined in Woodward's earlier study *Origins of the New South* (1951),[14] but his primary motivation in writing *The Strange Career* came from elsewhere. In a recurring theme in African American historiography, Woodward was inspired to revisit the past as a result of his personal convictions combined with contemporary developments in race relations.

Born in 1908 in the small village of Vanndale, Arkansas,

Vann Woodward's family had formerly owned slaves and his grandfather John Vann had served for four years in the Confederate army during the American Civil War, 1861–5. This conservative background belied Vann Woodward's own liberal upbringing. His parents were both educators with an enlightened left-of-centre perspective, as well as being committed Methodists. Intellectually he came of age in the 1930s during the years of Franklin Roosevelt's New Deal. In 1931–2 Vann Woodward's principled views on racial and political issues were highlighted by his involvement in the defence of Angelo Herndon, an African American Communist jailed for leading a demonstration against a reduction in poor relief for the unemployed. Shortly afterwards Vann Woodward was dismissed from his teaching post at Georgia Tech, leading him to take up a position at the University of North Carolina at Chapel Hill, prior to serving in naval intelligence during the Second World War.[15]

In the *Brown* v. *Board of Education* case of 1954, the United States Supreme Court, by a unanimous decision, ruled that racial segregation in education was unconstitutional, overturning the doctrine established by the 1896 case of *Plessy* v. *Ferguson* of 'separate but equal'. In an 8-1 majority decision the judges in the *Plessy* case had concluded that separate facilities for whites and blacks did not violate the equal citizenship rights of African Americans, as separation in itself did not imply superior or inferior treatment for either race. A landmark ruling, *Plessy* paved the way for the rapid spread of racial segregation under the law throughout the South by the early years of the twentieth century. Almost all aspects of daily life were affected, including seating in theatres, restaurants, public transport, schools, hospitals, shops factories, restrooms and even cemetery burial plots. Predictably, the facilities provided for African Americans were almost invariably grossly inferior to those laid on for their white counterparts.

By the time of the *Brown* case, and now employed at Johns Hopkins University, Vann Woodward's continuing racial liberalism and growing academic reputation were reflected in the fact that he wrote historical background briefs for Thurgood Marshall, the NAACP's lead attorney in the case. Building on this research, and encouraged by the court's verdict, Vann Woodward resolved to write a history of racial segregation in America to bring about a better public understanding of its origins and development. At a time when many white southerners were prepared to flout the law rather than accept the *Brown* decision, he hoped that his study might help lessen the intense opposition to integrated schooling.[16]

Vann Woodward argued that, contrary to popular belief, segregation was not a hallowed southern tradition but was actually an aberration of comparatively recent origin. Black slavery during the Antebellum period, 1787–1861, had constituted an extreme form of racial oppression but there had not been a physical separation, or segregation, of the races. On the contrary, the institution of slavery had necessitated daily contact between whites and blacks, and 'a degree of intimacy between the races unequalled, and often held distasteful, in other parts of the country'.[17]

Vann Woodward acknowledged that after the Civil War emancipation resulted in a greater physical distance between whites and blacks in the South. However, there was still considerable fluidity and flexibility in race relations in the region. The old slave-owning planter class, or Bourbon aristocracy as it was known, dominated political life in the region. Conservative Bourbon leaders, like Wade Hampton in South Carolina, and James George in Mississippi, retained paternalistic attitudes towards freed slaves. They envisaged an inclusive role for them in society, albeit on clearly unequal terms with whites, principally as servants and labourers.

This situation, Vann Woodward argued, persisted until the early 1890s, when changing political, social and economic conditions in the region brought about a hardening of white racial attitudes. New political leaders, like 'Pitchfork' Ben Tillman in South Carolina and James Vardaman in Mississippi, emerged, who held more extreme racial views. These spokesmen perceived African Americans not as benign childish dependents but as bestial in nature and a threat to white civilization. Reflecting these developments, state governments across the South began to pass laws requiring physical separation of the races that became a characteristic of life in the region for the next sixty years.

Given this, Vann Woodward acknowledged the fears of southern whites in the mid-1950s at the *Brown* decision but sought to demonstrate that such anxieties were groundless. The notion that without segregation racial co-existence in the region would be impossible was misconceived and derived, in part, from the lack of a true understanding of southern history. Indeed, the mid-nineteenth-century ancestors of those who advanced such an idea would have regarded it as absurd.

The impact of *The Strange Career* in intellectual circles was such that at the 1965 Selma to Montgomery March in Alabama, a civil rights demonstration in which Van Woodward participated, Martin Luther King publicly praised the book as 'the Bible of the Civil Rights Movement'. Unfortunately, as a southern white with a liberal outlook on race relations, Vann Woodward was a member of a minority group in the 1950s and 1960s. It was thus ironic that the most telling critique of the thesis that he advanced in *The Strange Career* came from another liberal southern white historian, Joel Williamson. A lecturer at Chapel Hill in the early 1960s, Williamson shared Vann Woodward's ideals but, at least in the short term, was less optimistic about their chances of being realized, given what he saw as 'the obdurate racism of the white South'.[18]

Williamson also had reservations about the Vann Woodward thesis on scholarly grounds. In *After Slavery: The Negro in South Carolina During Reconstruction* (1965) he found that segregation was common in the Palmetto state by the late 1860s and early 1870s, casting doubt on Vann Woodward's findings that it did not become widespread until the 1890s. This was also the conclusion reached by Vernon Lane Wharton, a southern liberal with a Methodist background, in an earlier study on Reconstruction Mississippi.[19]

Williamson argued that Vann Woodward had erred in placing too much emphasis on legal, or *de jure*, segregation. What mattered was when Jim Crow-ism first became common in practice, *de facto* segregation, with or without the force of law. In consequence, Vann Woodward had miscalculated the timing of the introduction of segregation in the South. This occurred not, as he had suggested, in the 1890s, but shortly after the end of the Civil War. In an important 1968 collection of essays, *The Origins of Segregation*, Williamson and other historians expressed their doubts about the Vann Woodward thesis, starting a historiographical debate that has continued into the twenty-first century.[20]

An unfortunate consequence of this development was that other aspects of segregation tended to be less well explored, though inevitably there were some exceptions. In a thoughtful essay, radical historian Barton J. Bernstein highlighted the flawed 'conservative sociological jurisprudence' in the 1896 *Plessy* v. *Ferguson* case. In *Jim Crow's Defense* (1965) I. A. Newby examined the reasons advanced by white southerners to justify racial segregation in the early years of the twentieth century. He found that these generally comprised doubtful social science theories and even more dubious racial concepts such as a 'consciousness of kind' and a 'call of the blood' that, it was argued, inexorably drew individuals to the society of members of his or her own race. Conversely, in an influential 1969 article August Meier and Elliott Rudwick drew attention to the surprising, and sustained, level of opposition by African Americans to the imposition of streetcar segregation in southern cities at the turn of the century.[21]

The growing public prominence given to black civil rights by the late 1940s combined with the subsequent rise of the post-war Civil Rights Movement encouraged a number of scholars to explore various aspects of the nation's racial history. In 1951 political scientist V. O. Key studied the political disfranchisement of African Americans in the 1890s, concluding that the campaigns were effectively a coup d'état led by the Bourbon planter aristocracy and centred on black belt counties with large African American populations.[22] Conversely, J. Abramovitz and William Chafe looked at the rise of the People's Party in the 1890s. The Populist Movement, as it was also known, had appealed to yeoman farmers in the southern and western United States and had notably been marked by instances of political co-operation between whites and blacks. Abramovitz and Chafe argued that this inter-racial alliance was doomed because of internal disunity, regardless of the actions of the planter aristocracy.[23]

New studies also began to appear on Booker T. Washington. In *Booker T. Washington: Educator and Inter-Racial Interpreter* (1949) and *Booker T. Washington and the Negro's Place in American Life* (1956) Basil Matthews and Samuel J. Spencer

respectively went further than earlier commentators in acknowledging the conservative nature of Washington's leadership, but
also concluded that his programme was the only realistic option
open to African Americans in the repressive racial climate of the
early twentieth century. Raised in Columbia, South Carolina,
Spencer was another example of a white southerner who was
prompted to question the region's racial values as a result of his
deeply held Christian beliefs.[24]

In 1963 historian August Meier's *Negro Thought in America,
1880–1915* constituted an important revisionist work on
Washington. A civil rights activist himself, Meier's study was
published at the height of Martin Luther King's career when the
Civil Rights Movement appeared to have gained an irresistible
momentum. Perhaps in part because of this, Meier was inclined to
be more critical of the shortcomings of Washington's patient,
gradualist philosophy. He drew on earlier neglected writings by
Du Bois that demonstrated the extent to which Washington had
used underhand tactics to silence his critics within the black
community. Such actions not only revealed a vindictive side to
Washington's personality but also, by unspoken implication,
contrasted sharply with the inclusive leadership style of Martin
Luther King, who went out of his way to maintain a public show
of unity in the civil rights coalition of the early 1960s.[25]

In the decades that followed the decline of the Civil Rights
Movement in the early 1970s existing topics of debate were rein-
vigorated by fresh discussion and new findings. Emma Lou
Thornbrough and Stephen Fox respectively provided biographical
studies on Timothy Thomas Fortune and William Monroe Trotter,
two turn-of-the-century black spokesmen, who offered a more
radical form of racial leadership than that provided by Booker T.
Washington.[26] Born in 1913 to a conservative Republican family
in Indiana, Thornbrough's work constituted an academic milestone, making her 'the first white woman to publish a scholarly
monograph in black history', a subject area to which she devoted
her career. Thornbrough's dedication reflected her personal interest in black civil rights as a member of the NAACP and may also
have been attributable to the fact that 'her own marginality as a
woman historian making her way in a male dominated profession
sensitized her to the situation that blacks faced as a minority'.[27]

In respect to Booker T. Washington the revisionism of Meier found its most mature expression in the work of Louis Harlan. A southerner born in 1922, Harlan was, by his own admission, a racist in early life. His outlook was, however, broadened by naval service during the Second World War when 'racial encounters with black people and white liberals' directed him 'on a path that diverged from' his 'southern heritage'. At the end of the war he made the life-changing decision to pursue a career as a historian, embarking on an MA degree at Vanderbilt University followed by PhD research at Johns Hopkins University on the topic of segregated public schooling in the South at the turn of the century. By the early 1950s he was working at a small college in rural Texas 'where race relations were so oppressive that the local blacks were still stepping off the sidewalk when whites passed by'. Harlan responded to this by helping to organize both white and black voters in support of liberal democratic candidates.[28]

These varied experiences may also explain Harlan's burgeoning interest in Booker T. Washington, a black leader who fought racial injustice at the turn of the century from his base at Tuskegee, a small country town in Alabama. From the mid-1960s through to the 1980s Harlan published a series of essays on Washington together with a detailed and scholarly two-volume biography. During the 1970s and 1980s he also headed a team of leading historians in the publication of *The Booker T. Washington Papers*, a fourteen-volume collection of the Tuskegeean's writings, speeches and private correspondence.[29] These works revealed the complex and contradictory nature of Washington. In a 'secret life' the Tuskegeean not only persecuted perceived rivals but also covertly supported anti-segregation lawsuits and penned outspoken anonymous editorials attacking racial segregation.

The painstaking quality of Harlan's research, combined with his prolific scholarly output, established him as unquestionably the leading modern authority on Washington by the 1980s. Although careful to present a balanced picture of his subject, it was also clear that Harlan himself was generally unsympathetic to the Tuskegeean's accommodationist philosophy. By the early 1990s, an era when increasingly conservative social values first apparent in the 1970s had become more firmly entrenched in the American public mind, there were signs that some researchers were starting to be critical of this negative outlook. Underpinning this belief was the feeling that Harlan was, to some extent, guilty of judging Washington by the values of the Civil Rights Movement of the 1960s rather than the standards of his day.

Virginia Denton, a southern educator and open admirer of the Tuskegeean, took Harlan to task for engaging in 'liberal revisionistic judgments' and evincing a 'general negativism towards the South'. Denton's partisan tone, combined with methodological weaknesses in her own research, blunted the impact of her attack. More notably, however, in 2001 the leading British historian Adam Fairclough, though acknowledging Harlan's scholarship, questioned the image of Washington that emerged from his writings as 'a despotic, devious, and rather sinister figure – and above all a failure'. Instead Fairclough suggested, Washington was 'a man unselfishly committed to the social, educational, and economic uplift of his race'. 'Judged by his best', he 'was an admirable leader'. This assessment was doubly significant in that Fairclough was not only an eminent scholar of international standing but also liberal minded in his political philosophy.[30]

The growing emphasis on economic inequalities by civil rights campaigners and Black Power advocates during the late 1960s and early 1970s encouraged a number of studies in the early 1970s that examined the problem from a historical perspective. By the late nineteenth century sharecropping had become the dominant form of agriculture in the South. Under this system planters provided black families with small landholdings, accommodation, food and supplies in return for a share of the proceeds of the crop, almost invariably cotton, at the end of the year. In an important, if unconvincing, journal article economic historian Joseph Reid argued that such arrangements constituted a natural free market compromise between the economic interests of former slaves and white landowners. Later studies, most notably by Roger Ransom, Richard Sutch, Jay Mandle, Daniel Novak and Peter Daniel demonstrated the flaws in such reasoning. These works graphically highlighted the chronic disadvantages suffered by black farmers in their dealings with white landowners. Routine and systematic use of fraudulent accounting and extortionate mark-ups enabled planters to deprive sharecroppers of the fruits of their labour. Worse still, many black farmers became trapped into a cycle of neo-slavery or debt peonage as in succeeding years they were compelled to labour without hope of any financial reward in a vain attempt to pay off ever mounting undischarged contractual obligations.[31]

The debate on the origins of segregation continued with undiminished vigour and enthusiasm from the 1970s through to the dawn of the new millennium. Research by subsequent scholars in the debate begun by Van Woodward and Williamson periodically reinforced the case advanced by both historians without ever providing any clear resolution of the issue. One reason for this was that the precise extent of the disagreement between the two men appeared to become blurred over time, with each making concessions to the other's point of view.

Taking heed of his critics, Vann Woodward modified his original hypothesis in revised second and third editions of *The Strange Career of Jim Crow* published in 1966 and 1974 respectively. He now accepted that there was evidence of a degree of segregation in the South in the decades after the Civil War but maintained that this did not become systematic and widespread until the 1890s. Similarly, in another major work, *The Crucible of Race* (1984), Williamson, although not abandoning his original argument, agreed with Vann Woodward in pinpointing the 1890s as marking a major deterioration in race relations in the South.[32]

A central problem in the debate was that the complexity and diversity of southern society in the late nineteenth century made it difficult for historians to make meaningful generalizations about the region as a whole. One factor was the issue of southern inconsistency. In the 1860s and 1870s whites insisted on racial separation in some areas of life but not in others. Throughout the South education was conducted on a segregated basis, yet it was still socially acceptable for white and black children to play together outside the classroom. Regional differences were another consideration. Deep South states like Mississippi and Alabama, with large black populations and a brutal racial history, even by southern standards, may have embraced segregation earlier than other regions, as Vann Woodward himself acknowledged.

A significant development came with the publication of

Howard Rabinowitz's *Race Relations in the Urban South, 1865–1890* (1978). In this study of five southern cities, Atlanta, Georgia; Montgomery, Alabama; Nashville, Tennessee; Raleigh, North Carolina; and Richmond, Virginia, Rabinowitz found that segregation was widespread in all these urban locations well before the 1890s.[33] While apparently providing strong supportive evidence for Williamson's views, the significance of Rabinowitz's findings was less clear-cut than it first appeared. In common with much of the United States, the South experienced growing urbanization in the second half of the nineteenth century, but in 1900 it was still predominantly rural. This consideration raised obvious doubts as to what extent urban centres could be seen as typical of the pattern of race relations in the region as a whole.

Rabinowitz's study also highlighted another complicating factor, the importance of the process of modernization within the region in the late nineteenth century, and the impact of such change on southern culture and society. Urbanization created the potential for daily social contact between whites and blacks – in transportation, commerce and public accommodations – on a scale without precedent in rural locations. In bringing about conditions of close physical proximity between the races it is possible that urban growth acted as a catalyst for the spread of segregation.

Confusingly, historian John Graves reached the opposite conclusion. In Arkansas he found that the impetus for segregation laws came from conservative rural districts. Urban Little Rock was more cosmopolitan and liberal in attitude and its citizens, both white and black, resented segregation being imposed upon them. In another challenge to existing thought he also argued that southern Atlantic states, like Virginia and the Carolinas, might have moved to widespread segregation more quickly than southern states further west. This was because the former had more developed social structures and legal systems, whereas states like Arkansas, even in the late nineteenth century, still retained some of the characteristics of a frontier society and thus retained a more fluid pattern of race relations.[34]

Edward Ayers looked at modernization from another viewpoint in *The Promise of the New South: Life After Reconstruction* (1992). In a chapter devoted to the issue of segregation he drew attention to the importance of the growth of railroad networks in the region in the late nineteenth century and the dilemmas this created for southern race relations. Prior to the development of the automobile the railroads provided an essential means of transportation for whites and blacks alike, creating endless possibilities for racial conflict. During the 1870s and 1880s the spread of railways in the South thus forced railroad companies to introduce segregated seating arrangements on trains to accommodate the wishes of white passengers.[35]

In a later 1990s study historian Grace Elizabeth Hale detected another explanation for the spread of segregation. She noted that between 1880 and 1900 the proportion of black farmers in the Deep South owning their own land rose from 3.8 per cent to 25 per cent. Belying claims by southern whites that blacks lacked the capacity for self-reliance, such gains ultimately posed a threat to continued white supremacy in the region if left unchecked. Whites thus 'created the culture of segregation in large part to counter black success, to make a myth of absolute racial difference, to stop the rising'. Moreover, at the same time as condemning blacks to a life of subordination, segregation reinforced concepts of whiteness, creating a 'new collective white identity across lines of gender and class and a new regional distinctiveness'.[36]

Other studies examined segregation from different perspectives. Charles Lofgren's *The Plessy Case: A Legal Historical Interpretation* (1987) provided the most authoritative full-length study of its subject. Pursuing a different line of enquiry, John Cell and George Frederickson sought to come to a greater understanding of segregation by making a comparative analysis of the Jim Crow South with the system of apartheid in South Africa. Born in 1934 to a conservative family, Frederickson had been a civil rights sympathizer since the 1950s. The work of the two historians reflected mounting international concern in the early 1980s at the political system in South Africa. Moreover, it provided a fresh scholarly perspective on an increasingly well-worn subject, but despite this it failed to spark off a lasting new line of historical enquiry.[37]

One reason for this was simply that few historians possessed a sufficiently detailed historical knowledge of both South Africa and the United States to engage in such research. Another problem was that, despite superficial similarities between the two countries, Cell and Frederickson both concluded that each had highly distinctive features. Generally speaking, in examining 'the structural and demographic differences between twentieth-century black-white relations in the two societies', the 'contrast was so great' as to suggest that 'there was little basis for a detailed comparison'.[38]

The 1970s onwards also saw new work on both the political disfranchisement of southern blacks in the late nineteenth century and race relations in the Populist movement of the 1890s. One important development was J. Morgan Kousser's *The Shaping of Southern Politics* (1974).[39] A former student of Vann Woodward, Kousser's research was in part inspired by his old mentor. In *Origins of the New South* Vann Woodward had broadly supported Key's view that the electoral disfranchisement of southern blacks in the 1890s was masterminded by the white planter aristocracy. However, in *The Strange Career of Jim Crow* he shifted his position, placing greater emphasis on working-class whites as the prime instigators. At the very least the issue clearly required further investigation to resolve which version of events was the more accurate.

Kousser's scholarly curiosity was reinforced by technological developments in the study of history. Both Key and Vann Woodward's findings had been based on intuitive reading of source materials. Kousser sought to base his research in hard statistical information obtained through the application of new techniques of quantitative computer analysis to newspaper, legislative and electoral records of the period. Large-scale 'number crunching' exercises of this sort had not been available to previous generations of scholars and in the early 1970s historians working across a wide range of fields hoped that analysis of such detailed, objective, numerical data might provide definitive answers, or at least a fresh perspective, to longstanding historiographical debates.

Ironically, Kousser's investigations supported Key's contention that conservative black belt planters were the prime movers of disfranchisement. Indeed, as 'members of a privileged élite this group were contemptuous of lower class, uneducated whites and disfranchised these as willingly as they did blacks'. In other respects, however, Kousser rebutted some of Key's earlier findings. Key had argued that the *de jure* disfranchisement of blacks in the 1890s replaced earlier *de facto* measures employed to achieve the same ends. In the 'Redemption' campaigns of the mid-1870s, white Democrats resorted to systematic use of fraud and intimidation to regain control of state governments in the South. During the 1880s, Key concluded, the new Democratic administrations simply resorted to the same tactics to perpetuate their domination before turning to legal proscription in the 1890s. Kousser's research demonstrated that this perception was over-simple. He found that Democratic administrations resorted to restrictive legislative measures as early as the 1880s.[40]

In *Blacks and the Populist Revolt: Ballots and Bigotry in the New South* (1977), historian Gerald Gaither concluded that the Populist movement was a sincere attempt to create a bi-racial, class-oriented, political party, but this failed because the planter class convinced poor whites that it constituted a betrayal of their Anglo-Saxon ancestry. In a 1989 article on Texas, historians Gregg Cantrell and D. Scott Barton broadly backed these findings. In the Lone Star state they concluded that biracial Populism failed because the comparatively enlightened racial outlook of some Populist leaders was unacceptable to their rank and file supporters.[41]

Looking at Populism in Kansas, William Chafe advanced another explanation for the failure of the movement. He concluded that, although both black and white farmers were attracted to the party, it was for different reasons. The prime concerns of white supporters were rural poverty and economic issues. Blacks attached greater importance to alleviating bigotry and achieving greater protection from racial violence. The attempt at a bi-racial Populist alliance in the state was thus flawed from the outset, because whites and blacks did not share common objectives. Moreover, black Kansans were ultimately unwilling to support an attack on upper-class white leaders who had previously given them partial protection from the worst excesses of racial violence.[42]

Historian Michael Perman's important 2001 study, *Struggle for Mastery: Disfranchisement in the South, 1888–1908*, provided the most authoritative modern account of the political exclusion of blacks in the region. The key development of the 1890s was, he concluded, a shift from legislation to constitutional revision. In the 1880s Democratic administrations passed laws that regulated the conduct of elections, a process of 'voter manipulation'. During the 1890s they adopted the bolder measure of passing amendments to state constitutions to exclude certain categories of voters altogether, a process of 'voter elimination'. He found that the prime movers of disfranchisement campaigns varied from state to state. In South Carolina and Mississippi it was upcountry yeoman farmers who initiated disfranchisement. Indeed, in the Mississippi black belt planters were initially opposed to this measure. At the same time in all states 'disfranchisement rarely, if ever, happened unless the Democrats of the black belt concurred'. He also noted that that although some Reformer Democrats were happy to exclude ignorant white voters as well as blacks, in every state the Disfranchisers 'went to some pains, and usually a good deal of embarrassment, to concoct schemes for including otherwise vulnerable, illiterate and poor whites'.[43]

Although informative, the continuing debates on segregation and disfranchisement were not unexpected. A less predictable development of the 1980s and 1990s was the revival of interest in lynching. The impetus for this came in an unexpected manner. The rise of the feminist movement in the United States during the late 1960s and early 1970s prompted an understandable growth of interest in women's history. In 1970 Afreda M. Duster edited a new edition of *Crusade for Justice*, the autobiography of Ida B. Wells. In the same vein, in *Revolt Against Chivalry* (1979) historian Jacquelyn Dowd Hall embarked on a study of Jessie Daniel Ames, a leading southern anti-lynching campaigner of the 1930s. Although primarily intended as a biography, in a key chapter in the book Hall examined the causes of lynching. This was necessary because, as she observed, despite the central place occupied by lynching 'in the southern imagination and in the idea of the South in the rest of the country', historians had 'paid remarkably little attention to the phenomenon'. Indeed, there had been little academic debate of any kind on the subject since the sociological studies of Raper and Dolland in the 1930s.[44]

Moreover, Hall added a fresh dimension to the subject by

providing a gendered perspective. Lynching derived from male guilt over inter-racial sexual relations, or miscegenation, combined with 'the veiled hostility toward women in a patriarchal society' and 'the myths of black sexuality'. It 'served as a dramatization of hierarchical power relationships based both on gender and on race'. In short, lynching not only oppressed blacks but also white women by reinforcing their dependency on male protection.[45]

In the 1990s Glenda Gilmore supported this conclusion in an important study on gender and white supremacy in North Carolina. The new climate of white supremacy in the state at the turn of the century was primarily intended to subjugate blacks, she argued, but 'domination of white women became a by-product'. Exploiting the myth of the black rapist, southern white men 'invoked danger and restriction' at a time when white women were beginning to seek 'pleasure and freedom'. More specifically, new hardline attitudes in race relations were the result of 'growing assertiveness among white women' combined with 'urban and industrial social pressure' and mounting evidence of black economic success.[46]

Hall's study was one of the first works to consider the relationship between race and gender. It also prompted fresh interest among historians in lynching. In *Crucible of Race*, Joel Williamson revisited the psychological motives for lynching. Echoing Walter White, he found one explanation in repressed male sexuality. By the 1890s southern white concepts of honour and chivalry had 'pedestalized white women'. They were perceived as pure, chaste beings without sexual desire, who only submitted to the carnal demands of their husbands out of love and duty. This created feelings of guilt in white men who, in hunting down alleged black rapists, restored 'their own self image as protectors and used blacks as surrogates to be punished for their own sexual desires'.

This pathological behaviour was reinforced by economic recession. In the mid-1890s agricultural prices in the South slumped, making it harder for male white southerners to fulfil their traditional role of family providers and protectors. 'It seems fully possible', Williamson concluded, that 'the rage against the black beast rapist was a kind of psychic compensation. If white men could not provide for their women materially as they had done before, they could certainly protect them from a much more awful threat – the outrage of their purity'.[47]

From the 1960s onwards, and in some cases even earlier, psychological analysis was increasingly used by historians in a wide range of different fields to try to achieve a deeper under-standing of the past. Almost always interesting, this approach was typically fraught with methodological problems. Since this view focused on repressed emotions that lynchers themselves were not fully aware of, it was impossible to advance tangible evidence in support of such theories. Moreover, generalized observations about human behaviour did not take account of regional diversity. Lynchings did not occur in an even pattern across the South. There was a much higher incidence of the crime in some states, most notably Georgia and Mississippi, than others, but there is no reason to believe that whites in these areas were more psychologically damaged than their counterparts elsewhere.

Edward Ayers explored this issue of regional variation. He concluded that lynchings most commonly occurred in areas of low population density that experienced a large rise in their black population between 1880 and 1910. This included the cotton uplands of Mississippi, Louisiana, Arkansas and Texas and the Gulf Plain from Florida to Texas. Counties in these areas were characterized by 'few towns, weak law enforcement, poor communications with the outside and high levels of transiency among both races'. These conditions 'fostered the fear and inse-curity that fed lynching' and 'removed the few checks that helped dissuade would-be lynchers elsewhere'. Significantly, Ayers found that lynch victims were likely to be newcomers to an area or social outsiders, 'blacks with no white to vouch for them' and 'no reputation in the neighborhood'. William Fitzhugh Brundage reinforced this view in a leading important regional study. He found that one in five of recorded lynch victims in Georgia between 1880 and 1930 were migrant labourers, and for Virginia the proportion was one in three. The reason for this was that 'blacks who had a nomadic life as laborers in a rural industry – railroad workers, miners, lumber and turpentine hands for example – kindled hostility even without committing any crime'.[48]

By the early 1990s a growing number of works were

published on lynching. Dominic Capeci, Nancy MacLean, James McGovern and Howard Smead provided case studies of individual lynchings. In a more general overview of the subject sociologists Stewart Tolney and E. M. Beck emphasized economic self-interest as a motive for lynching. James Allen produced a collection of lynching photography that could be used in conjunction with an internet website devoted to the same subject. In 2002 Philip Dray and Christopher Waldrep added chronological narrative-based studies. Two years later Dora Apel, Jonathan Markowitz and Michael J. Pfeifer contributed works that focused on the imagery, legacy and cross-regional comparisons of the crime.[49]

These developments notwithstanding, in the first years of the twenty-first century important questions about lynching were still left unanswered. Almost all research had been concentrated on lynch mobs that achieved their objective. Little investigation has been carried out on unsuccessful lynchings. There was thus insufficient understanding of how and why state law enforcement officers were able to prevent lynchings in some instances and not others. Equally, it remained unclear why some blacks became lynch victims whereas others, in seemingly similar circumstances, did not.

The spate of research on lynching during the 1980s and 1990s was accompanied by new scholarly studies on the related subject of the treatment afforded to African Americans within the southern legal system in the late nineteenth century and early twentieth century. Sadly, if not unexpectedly, such works demonstrated that southern courts and penal institutions of the period were often only marginally better than vigilante lynch mobs in adhering to even the most basic requirements of natural justice.

Looking at Kentucky, a border state with, by southern standards, no record of racial extremism, historian George C. Wright calculated that at least 229 lawful executions were carried out by the state between 1872 and 1940. African Americans accounted for 10 per cent of the state's population but comprised 57 per cent of those executed. It was not unusual for the process of trial, sentencing and execution to be carried out in a matter of hours. In one 1906 case these were all accomplished within just sixty-two minutes. In some instances judges even dissuaded lynch mobs by the promise that retribution would be as swift, if not quicker, through the courts. To avoid unnecessary delay scaffolds were sometimes constructed outside a courthouse before the trial had even began.[50]

The fate of southern blacks convicted of lesser crimes in the courts could be equally appalling, albeit in a different way. In the 1880s the leasing of convict labour, especially in mining, became widespread throughout the South. By 1890 some 27,000 convicts in the region, most particularly in Alabama, Georgia, Florida and Tennessee, were put to work in this manner. Ninety per cent of these were African Americans. Petty theft and other minor misdemeanours, in cases involving black defendants, were often punished by sentences of months, if not years, of hard labour on a chain gang.

More than just the reintroduction of slavery by other means, chain gangs provided southern states with a captive labour force for capitalist industrial development within the region. Prisoners could be put to work clearing dangerous swamps or in primitive, hazardous mines in conditions that free workers would not tolerate. 'Convict labor', as Edward Ayers has observed, 'depended upon both the heritage of slavery and the allure of industrial capitalism'. The attitude of state authorities to the health and well-being of convicts was aptly summed up in the title of the most authoritative overview of convict leasing in the South by Matthew Mancini, *One Dies, Get Another*. In *Worse Than Slavery: Parchman Farm and the Ordeal of Jim Crow Justice* (1996) and *Black Prisoners and Their World* (2000), historians David M. Oshinsky and Mary Ellen Curtin provided excellent, though depressing, regional studies of the penal system in Mississippi and Alabama respectively.[51]

Such works on the day-to-day existence of black convicts reflected a broader development in African American historiography of the late 1980s and the 1990s, which saw historians manifest a greater interest in the daily experiences of ordinary black communities in the South. In keeping with this trend Andrew Manis studied working-class African Americans in Birmingham, Alabama during the 1950s and 1960s, while Robin D. G. Kelley looked at the everyday life of southern blacks in the 1930s. In two other outstanding groundbreaking studies, *Dark*

Journey (1989) and *Trouble in Mind* (1998), historians Neil R. McMillen and Leon Litwack rendered a similar service for turn-of-the-century black communities, respectively examining Mississippi in particular and the South as a whole.[52]

In the case of Litwack, however, this work was less the indication of a new departure than the culmination of almost lifelong interest in the field. Born in 1929 to liberal Jewish parents, Litwack was raised in Santa Barbara, California, and even in high school demonstrated a fascination with African American literature and the Blues. A radical student activist at the University of California in the 1960s, his principal work as a historian prior to *Trouble in Mind* included seminal studies on segregation in the northern states between 1830 and 1860 and the experiences of southern blacks during the Civil War and Reconstruction Era, 1861–77.[53]

Research on women also proceeded apace. In addition to the work of Dowd Hall and Gilmore, historians Linda O. McMurry and Patricia Schecter provided new biographical studies on Ida B. Wells. The National Association of Colored Women (NACW), an organization co-founded by Wells in 1896 to promote self-help in African American communities, also began to attract serious academic attention. Diverse scholars such as Stephanie J. Shaw, Deborah Gray White and Floris Barnett Cash highlighted the work of the Association as a pioneering form of civil rights activity in the early twentieth century.[54] The fact that the NACW was run by women made it more effective by making it appear less threatening to contemporary southern whites. Unfortunately, this same consideration also contributed to its being all but ignored by historians prior to the 1990s, and at the start of the new millennium there was still no definitive full-length academic study on the history of the NACW. In what is a recurring theme in historiography, research of the 1990s was thus as significant in highlighting new areas requiring further investigation as it was in providing deeper understanding to existing debates.

Notes

1 Glenda Elizabeth Gilmore, *Gender and Jim Crow: Women and the Politics of White Supremacy in North Carolina, 1896–1920* (Chapel Hill, North Carolina, 1996), p. 225.

2 Booker T. Washington, *The Story of My Life and Work* (New York, 1900); Booker T. Washington, *Up From Slavery* (New York, 1901). A more detailed account of these two works can be found in Kevern Verney, *The Art of the Possible: Booker T. Washington and Black Leadership in the United States, 1881–1925* (New York, 2001), pp. 127–42.

3 W. E. B. Du Bois, 'Of Mr. Booker T. Washington and Others', in W. E. B. Du Bois, *The Souls of Black Folk* (New York, 1903).

4 Max Bennett Thrasher, *Tuskegee: Its Story and Its Work* (New York, 1901); Emmett J. Scott and Lyman Beecher, *Booker T. Washington: Builder of a Civilization* (London, 1916).

5 Adam Fairclough, *Better Day Coming: Blacks and Equality, 1890–2000* (New York, 2001), p. 24.

6 Ida B. Wells, *Southern Horrors: Lynch Law in All Its Phases* (New York, 1892); Ida B. Wells, *A Red Record: Tabulated Statistics and Alleged Causes of Lynchings in the United States, 1892–1894* (Chicago, 1895).

7 Fairclough, *Better Day Coming*, pp. 31–3.

8 Walter White, *Rope and Faggot: A Biography of Judge Lynch* (New York, 1929).

9 White, *Rope and Faggot*, pp. 57–9, 61.

10 Arthur Raper, *The Tragedy of Lynching* (Chapel Hill, North Carolina, 1933).

11 William Fitzhugh Brundage, *Lynching in the New South: Georgia and Virginia, 1880–1930* (Urbana, Illinois, 1993), p. 11.

12 John Dollard, *Caste and Class in a Small Southern Town* (New Haven, 1937); John Dollard, *Frustration and Aggression* (New Haven, 1939).

13 C. Vann Woodward, *The Strange Career of Jim Crow* (New York, 1955).

14 C. Vann Woodward, *Origins of the New South, 1877–1913* (Baton Rouge, Louisiana, 1951).

15 August Meier and Elliott Rudwick, *Black History and the Historical Profession, 1915–1980* (Urbana, Illinois, 1986), pp. 111–12; Lawrence N. Powell et al., 'C. Vann Woodward, 1908–1999: In Memoriam', *Journal of Southern History* (66, 2000), pp. 208–9; William Palmer, *Engagement With the Past: The Lives and Works of the World War II Generation of Historians* (Lexington, Kentucky, 2001), pp. 14, 40–1.

16 Powell et al., 'C. Vann Woodward', pp. 209, 212; Palmer, *Engagement With the Past*, p. 106; Joel Williamson, 'Wounds Not Scars: Lynching, the National Conscience and the American Historian', *Journal of American History* (83, 1997), p. 1230.

17 C. Vann Woodward, *The Strange Career of Jim Crow*, revised 3rd edn (New York, 1974), p. 12.

18 Powell et al., 'C. Vann Woodward', p. 211; Meier and Rudwick, *Black History and the Historical Profession*, p. 168.

19 Joel Williamson, *After Slavery: The Negro in South Carolina During Reconstruction, 1861–1877* (Chapel Hill, North Carolina, 1965), pp. 274–99; Williamson, 'Wounds Not Scars', p. 1233; Vernon Lane Wharton, *The Negro in Mississippi, 1865–1890* (Chapel Hill, North Carolina, 1947).

20 Joel Williamson (ed.), *The Origins of Segregation* (Boston, 1968).

21 Barton J. Bernstein, '*Plessy v. Ferguson*: Conservative Sociological Jurisprudence', *Journal of Negro History* (48, 1963); I. A. Newby, *Jim Crow's Defense: Anti-Negro Thought in America, 1900–1930* (Baton Rouge,

Louisiana, 1965), pp. 50–1; August Meier and Elliott Rudwick, 'The Boycott Movement Against Jim Crow Street Cars in the South, 1900–1916', *Journal of American History* (55, 1969).

22 V. O. Key, *Southern Politics in State and Nation* (New York, 1949).

23 Jack Abramovitz, 'The Negro in the Populist Movement', *Journal of Negro History* (38, 1953); William H. Chafe, 'The Negro and Populism: A Kansas Case Study', *Journal of Southern History* (34, 1968).

24 Basil Matthews, *Booker T. Washington: Educator and Inter-Racial Interpreter* (Cambridge, Massachusetts, 1949); Samuel J. Spencer, *Booker T. Washington and the Negro's Place in American Life* (Boston, 1956); Meier and Rudwick, *Black History and the Historical Profession*, fn. p. 149.

25 August Meier, *Negro Thought in America, 1880–1915* (Ann Arbor, Michigan, 1963).

26 Emma Lou Thornbrough, *T. Thomas Fortune: Militant Journalist* (Chicago, 1972); Stephen R. Fox, *The Guardian of Boston: William Monroe Trotter* (New York, 1970).

27 Meier and Rudwick, *Black History and the Historical Profession*, pp. 149–50; Wilson J. Moses, 'Emma Lou Thornbrough's Place in American Historiography', *Indiana Magazine of History* (91, 1995).

28 Louis R. Harlan, *All At Sea: Coming of Age in World War II* (Urbana, Illinois, 1996), pp. 15, 26; Meier and Rudwick, *Black History and the Historical Profession*, pp. 148–9.

29 Louis R. Harlan, *Booker T. Washington: The Making of a Black Leader, 1856–1901* (Oxford, 1972); Louis R. Harlan, *Booker T. Washington: The Wizard of Tuskegee, 1901–1915* (New York, 1983); Raymond W. Smock (ed.), *Booker T. Washington in Perspective: Essays of Louis R. Harlan* (Jackson, Mississippi, 1988); Louis R. Harlan et al. (eds), *The Booker T. Washington Papers*, 14 vols (Urbana, Illinois, 1972–89).

30 Virginia Lantz Denton, *Booker T. Washington and the Adult Education Movement* (Gainesville, Florida, 1993), p. 165; Fairclough, *Better Day Coming*, p. 60.

31 Joseph D. Reid, 'Sharecropping as an Understandable Market Response: The Post-Bellum South', *Journal of Economic History* (33, 1973); Roger L. Ransom and Richard Sutch, *One Kind of Freedom: The Economic Consequences of Emancipation* (Cambridge, 1977); Jay R. Mandle, *The Roots of Black Poverty: The Southern Plantation Economy After the Civil War* (Durham, North Carolina, 1978); Daniel A. Novak, *The Wheel of Servitude: Black Forced Labor After Slavery* (Lexington, Kentucky, 1978); Peter Daniel, *The Shadow of Slavery: Peonage in the South, 1901–1969* (Urbana, Illinois, 1990).

32 Joel Williamson, *The Crucible of Race: Black-White Relations in the American South Since Emancipation* (New York, 1984). An abridged version of this work was published as Joel Williamson, *Rage For Order: Black-White Relations in the American South Since Emancipation* (New York, 1986).

33 Howard N. Rabinowitz, *Race Relations in the Urban South, 1865–1890* (New York, 1978).

34 John William Graves, 'Jim Crow in Arkansas: A Reconsideration of Urban Race Relations in the Post-Reconstruction South', *Journal of Southern History* (55, 1989); John William Graves, *Town and Country: Race Relations*

in an Urban-Rural Context, Arkansas, 1865–1905 (Fayetteville, Arkansas, 1990).

35 Edward L. Ayers, *The Promise of the New South: Life After Reconstruction* (New York, 1992), pp. 136–45.

36 Grace Elizabeth Hale, *Making Whiteness: The Culture of Segregation in the South, 1890–1940* (New York, 1998), pp. 9, 21.

37 Charles A. Lofgren, *The Plessy Case: A Legal-Historical Interpretation* (New York, 1987); John Cell, *The Highest Stages of White Supremacy: The Origins of Segregation in South Africa and the American South* (Cambridge, 1982); George M. Frederickson, *White Supremacy: A Comparative Study in American and South African History* (New York, 1981); George M. Frederickson, *Black Liberation: A Comparative History of Black Ideologies in the United States and South Africa* (New York, 1995); Meier and Rudwick, *Black History and the Historical Profession*, p. 189.

38 Frederickson, *Black Liberation*, p. 5.

39 J. Morgan Kousser, *The Shaping of Southern Politics: Suffrage Restriction and the Establishment of the One-Party South, 1880–1910* (New Haven, 1974).

40 Michael Perman, *Struggle for Mastery: Disfranchisement in the South, 1888–1908* (Chapel Hill, North Carolina, 2001), p. 5.

41 Gerald H. Gaither, *Blacks and the Populist Revolt: Ballots and Bigotry in the New South* (Alabama, 1977); Gregg Cantrell and D. Scott Barton, 'Texas Populists and the Failure of Biracial Politics', *Journal of Southern History* (55, 1989).

42 Chafe, 'The Negro and Populism', pp. 402–19.

43 Perman, *Struggle for Mastery*, pp. 5–6, 324–5.

44 Alfreda M. Duster (ed.), *Crusade for Justice: The Autobiography of Ida B. Wells* (Chicago, 1970); Jacquelyn Dowd Hall, *Revolt Against Chivalry: Jessie Daniel Ames and the Women's Campaign Against Lynching* (New York, 1979), p. 137.

45 Hall, *Revolt Against Chivalry*, p. 156.

46 Gilmore, *Gender and Jim Crow*, pp. xx, 96.

47 Williamson, *Crucible of Race*, pp. 306–9.

48 Ayers, *Promise of the New South*, pp. 156–7; Brundage, *Lynching in the New South*, p. 81.

49 Dominic J. Capeci, *The Lynching of Cleo Wright* (Lexington, Kentucky, 1998); Nancy MacLean, 'The Leo Frank Case Reconsidered: Gender and Sexual Politics in the Making of Reactionary Populism', *Journal of American History* (77, 1991); other versions of this article can be found in William Fitzhugh Brundage (ed.), *Under Sentence of Death: Lynching in the South* (Chapel Hill, North Carolina, 1997), pp. 158–88, and Jane Dailey, Glenda Elizabeth Gilmore and Bryant Simon (eds), *Jumpin' Jim Crow: Southern Politics From Civil War to Civil Rights* (Princeton, New Jersey, 2000), pp. 183–218; James R. McGovern, *Anatomy of a Lynching: The Killing of Claude Neal* (Baton Rouge, Louisiana, 1982); Howard Smead, *Blood Justice: The Lynching of Mack Charles Parker* (New York, 1986); Stewart E. Tolney and E. M. Beck, *A Festival of Violence: An Analysis of Southern Lynchings, 1882–1930* (Urbana, Illinois, 1995); James Allen, *Without Sanctuary: Lynching Photography in America* (Santa Fe, 2000); Philip Dray, *At the Hands of Persons Unknown: The Lynching of Black America* (New York,

2002); Christopher Waldrep, *The Many Faces of Judge Lynch: Extralegal Violence and Punishment in America* (London, 2002); Dora Apel, *Imagery of Lynching: Black Men, White Women, and the Mob* (Piscataway, New Jersey, 2004); Jonathan Markowitz, *Legacies of Lynching: Racial Violence and Memory* (Minneapolis, Minnesota, 2004); Michael J. Pfeifer, *Rough Justice: Lynching and American Society, 1874–1947* (Urbana, Illinois, 2004).

50 George C. Wright, 'By the Book: The Legal Executions of Kentucky Blacks', in Brundage, *Under Sentence of Death*, pp. 252–3, 256–7; George C. Wright, *Racial Violence in Kentucky, 1865–1940: Lynchings, Mob Rule and Legal Lynchings* (Baton Rouge, Louisiana, 1990).

51 Edward L. Ayers, *Vengeance and Justice: Crime and Punishment in the Nineteenth Century American South* (New York, 1984), p. 192; Matthew J. Mancini, *One Dies, Get Another: Convict Leasing in the American South, 1866–1928* (Columbia, South Carolina, 1996); David M. Oshinsky, *Worse Than Slavery: Parchman Farm and the Ordeal of Jim Crow Justice* (New York, 1996) and Mary Ellen Curtin, *Black Prisoners and Their World, Alabama, 1865–1900* (Richmond, Virginia, 2000).

52 Andrew M. Manis, *A Fire You Can't Put Out: The Civil Rights Life of Birmingham's Reverend Fred Shuttlesworth* (Tuscaloosa, Alabama, 1999); Robin D. G. Kelley, ' "We Are Not What We Seem": Rethinking Black Working Class Opposition in the Jim Crow South', *Journal of American History* (80, 1993); Leon Litwack, *Trouble in Mind: Black Southerners in the Age of Jim Crow* (New York, 1998); Neil R. McMillen, *Dark Journey: Black Mississippians in the Age of Jim Crow* (Urbana, Illinois, 1989).

53 Meier and Rudwick, *Black History and the Historical Profession*, p. 143; Leon Litwack, *North of Slavery* (Chicago, 1961); Leon Litwack, *Been in the Storm So Long* (New York, 1980).

54 Linda O. McMurry, *To Keep the Waters Troubled: The Life of Ida B. Wells* (New York, 1998); Patricia Schecter, *Ida B. Wells-Barnett and American Reform* (Chapel Hill, North Carolina, 2001); Stephanie J. Shaw, 'Black Club Women and the Creation of the National Association of Colored Women', in Darlene Clark Hine, Wilma King and Linda Reed (eds), *We Specialize in the Impossible: A Reader in Black Women's History* (New York, 1995); Deborah Gray White, *Too Heavy a Load: Black Women in Defense of Themselves, 1894–1994* (New York, 1999), pp. 70–6; Floris Barnett Cash, *African American Women and Social Action: The Clubwomen and Volunteerism from Jim Crow to the New Deal, 1896–1936* (Westport, Connecticut, 2001).

2

The Great Migration and the 'New Negro', 1915–1930

Before the 1950s mainstream scholars typically showed little interest in African American history. However, as with most general observations, there were some exceptions to the rule. This was particularly the case when incidents and events involving African Americans for some reason engaged the interest of the American public as a whole. Academic studies published on lynching during the 1920s and 1930s thus reflected heightened public awareness of the crime in these decades as a result of both the gruesome and sensationalist accounts of lynchings that periodically appeared in the press and the NAACP's long-term campaign to secure the passage of a federal anti-lynching law.[1]

An even greater concern was the unprecedented growth of the Ku Klux Klan in the 1920s with the 'Invisible Empire', as it was known, acquiring some five million members by the early 1920s and a powerful network of branches, or Klaverns, in many northern and western states as well as the South. The most notable early manifestation of scholarly interest in this phenomenon came with the 1924 publication of *The Ku Klux Klan: A Study of the American Mind* by sociologist John Moffatt Mecklin. In a key work Mecklin advanced what for the next fifty years became the standard scholarly explanation for the rise of the 1920s Klan. The organization's success, he argued, lay in its appeal to a range of common prejudices that included not just its traditional antipathy to African Americans but also anti-Catholicism, anti-Semitism and xenophobia. The particular bigotries stressed by individual Klaverns reflected local anxieties.

These ranged from fears over immigration in the North to Protestant fundamentalist distrust of other faiths and denominations in the West and black–white racial tensions in the South.[2]

The 'Great Migration' of 1915–25, during which some 1.25 million blacks left the South to settle in major urban centres of the North like New York and Chicago, was another issue that attracted the attention of white Americans. In the South, planters feared that they would be left with insufficient labourers to farm their lands. In the North, industrialists may have welcomed the migrants, as a vital addition to the expanding factory workforce, but ordinary city dwellers were shocked at the sudden growth in urban black populations, prompting heightened racial tensions and increased discrimination and segregation.

W. E. B. Du Bois provided one of the first serious academic studies on black migrants in *The Philadelphia Negro* (1899), a work that serves as a timely reminder that a black population drift to the cities was taking place well before the Great Migration years, if not on such an epic scale. A multi-talented scholar, Du Bois chose to approach the subject from a sociological, rather than a historical, perspective.[3] Moreover, he viewed Philadelphia's black community in largely 'pathological' terms, focusing on the social problems that the newcomers experienced. In part Du Bois emphasized the damaging aspects of city life as a means of countering suggestions by conservative sociologists and anthropologists that African Americans were innately inferior to whites and thus were personally responsible for any disadvantages they experienced in their daily lives. However, in emphasizing their discouraging surroundings he unwittingly contributed to the portrayal of 'black urban life as a world warped by prejudice and disoriented by the impact of urbanization'.[4]

These characteristics were also typical of the first studies on the Great Migration that appeared at the end of the First World War through to the 1930s. In 1918 the father of black history, Carter G. Woodson, published *A Century of Negro Migration*, and in 1919–20 Booker T. Washington's former personal assistant, Emmett J. Scott, published collected letters of black migrants and *Negro Migration During the War*. However, most authors on the migration, such as Thomas J. Woofter, Charles S. Johnson, Louise V. Kennedy, Edward E. Lewis, Clyde V. Kiser and E. Franklin Frazier, were sociologists and anthropologists rather than historians.[5]

Indeed, as the modern urban historian Kenneth L. Kusmer has observed, the subject of black city life 'can scarcely be said to have existed prior to the mid-1960s' as 'a topic of historical research'. In fact, before the publication of Arthur Schlesinger Sr's important study *The Rise of the City, 1878–1898* in 1933, the American historical profession showed little interest in urban history at all.[6] In part this was because the thinking of historians in the early decades of the twentieth century was still dominated by the enormously influential Turner thesis. Researching the history of the West in the 1890s, historian Frederick Jackson Turner had concluded that it was the frontier experience of the nineteenth century, rather than industrialization or urbanization that had been the primary force in shaping American culture and history.[7] One consequence of this preoccupation was that early studies on the black migration were generally lacking in historical perspective. Admittedly, scholars in the field usually took care to place the migration in a larger historical context, but such discussion almost invariably took the form of a 'brief backdrop' rather than sustained analysis integrated into the main body of the text. Black migration as a long-term historical process thus received little attention.[8]

Similarly, early studies of black migration were generally pathological in tone. This tendency was most powerfully expressed in E. Franklin Frazier's *The Negro Family in Chicago* (1932) and *The Negro Family in the United States* (1939). A black sociologist, Frazier, evoked a depressing picture of black family life disintegrating under the pressures of urban environments. In retrospect, such conclusions appear unduly negative and overstated. They are also indicative of other shortcomings in the first scholarly works on the migration. Specifically, pioneering researchers in the field tended to concentrate too much on conditions in the North rather than the southern communities the migrants left behind. Moreover, the environments in the largest and best-known black ghetto neighbourhoods, such as Harlem in New York and the South Side in Chicago, were assumed to be typical of black urban life, ignoring the considerable diversity of experience in individual cities.[9] In reality, Chicago, as a centre of the meatpacking industry and a gateway to the West, had its own distinctive history and social and economic character that was different from that of Detroit, centre for the rapidly developing automobile industry, or Pittsburgh, famed for its steel production.

Other than migration studies, the most important works on the African American experience in the inter-war years took the form of autobiographical publications. In the absence of any significant interest from professional scholars or biographers, black and white civil rights activists chronicled their own life experiences and contributions to the black freedom struggle. In *The Walls Came Tumbling Down* (1947) Mary White Ovington reflected on her work as a founder member of the National Association for the Advancement of Colored People (NAACP) in 1909 and leading officeholder within the Association for almost forty years. The NAACP's first black Executive Secretary, James Weldon Johnson, published his autobiographical reminiscences in *Along This Way* (1933), as did his successor, Walter White, in *A Man Called White* (1949). Never one to underestimate the importance of his place in history, W. E. B. Du Bois recounted his life experiences in *Darkwater* (1920) and *Dusk of Dawn* (1940).[10]

Collectively, these accounts were informative in providing insider insights into the NAACP and in highlighting the Association's achievements and the adverse conditions in which it was forced to operate. Their principal shortcomings were those of most autobiographies. They described events from the viewpoint of individuals rather than providing a holistic perspective, and, either consciously or unconsciously, tended to magnify the role played by the author in question. Penned by NAACP spokespersons, they also revealed little about weaknesses and divisions within the Association. These several failings were most pronounced in the autobiography of Walter White, which reads more like an apologia for the NAACP and White himself, though not necessarily in that order, than an accurate and honest collection of reminiscences.

By the 1950s and 1960s burgeoning scholarly interest in black history, stimulated by the rise of Martin Luther King and the post-war Civil Rights Movement, was reflected in a number of new works on black leaders of the inter-war period. In *Black*

Moses (1955), historian E. David Cronon provided one of the first serious full-length academic studies of the Black Nationalist leader of the 1920s Marcus Garvey. Cronon's generally negative perceptions of Garvey and his UNIA movement were encouraged by a number of factors. In the first instance the Jamaican's belief in racial separatism appeared pessimistic and misguided in the light of the optimistic integrationist philosophy of the emerging Civil Rights Movement of the 1950s. Moreover, Cronon was also influenced by the still fresh memories of the Second World War. He perceived Garvey's Universal Negro Improvement Association (UNIA) as a dangerous extremist right-wing organization akin to the fascist movements that had emerged in Europe during the inter-war period. This view was reinforced by the fact that in the 1930s, a time when many people in Britain and the United States had sympathetic attitudes towards fascism, Garvey himself claimed that he and the UNIA were the first fascists and that Mussolini had copied his ideas.[11]

In 1959 Francis Broderick's *W. E. B. Du Bois: Negro Leader in Time of Crisis* achieved the distinction of being 'the first scholarly biography' of the eminent African American scholar and civil rights activist. This privileged monopoly position was ended the following year with the publication of Elliott Rudwick's *W. E. B. Du Bois: A Study in Minority Group Leadership*. These monographs were doubly significant in that they were not only groundbreaking works in their field but the two authors were part of a new generation of historians whose early formative life experiences had been shaped by the liberal New Deal reformism of the 1930s and the Second World War. Born in 1922, Broderick was an Irish American Catholic who came from a family of ardent New Deal supporters in New York. Rudwick, born in 1927, was 'raised in a New Deal-oriented non-ideological working class Philadelphia family'. Serving in the navy during the war, he was disturbed at the unequal segregated treatment afforded to African American conscripts.[12]

By the 1960s studies also began to appear on the NAACP. In *Caucasians Only* (1967) Clement E. Vose examined one of the Association's earliest breakthroughs in its courtroom struggles against state laws and city ordinances that sought to enforce residential segregation. The same year Charles Flint Kellogg took a broader perspective, providing the standard academic history of the NAACP during the first decade of its existence.[13]

Kellogg, born in 1909, was of an older generation than Broderick and Rudwick. His work on the NAACP was linked to his deeply religious family background and missionary-oriented concern for the welfare and education of non-white races. An ordained Episcopal minister, Kellogg even worked for a time as a missionary teacher in China. His scholarly interest in the NAACP was also prompted by experiences closer to home. He was raised in the small town of Great Barrington, Massachusetts, the birthplace of Du Bois and where, in the 1920s and 1930s, Du Bois still retained a vacation home. During Kellogg's childhood years, visits by leading NAACP officials were commonplace in Great Barrington and a recurring source of local interest.[14]

Du Bois himself provided new insights on the NAACP in the last of his three autobiographies, which was not published in the West until five years after his death.[15] This work was more controversial than his earlier recollections of his life and in it he highlighted personality clashes and rivalries in the NAACP during the late 1920s and early 1930s, principally between Walter White and other leading NAACP officeholders, especially Du Bois himself. This candour can be attributed to a number of factors. Writing in his nineties and aware of his impending mortality, Du Bois was doubtless keen to document for posterity the story of his turbulent relationship with the NAACP from his point of view. The events in question were of the distant past and thus would have no obvious harmful impact on the present-day work of the Association. Moreover, most of the individual NAACP officeholders described by Du Bois, including Walter White, were long since deceased and thus no longer vulnerable to hurt feelings, and, perhaps more to the point, unable to exercise the right of reply.

Another important development of the 1960s and early 1970s was the appearance of fresh studies on the Great Migration. In contrast to earlier accounts, many of the new works were written by historians.[16] In part this was because the American historical profession now attached greater importance to the study of the nation's urban past. Generational change was another factor. The historian Gilbert Osofsky, author of a leading

1966 study on Harlem, was born in 1935. His politically left-wing Jewish family background gave him 'an intellectual fascination with anti-Semitism and other kinds of oppression against minority groups'. Allan Spear, who published a similar study on black Chicago the following year, was born in 1937. He had personal experience of 'dual marginality', being both Jewish and gay, which gave him empathy for those 'outside the mainstream' and led him to become an active participant in the black civil rights struggle at university.[17]

At the same time it was more than just personal or family background that attracted scholars to the study of black urban history. Growing awareness of the problems of the nation's inner cities combined with recurring ghetto race riots meant that research in the field had obvious contemporary relevance. This consideration also helped shape the analytical framework adopted by researchers. On the positive side, the new studies generally benefited from deeper historical awareness. Historians like Osofsky and Spear thus placed the exodus from the South between 1915 and 1925 in the context of rising levels of black migration in the decades preceding the First World War. Similarly, scholars sought to better understand the dynamics of ghetto formation, examining how housing patterns together with discriminatory racial practices led to the development of racially segregated communities in northern cities.[18]

Although generally written from a well-intentioned, liberal perspective, the disadvantage of this approach was that it tended to portray black migrants as 'passive objects of external forces beyond their control'. It also paid insufficient attention to the impact of the Great Migration on black class structure and the development of urban working-class black consciousness.[19] This was despite the fact that one of the most notable developments in many fields of historical research during the 1960s was the rise of the 'new social history', looking at the past from the 'bottom up', from the perspective of the most disadvantaged groups in society. Before the 1980s the consideration of class structures within black society generally received limited attention in the study of African American history.

The rapid growth of the Black Power Movement during the late 1960s and early 1970s contributed to a number of significant historiographical developments. The Black Nationalist philosophy espoused by some militant African American spokespersons encouraged fresh interest in Marcus Garvey's UNIA organization of the 1920s. Amy Jacques Garvey, former wife of the Jamaican leader, published selections of his speeches and ideas. Historians E. David Cronon and John H. Clarke edited collections of selected writings by admirers and opponents of Garvey. Most significant of all, fellow historians Theodore Vincent and Tony Martin contributed two new full-length scholarly monographs on Garvey and the UNIA.[20] In contrast to Cronon's earlier 1955 biography, they were both clearly sympathetic to the Jamaican, viewing him not as a forerunner of fascism but as a visionary race leader committed to the Black Power objectives of racial pride, self-help and Third World decolonization. Painfully aware of the strong-arm tactics used against Black Power radicals by political authorities and law enforcement agencies, they argued that Garvey's downfall was more the result of persecution by US and colonial authorities than any internal weaknesses within the UNIA or shortcomings in Garvey's philosophy.

The emphasis on cultural awareness and achievement during the Black Power era highlighted the fact that African American cultural history remained a largely neglected area of twentieth-century black history. African American historian Nathan Huggins began the process of remedying this omission in *Harlem Renaissance* (1971), a study of the black literary and artistic cultural flowering of the 1920s centred on New York. Fellow African American scholar David Levering Lewis followed up this line of investigation in a later groundbreaking study *When Harlem Was in Vogue* (1981).[21]

Lewis's career affords useful insights into the factors that shape historiographical advances. Born in 1936 and initially trained as a Europeanist, he was drawn to the field of African American history by chance when approached by Penguin Books in the late 1960s to write a biography of Martin Luther King. Having completed this project, he was stuck by the paucity of published scholarly work on the Harlem Renaissance, prompting *When Harlem Was in Vogue*. Although he never abandoned his earlier interest in Europe, thereafter he became best known for his publications on African American history.[22]

By the late 1970s the Black Power Movement had suffered a decline in popularity. Despite this the Harlem Renaissance became an increasingly attractive topic for researchers in the decades that followed. This development reflected the fact that by the 1980s and 1990s cultural history had become a major subject of interest for scholars across a wide range of fields. Moreover, the pioneering works of Huggins and Lewis acted as a catalyst for subsequent debate which acquired a self-sustaining momentum.

Although Huggins and Lewis demonstrated an obvious enthusiasm for their subject, both scholars had come to the reluctant conclusion that the Renaissance was ultimately unsuccessful in achieving its highest aspirations. Specifically, leading lights of the Renaissance, like Langston Hughes, Claude McKay, Jean Toomer and Zora Neale Hurston, had hoped that their work would inspire racial pride and solidarity among African Americans as a whole. At the same time, faced with such irrefutable evidence of black cultural creativity, white Americans would be forced to confront their racial prejudices, leading to more equal treatment for African Americans in US society.

By the onset of the Great Depression at the end of the 1920s it had become clear that these far-reaching objectives had not been realized. In an influential 1937 article the African American scholar and leading inspiration of the Renaissance, Alain Locke, famously recorded what appeared to be a virtual obituary for the movement. 'Eleven brief years ago Harlem was full of the thrill and ferment of sudden progress and prosperity', he reflected, but now 'with the same Harlem prostrate in the grip of the depression and throes of social unrest, we confront the sobering facts of a serious relapse and premature setback, indeed, find it hard to believe that the rosy enthusiasm and hopes of 1925 were more than the bright illusions of a cruelly deceptive mirage.' The sad truth was that ultimately there was 'no cure or saving magic in poetry and art, an emerging generation of talent, or international prestige and inter-racial recognition, for unemployment or precarious marginal employment'.[23]

Huggins and Lewis broadly agreed with this gloomy prognosis. Others did not. In 1987 black cultural historian Houston Baker robustly challenged their perception of the Renaissance in an important extended essay, *Modernism and the Harlem*

Renaissance.[24] Baker argued that to see the Renaissance as a failure was an unjust and highly subjective concept. In their life and work Renaissance artists had successfully affirmed their creativity and humanity to the full within the constraints of a racist society. In doing so they kept alive a longstanding African American tradition that could be traced back to the rich and diverse culture developed by black slaves before the Civil War as a means of maintaining their pride and self-identity.

Baker's thesis, though not commanding universal acceptance, had a significant impact on the analytical framework of subsequent debate. In perhaps the most insightful study of the Renaissance of the 1990s, historian George Hutchinson questioned the thinking of both the revisionist Baker and more traditional studies. Implicitly rebuking the former for being overly ideological in approach, he argued that Renaissance artists 'by and large, were not tricksters, guerrilla warriors, assimilationists, or dupes in their dealings with white intellectuals'. At the same time, it was 'hard to know how to respond' to earlier critiques that sought to evaluate the 'success of an artistic movement' by 'its effectiveness in ending centuries of oppression'.[25]

Seeking a 'recovery of historical complexity', Hutchinson also rebutted other commonly held perceptions of the Renaissance, namely that white patrons steered the direction of the movement towards 'the primitive and exotic', and that the onset of the Great Depression in 1929 killed off the Renaissance, as patronizing white benefactors 'suddenly lost all interest in the vogue'. On the contrary, black writers of the 1920s continued to publish during the Depression but, in common with other American authors, adopted new themes in their work reflecting the changed social conditions. 'The thirties witnessed a turn away from stress on race in favor of class and a critique of capitalism – all in the form of a sharper-edged social radicalism.'[26]

Adopting an alternative line of enquiry, music historians Samuel A. Floyd and Jon Michael Spencer drew attention to a hitherto neglected aspect of the Renaissance, challenging the general perception of it as a predominantly literary movement. Spencer in particular argued that the work of black Renaissance composers like Henry Burleigh (1866–1949) and William Grant Still (1895–1978) deserved greater recognition. Moreover, their work constituted not a temporary achievement, but a lasting breakthrough that made it easier for subsequent generations of African American composers to pursue their careers without being stigmatized as race artists. In respect to music, the traditional view of the Renaissance as a failure was thus misconceived.[27]

Scholarly research on the Great Migration also went in different directions from the 1970s onwards. Historians like Peter Gottlieb, James R. Grossman, Kenneth Kusmer, Joe William Trotter, Richard Thomas and Kimberley Phillips explored the relationship between the migration and the emergence of an urban black working class and placed more emphasis on the active role of migrants themselves in the migratory process.[28] Whereas studies of the 1960s and earlier 1970s had concluded that the migrants who participated in the exodus from the South had generally experienced a modest but significant improvement in their quality of life in their new homes, later researchers were inclined to be less optimistic.

Writing in decades when evidence of seemingly intractable problems of crime and social deprivation were all too apparent in America's urban black ghettos, scholars of the 1980s and 1990s were, perhaps, inclined to take a more gloomy view of the prospects of black city dwellers of an earlier generation. In respect to Pittsburgh, Peter Gottlieb concluded that the aspirations of black migrants to 'improve their economic status in the short-term' and 'secure permanent access to the mainstream of advancing northern industrial labor' had been 'dashed' as soon 'as the mid-1920s, if not earlier'.[29] In Detroit historian Richard Thomas reflected that 'the average black factory worker must have wondered whether the trip north was worth the train ticket', as, although migrants 'earned more money', the 'higher rents ate most of it up'. Moreover, the 'harsh foreman probably had much in common with southern plantation overseers. Both concerned themselves only with the productivity of black labor and cared little for black workers as human beings.'[30]

In two important general overviews of the migration, *Black Migration, Movement North, 1900–1920* (1976) and *Farewell – We're Good and Gone: The Great Black Migration* (1989), historians Florette Henri and Carole Marks respectively reached similarly depressing conclusions.[31] The commendable scholarship of Henri and Marks excepted, much of the best work on the experience of black migrants in the North published during the 1980s and 1990s took the form of detailed studies of individual cities, often over short chronological terms. This trend made it difficult for scholars to enter into a holistic analysis of the migration because, as already been noted, different cities had strong individual characteristics. Lamenting the lack of more broad-based research, leading urban historian Kenneth L. Kusmer thus urged his fellow scholars to 'resist the tendency to focus on too narrow a time period or subject matter' and recognize the 'need to begin to compare and contrast blacks in a variety of cities in a more systematic way'. In a welcome contribution of a different kind, 1974 and 1982 studies by Nancy J. Weiss and Jesse Thomas Moore respectively provided the first detailed scholarly histories of the National Urban League (NUL). Created in 1910–11 from two earlier groups, the National League for the Protection of Colored Women and the Committee for Improving the Industrial Conditions of Negroes in New York, the NUL concentrated on promoting practical economic self-help, most particularly in the rapidly expanding black urban ghettos of the North. [32]

A number of studies focused on the particular experience of West Indian immigrants to the United States, examining their relationship with existing black urban communities and recent southern migrants. Historians Patrick Renshaw and David J. Hellwig highlighted the justified reputation of West Indian settlers for success in business and ethnic and family solidarity, factors that made them both a source of resentment and admiration for native black Americans.[33] Academic researchers manifested a similar ambivalence in outlook. In a controversial 1984 publication, *The Crisis of the Negro Intellectual*, black historian Harold Cruse criticized West Indian immigrants for being conservative in thought and unable to understand the nature of American race relations. Winston James's *Holding Aloft the Banner of Ethiopia: Caribbean Radicalism in Early Twentieth Century America* (1998) came to the opposite conclusion. In easily the most detailed study to date on West Indian immigration to the United States in this period, James was sharply critical of Cruse's findings and praised the major contribution made by

West Indian settlers to African American society.[34]

The most famous West Indian immigrant of the period, Marcus Garvey, continued to attract the attention of scholars from the late 1970s through to the 1990s and beyond. In 1978 two works by Randall Burkett examined the appeal of Garveyism from a religious perspective, whereas in 1980 Emory Tolbert's *The UNIA and Black Los Angeles* provided a case study on the grassroots organization of the movement.[35] In the 1980s the publication of the first volumes of *The Marcus Garvey and UNIA Papers*, compiled by historian Robert Hill with the assistance of an editorial team of eminent fellow academics, constituted certainly the most important and ambitious scholarly initiative ever undertaken on the Garvey movement. Continuing throughout the 1980s and the 1990s, the anticipated ten-volume series was comprised of a hitherto largely unpublished collection of primary source materials on Garvey.[36] These were all the more valuable in that in earlier decades the incomplete and scattered nature of surviving archive materials on Garvey and the UNIA had been a major obstacle to scholars wishing to research the movement. The liberal funding needed to undertake the project also constituted impressive tangible evidence, if such was needed, that African American history had acquired mainstream academic respectability.

Significantly, the final three volumes of *The Garvey Papers* were earmarked for the publication of source materials on the Garvey movement outside the United States. Earlier works on Garveyism had focused predominantly on the organization of the UNIA in the United States. This was also the case with historian Judith Stein's important 1986 work *The World of Marcus Garvey*.[37] Writing a decade after the heyday of Black Power, Stein surpassed earlier Garvey scholars in her balanced approach, paying due recognition to both the Jamaican's strengths and weaknesses in equal measure. Stein's study notwithstanding, a notable feature of 1980s and early 1990s publications on Garveyism, most particularly by Rupert Lewis, was the extent to which they concentrated on the movement as an international phenomenon, looking at its organization in Africa and the Caribbean.[38] This was in line with scholarly research on other periods of twentieth-century African American history that also started to view the black freedom struggle from a more global perspective in the 1980s and 1990s.

Despite the ongoing publication of *The Garvey Papers*, the Jamaican received comparatively little attention from historians from the early 1990s onwards. One possible reason for this neglect was that although scholars at this time showed increasing interest in African American history of the 1920s and 1930s, it was often with the objective of looking for the early origins of post-war civil rights protest rather than to study Black Nationalist alternatives to the Civil Rights Movement. Particularly disappointing was the lack of published research on the role of women in the Garvey movement, despite both growing interest by historians of twentieth-century African American history in the contribution made by women campaigners and the prominent positions occupied by women in Garvey's UNIA organization. On the positive side, Ula Yvette Taylor's 2002 biography, *The Veiled Garvey: The Life and Times of Amy Jacques Garvey*, was possibly an early indication that this situation was about to change in the first decade of the twenty-first century.[39]

More predictably, the steady expansion of scholarly research on the inter-war years from the 1970s onwards resulted in a variety of fresh studies on the NAACP and its leadership. In 1970 historian Philip S. Foner contributed two volumes of selected speeches and addresses by W. E. B. Du Bois.[40] Born in 1910, the Jewish New Yorker Foner was drawn to black history because of his concern at the distorted and inadequate treatment of African Americans in existing studies of the 1930s and 1940s. A political radical who moved in communist circles, he also had a natural empathy for Du Bois's increasingly left-wing philosophy in later life. This was also the case with the Marxist Herbert Aptheker, born in 1915, who during the 1970s and early 1980s published a wide variety of selected writings by Du Bois, most notably three volumes of correspondence.[41]

In 1972 and 1973 William B. Hixon Jr, B. Joyce Ross and Eugene Levy, respectively, provided biographical studies of three other early NAACP stalwarts, Moorfield Storey, Joel Spingarn and James Weldon Johnson.[42] Taking a different approach, Elliott Rudwick and August Meier's *Along the Color Line: Explorations in the Black Experience* (1976) included two seminal essays on the early administrative history of the NAACP.[43] In particular they sought to examine the process by which the Association evolved from being a white dominated organization to one run predominantly by blacks themselves, a line of investigation that reflected the emphasis of Black Power radicals of the late 1960s and early 1970s on the need for African Americans to assume full leadership responsibilities in civil rights groups.

Leading scholarly authorities on the NAACP, in the early 1980s Meier and Rudwick headed a team of eminent historians in launching the publication of an extensive selection of the Association's archival records on microfilm. In what remains an ongoing project, the selection and editing of *The NAACP Papers* constituted an enormous undertaking, as the centralized, bureaucratic, tendencies of the Association ensured that a staggering proportion of its records and files had remained largely intact. From a scholarly perspective this was both a blessing and a burden. A blessing because the full collection of the NAACP papers comprised a treasure trove of primary source materials on twentieth-century African American history rivalled only by the Booker T. Washington papers housed in the Library of Congress. A burden because the sheer volume of material available made any attempt to study it in its entirety a task of heroic proportions.[44]

This dilemma was reflected in the nature of the work published on the Association during the 1980s and 1990s. Opting for prudence rather than valour, historians collectively resisted the temptation to write a comprehensive history of the NAACP, instead preferring to examine the lives of key individuals or particular aspects of the Association's work. In 1980 historian Robert L. Zangrando examined the NAACP's prolonged anti-lynching campaign. In *A Mob Intent on Death* (1988) fellow scholar Robert Cortner looked at the Association's legal involvement in the courtroom struggles resulting from the notorious 1919 race riot in Elaine, Arkansas, while Kenneth Goings charted its successful attempt to block the appointment of a segregationist southern judge to the United States Supreme Court in 1930. In 1993 August Meier and John H. Bracey provided a broad overview of the NAACP's history from its formation in 1909 through to the mid-1960s but wisely, if disappointingly, opted for the charcoal sketch depiction of a journal article rather than the richly detailed canvas in oils perspective of a full-length monograph.[45]

In respect to individuals, Sheldon Avery and Carolyn Wedin added biographical studies on NAACP Field Secretary William Pickens and leading Board member Mary White Ovington respectively. It was however W. E. B. Du Bois, as always, who was the NAACP spokesperson to attract the most scholarly attention. In *W. E. B. Du Bois: Black Radical Democrat* (1986) African American scholar Manning Marable provided an updated biography of his subject. A political radical, like Aptheker and Foner, Marable was drawn to Du Bois's left-wing views and pointed up the continuities in Du Bois's socialist values in later life and his philosophy in earlier years. In the early 1990s historians Mark Ellis and William Jordan debated the motives and actions of *The Crisis*'s editor during the First World War, and in 1993 and 2000 David Levering Lewis contributed an extensively researched two-volume study of Du Bois that constituted the most detailed and authoritative biography yet written on him. Then in 2002 historian Raymond Wolters added a thoughtful new study on Du Bois's strained relationships with fellow race leaders like Booker T. Washington and Marcus Garvey.[46]

In the first years of the twenty-first century scholarly interest in the NAACP appeared if anything to be gaining increased momentum with the 2002 publication of the first detailed account of the Association's work during the 1920s, by Mark Robert Schneider, and the first scholarly biography of Walter White the following year by Kenneth Janken. In part these works built on earlier studies of the 1980s and 1990s but they were also an indication of the growing recognition by historians that, despite the advances that had been made in earlier decades, the inter-war years and the efforts of the NAACP in particular in this period were still under-researched areas of African American history. Moreover, much of the best work on the grassroots organization of the Association was embedded in more wide-ranging texts or detailed state or local studies targeted at specialist researchers rather than more general readers.[47]

In one of the major historiographical developments of the decade the 1990s also saw a proliferation of major new academic studies on the Ku Klux Klan. In earlier years the unsophisticated image of the Invisible Empire combined with its violent excesses during the heyday of the Civil Rights Movement made the organization an unattractive subject for research by scholars. Indeed, since the publication of Moffatt Mecklin's pioneering 1924 work historians had done singularly little to address the need for detailed studies on the 1920s Klan.

Inevitably, there was the occasional exception. In 1966 Charles Alexander's *The Ku Klux Klan in the Southwest* looked at the Invisible Empire in Texas, Oklahoma, Arkansas and Louisiana, but his work attracted only limited scholarly attention. The following year Kenneth Jackson's *The Ku Klux Klan in the City, 1915–1930* focused on the growth of the Klan in major urban centres like Chicago.[48] However, though favourably received, Jackson's study failed to inspire further publications on the subject. There continued to be a paucity of academic publications on the 1920s Klan.

It is interesting to ask why this situation changed so dramatically in the 1990s. Possibly one factor was that by this time the Klan was all but defunct as an organization and the violent outrages of the 1950s and 1960s were events of the past, encouraging scholars to take a more dispassionate view of the Klan in its earlier historical incarnations. The growth of academic interest in the 1920s Klan was also consistent with the increasing awareness by historians in the 1990s that existing accounts of the Civil Rights Movement of the 1950s and 1960s had paid insufficient attention to the segregationist opponents of the black freedom struggle.[49]

Whatever the reason, in the early 1990s a new generation of Revisionist historians suddenly emerged to challenge the traditionally held negative perceptions of the 1920s Klan that dated back to Moffatt Mecklin.[50] Scholars like William Jenkins, Shawn Lay and Leonard Moore pointed out that in some areas, such as Indiana, the Klan thrived despite the virtual absence of ethnic and religious minorities. Popular prejudice and bigotry were thus insufficient explanations for the organization's success. Instead the Klan flourished because it appealed to the traditional conservative values of mainstream America. These included Protestantism, Prohibition and a desire to protect the sanctity of marriage and family life. In addition the Klan provided a means to promote worthy local causes and reassert community control over the political decision making process.

At the same time, Revisionist historians were careful still to condemn the Klan for its more ugly characteristics. Moreover, the new researchers, as they themselves stressed, typically came from impeccably liberal personal backgrounds. Shawn Lay reminded readers that he was 'a devout Roman Catholic' who was 'married to a woman of color and committed to a variety of progressive causes'.[51] Similarly, in his edited collection of Revisionist essays, *The Invisible Empire in the West* (1992), Lay noted that the contributors included 'two Roman Catholics, two Jews, a Greek American, and two ardent proponents of liberal causes – hardly the type of jury that the Klan would choose to stand in historical judgment'.[52]

Despite these considerations not all historians were happy to accept Revisionist findings. An unfortunate, albeit unintentional, consequence of the new thinking was that it appeared to present the Klan in a sympathetic light. Instead of being an organization of embittered extremists the Klan was seemingly afforded mainstream status and respectability. Its membership consisted predominantly of ordinary middle-class and working-class white Americans. In short, the 'Klan of the twenties might be best understood as a populist organization rather than a nativist one'.[53] Some historians were also concerned by the possible methodological shortcomings of Revisionist researchers. Nancy MacLean thus noted that Revisionist studies often focused on the Klan in northern or western locations where its members were more restrained in conduct.[54]

Examining the role of women in the Klan, Kathleen Blee demonstrated that although Klan members did not always resort to violence they sometimes engaged in other tactics that were equally unacceptable and damaging for the victims involved. Klanswomen organized 'poison squads', which spread malicious gossip about individuals they disliked, or organized consumer boycotts designed to drive small businessmen out of the community or engineer their economic ruin.[55]

Surprisingly, as has already been indicated, few of the studies of the 1990s surveyed the activities of the Klan in the South. This was despite the fact that Charles Alexander's earlier work on the Klan in the South-West had appeared to pre-empt a number of later Revisionist arguments, concluding that the principal appeal of the Klan in the region derived from its championing of law and order issues and traditional moral values. Looking at Alabama, historian Glen Feldman broadly supported Revisionist findings. The Klan in the state 'represented a political mouthpiece for plain folk in their struggle against entrenched elites'. At the same time Alabama Klansmen habitually engaged in vigilantism against African Americans and moral nonconformists alike. Consequently, 'Alabama's experience, and perhaps that of the South as a whole, may have differed from that of the rest of the nation with respect to violence.' In Florida independent researcher and journalist Michael Newton found further disturbing evidence of widespread violence fuelled by racial and religious bigotry.[56] Simply put, Revisionist findings notwithstanding, African Americans living in the 1920s had every reason to be alarmed by the Klan's revival.

Notes

1 See chapter 1, pp. 13–15.
2 John Moffatt Mecklin, *The Ku Klux Klan: A Study of the American Mind* (New York, 1924).
3 W. E. B. Du Bois, *The Philadelphia Negro: A Social Study* (Philadelphia, 1899).
4 Kenneth L. Kusmer, 'The Black Urban Experience in American History', in Darlene Clark Hine (ed.), *The State of Afro-American History: Past, Present, and Future* (Baton Rouge, Louisiana, 1986), p. 95.
5 Carter G. Woodson, *A Century of Negro Migration* (New York, 1918); Emmett J. Scott, 'Letters of Negro Migrants of 1916–1918', *Journal of Negro History*, (4, 1919), pp. 290–340, 412–65; Emmett J. Scott, *Negro Migration During the War* (New York, 1920); Thomas J. Woofter, *Negro Migration* (New York, 1920); Charles S. Johnson, *The Negro in Chicago: A Study of Race Relations and a Race Riot* (Chicago, 1922); Louise V. Kennedy, *The Negro Peasant Turns Cityward: Effects of Recent Migrations to Northern Cities* (New York, 1930); Edward E. Lewis, *The Mobility of the Negro* (New York, 1931); Clyde V. Kiser, *Sea Island to City: A Study of St Helena Islanders in Harlem and Other Urban Centers* (New York, 1931); E. Franklin Frazier, *The Negro Family in Chicago* (Chicago, 1932); Kusmer, 'The Black Urban Experience', p. 91; Joe William Trotter Jr, 'Black Migration in Historical Perspective: A Review of the Literature', in Joe William Trotter Jr (ed.), *The Great Migration in Historical Perspective: New Dimensions of*

Race, Class, and Gender (Bloomington, Indiana, 1991), p. 1.

6 Kusmer, 'The Black Urban Experience', pp. 91, 95.

7 Frederick Jackson Turner, 'The Significance of the Frontier in American History', reprinted in Frederick Jackson Turner, *The Frontier in American History* (New York, 1920).

8 Kusmer, 'The Black Urban Experience', pp. 91–2; Trotter, 'Black Migration in Historical Perspective', p. 5.

9 Frazier, *The Negro Family in Chicago*; E. Franklin Frazier, *The Negro Family in the United States* (Chicago, 1939); Kusmer, 'The Black Urban Experience', pp. 93–4; Trotter, 'Black Migration in Historical Persepctive', p. 9. For subsequent studies on the Great Migration see pp. 43–4, 48–9.

10 Mary White Ovington, *The Walls Came Tumbling Down* (New York, 1947); James Weldon Johnson, *Along This Way: The Autobiography of James Weldon Johnson* (New York, 1933); Walter White, *A Man Called White: The Autobiography of Walter White* (New York, 1949); W. E. B. Du Bois, *Darkwater: Voices From Within the Veil* (New York, 1920); W. E. B. Du Bois, *Dusk of Dawn: An Essay Toward an Autobiography of a Race Concept* (New York, 1940). For more recent accounts of the NAACP see pp. 42–3, 51–3.

11 E. David Cronon, *Black Moses: The Story of Marcus Garvey and the Universal Negro Improvement Association* (Madison, Wisconsin, 1955). For later works on Garveyism see pp. 44–5, 50–1.

12 Francis L. Broderick, *W. E. B. Du Bois: Negro Leader in Time of Crisis* (Stanford, 1959); Elliott Rudwick, *W. E. B. Du Bois: A Study in Minority Group Leadership* (Philadelphia, 1960); August Meier and Elliott Rudwick, *Black History and the Historical Profession, 1915–1980* (Urbana, Illinois, 1986), pp. 145–6.

13 Clement E. Vose, *Caucasians Only: The Supreme Court, the NAACP and the Restrictive Covenant Cases* (Berkeley, California, 1967); Charles Flint Kellogg, *NAACP: A History of the National Association for the Advancement of Colored People, Volume I, 1909–1920* (Baltimore, Maryland, 1967). Kellogg's death in 1980 prevented him from completing a projected second volume of history on the NAACP.

14 Meier and Rudwick, *Black History and the Historical Profession*, p. 150.

15 W. E. B. Du Bois, *The Autobiography of W. E. B. Du Bois: A Soliloquy on Viewing My Life from the Last Decade of Its First Century* (New York, 1968).

16 Gilbert Osofsky, *Harlem: The Making of a Ghetto, Negro New York, 1890-1930* (New York, 1966); Allan H. Spear, *Black Chicago: The Making of a Negro Ghetto, 1890–1920* (Chicago, 1967); William M. Tuttle, *Race Riot: Chicago in the Red Summer of 1919* (New York, 1970); Kusmer, 'The Black Urban Experience', pp. 97–8; Trotter, 'Black Migration in Historical Perspective', p. 13.

17 Meier and Rudwick, *Black History and the Historical Profession*, pp. 165–6.

18 Trotter, 'Black Migration in Historical Perspective', p. 13.

19 Trotter, 'Black Migration in Historical Perspective', pp. 13–14.

20 Amy Jacques Garvey (ed.), *Philosophy and Opinions of Marcus Garvey, Or Africa for the Africans* (New York, 1967); E. U. Essien-Udom and Amy Jacques Garvey (eds), *More Philosophy and Opinions of Marcus Garvey* (New

York, 1977); E. David Cronon (ed.), *Great Lives Observed: Marcus Garvey* (Englewood Cliffs, New Jersey, 1973); John H. Clarke (ed.), *Marcus Garvey and the Vision of Africa* (New York, 1974); Theodore Vincent, *Black Power and the Garvey Movement* (Berkeley, California, 1971); Tony Martin, *Race First: The Ideological and Organizational Struggles of Marcus Garvey and the Universal Negro Improvement Association* (Westport, Connecticut, 1976).

21 Nathan Irvin Huggins, *Harlem Renaissance* (New York, 1971); David Levering Lewis, *When Harlem Was in Vogue* (New York, 1981).

22 Meier and Rudwick, *Black History and the Historical Profession*, pp. 220–1.

23 Alain Locke, 'Harlem: Dark Weather Vane', *Survey Graphic* (25, 1936), p. 457.

24 Houston Baker, *Modernism and the Harlem Renaissance* (New York, 1987).

25 George Hutchinson, *The Harlem Renaissance in Black and White* (London, 1995), pp. 16, 22.

26 Hutchinson, *The Harlem Renaissance*, pp. 16, 435, 437.

27 Samuel A. Floyd (ed.), *Black Music in the Harlem Renaissance: A Collection of Essays* (New York, 1990); Jon Michael Spencer, *The New Negroes and Their Music* (Knoxville, Tennessee, 1997).

28 Peter Gottlieb, *Making Their Own Way: Southern Blacks' Migration to Pittsburgh, 1916–1930* (Urbana, Illinois, 1987); James R. Grossman, *Land of Hope: Chicago, Black Southerners and the Great Migration* (Urbana, Illinois, 1989); Kenneth L. Kusmer, *A Ghetto Takes Shape: Black Cleveland, 1870-1930* (Urbana, Illinois, 1976); Joe William Trotter Jr, *Black Milwaukee: The Making of an Industrial Proletariat, 1915–1945* (Urbana, Illinois, 1985); Richard W. Thomas, *Life For Us Is What We Make It: Building Black Community in Detroit, 1915–1945* (Bloomington, Indiana, 1992); Kimberley L. Phillips, *Alabama-North, African American Migrants: Community and Working Class Activism in Cleveland, 1915–45* (Urbana, Illinois, 1999).

29 Gottlieb, *Making Their Own Way*, p. 222.

30 Thomas, *Life For Us Is What We Make It*, p. 108.

31 Florette Henri, *Black Migration, Movement North, 1900-1920: The Road from Myth to Man* (New York, 1976); Carole Marks, *Farewell – We're Good and Gone: The Great Black Migration* (Bloomington, Indiana, 1989).

32 Kusmer, 'The Black Urban Experience', p. 105; Nancy J. Weiss, *The National Urban League, 1910–1940* (New York, 1974); Jesse Thomas Moore, *Search for Equality: The National Urban League, 1910–61* (Philadelphia, 1982).

33 Patrick Renshaw, 'The Black Ghetto, 1890-1940', *Journal of American Studies* (8, 1974), pp. 41–59; David J. Hellwig, 'Black Meets Black: Afro-American Reactions to West Indian Immigrants in the 1920s', *South Atlantic Quarterly* (77, 1978), pp. 206–24.

34 Harold Cruse, *The Crisis of the Negro Intellectual* (New York, 1984); Winston James, *Holding Aloft the Banner of Ethiopia: Caribbean Radicalism in Early Twentieth-Century America* (London, 1998).

35 Randall K. Burkett, *Garveyism as a Religious Movement: The Institutionalisation of a Black Civil Religion* (London, 1978); Randall K. Burkett, *Black Redemption: Churchmen Speak for the Garvey Movement*

(London, 1978); Emory J. Tolbert, *The UNIA and Black Los Angeles: Ideology and Community in the American Garvey Movement* (Los Angeles, 1980).

36 Robert Hill et al. (eds), *The Marcus Garvey and Universal Negro Improvement Association Papers* (Berkeley, California, 1983–).

37 Judith Stein, *The World of Marcus Garvey: Race and Class in Modern Society* (Baton Rouge, Louisiana, 1986).

38 Rupert Lewis and Maureen Warner Lewis (eds), *Garvey, Africa, Europe, the Americas* (Jamaica, 1986); Rupert Lewis, *Marcus Garvey: Anti-Colonial Champion* (London, 1987); Rupert Lewis and Patrick Brian (eds), *Garvey: His Work and Impact* (Trenton, New Jersey, 1991).

39 Ula Yvette Taylor, *The Veiled Garvey: The Life and Times of Amy Jacques Garvey* (Chapel Hill, North Carolina, 2002).

40 Philip S. Foner (ed.), *W. E. B. Du Bois Speaks: Speeches and Addresses, 1890-1919* (New York, 1970); Philip S. Foner, *W. E. B. Du Bois Speaks: Speeches and Addresses, 1920–1963* (New York, 1970).

41 Meier and Rudwick, *Black History and the Historical Profession*, pp. 107–10; Herbert Aptheker (ed.), *The Correspondence of W. E. B. Du Bois*, 3 vols (Amherst, Massachusetts, 1973–78); Herbert Aptheker (ed.), *W. E. B. Du Bois, Against Racism: Unpublished Essays, Papers, Addresses, 1887–1961* (Amherst, Massachusetts, 1985); Herbert Aptheker (ed.), *Writings in Periodicals Edited by W. E. B. Du Bois: Selections from* The Horizon (New York, 1985).

42 William B. Hixon Jr, *Moorfield Storey and the Abolitionist Tradition* (New York, 1972); B. Joyce Ross, *J. E. Spingarn and the Rise of the NAACP, 1911–1939* (New York, 1972); Eugene Levy, *James Weldon Johnson: Black Leader, Black Voice* (Chicago, 1973).

43 Elliott Rudwick and August Meier, 'The Rise of the Black Secretariat in the NAACP, 1909–35', and August Meier and Elliott Rudwick, 'Attorneys Black and White: A Case Study of Race Relations Within the NAACP', both in August Meier and Elliott Rudwick, *Along the Color Line: Explorations in the Black Experience* (Urbana, Illinois, 1976). An earlier version of the latter paper can be found in the *Journal of American History* (41, 1976), pp. 913–46.

44 August Meier, Elliott Rudwick et al., *Papers of the National Association for the Advancement of Colored People, 1909–1972* (Microfilm: University Publications of America, Inc., 1982–). A copy of this collection is housed in the Microfilm Reading Room of the Cambridge University Library, England.

45 Robert L. Zangrando, *The NAACP Crusade Against Lynching, 1909–1950* (Philadelphia, 1980); Robert Cortner, *A Mob Intent on Death: The NAACP and the Arkansas Riot Cases* (Middletown, Connecticut, 1988); Kenneth W. Goings, *The NAACP Comes of Age: The Defeat of Judge John J. Parker* (Bloomington, Indiana, 1990); August Meier and John H. Bracey, 'The NAACP as a Reform Movement, 1909–1965: "To Reach the Conscience of America"', *Journal of Southern History* (59, 1993.

46 Sheldon Avery, *Up From Washington: William Pickens and the Negro Struggle for Equality, 1900–1954* (Newark, Delaware, 1989); Carolyn Wedin, *Inheritors of the Spirit: Mary White Ovington and the Founding of the*

NAACP (New York, 1998); Manning Marable, *W. E. B. Du Bois: Black Radical Democrat* (Boston, 1986); Mark Ellis, '"Closing Ranks" and "Seeking Honors": W. E. B. Du Bois in World War I', *Journal of American History* (79, 1992); William Jordan, '"The Damnable Dilemma": African American Accommodation and Protest During World War I', *Journal of American History* (81, 1995); Mark Ellis, 'W. E. B. Du Bois and the Formation of Black Opinion in World War I: A Commentary on "The Damnable Dilemma"', *Journal of American History* (81, 1995); David Levering Lewis, *W. E. B. Du Bois: Biography of a Race, 1868–1919* (New York, 1993); David Levering Lewis, *W. E. B. Du Bois: The Fight For Equality and the American Century, 1919–1963* (New York, 2000); Raymond Wolters, *Du Bois and His Rivals* (Columbia, Missouri, 2002).

47 Mark Robert Schneider, *'We Return Fighting': The Civil Rights Movement in the Jazz Age* (Boston, 2002); Kenneth Robert Janken, *White: The Biography of Walter White, Mr. NAACP* (New York, 2003). Good analysis of the work of the NAACP at local level is provided in Raymond Gavins, 'The NAACP in North Carolina during the Age of Segregation', in Armstead L. Robinson and Patricia Sullivan (eds), *New Directions in Civil Rights Studies* (Charlottesville, Virginia, 1991), pp. 105–25; and Adam Fairclough, *Race and Democracy: The Civil Rights Struggle in Louisiana, 1915–1972* (Athens, Georgia, 1995).

48 Charles C. Alexander, *The Ku Klux Klan in the Southwest* (Lexington, Kentucky, 1966); Kenneth T. Jackson, *The Ku Klux Klan in the City, 1915–1930* (New York, 1967).

49 See chapter 4, pp. 104–60.

50 William D. Jenkins, *Steel Valley Klan: The Ku Klux Klan in Ohio's Mahoning Valley* (Kent, Ohio, 1996); Shawn Lay (ed.), *The Invisible Empire in the West: Toward a New Historical Appraisal of the Ku Klux Klan of the 1920s* (Urbana, Illinois, 1992); Shawn Lay, *Hooded Knights of the Niagara: The Ku Klux Klan in Buffalo, New York* (New York, 1995); Leonard J. Moore, *Citizen Klansmen: The Ku Klux Klan in Indiana, 1921–1928* (Chapel Hill, North Carolina, 1991).

51 Lay, *Hooded Knights of the Niagara*, p. 8.

52 Lay, *Invisible Empire in the West*, p. 12.

53 Leonard J. Moore, 'Historical Interpretations of the 1920s Klan: The Traditional View and Recent Revisions', in Lay, *Invisible Empire in the West*, p. 19.

54 Nancy MacLean, *Behind the Mask of Chivalry: The Making of the Second Ku Klux Klan* (New York, 1994), p. xiii.

55 Kathleen M. Blee, *Women of the Klan: Racism and Gender in the 1920s* (Berkeley, California, 1991), p. 3.

56 Glen Feldman, *Politics, Society and the Klan in Alabama, 1915–1949* (Tuscaloosa, Alabama, 1999), pp. 7–8; Michael Newton, *The Invisible Empire: The Ku Klux Klan in Florida* (Gainesville, Florida, 2001), pp. 49–53.

3

The Great Depression and the Second World War, 1930–1945

The study of African American history, as has been noted earlier, first became a focus of interest for mainstream historians in the late 1950s and early 1960s. Previously, in the 1930s and 1940s, the subject had been seen as being of importance or interest only to black scholars. The few white historians who researched or published in the field were perceived either as eccentric, like August Meier, or driven by obsessive ideological conviction, such as the Marxist Herbert Aptheker. The historiography of the black experience for this time period has followed a similar pattern. Initially, Martin Luther King and the Civil Rights Movement of 1955–68 was easily the most popular area of interest for researchers in the field, with the 1930s and the Second World War confined to the role of a poor relation. This imbalance is now not as great as it once was. Although the outpouring of work on the 1950s and 1960s remains considerable, there is greater interest by historians in studying developments in race relations in the preceding two decades.

There are a number of reasons why earlier scholars neglected the 1930s and early 1940s. When African American history began to command more serious attention in the mid-1960s, the generation of historians who, as young adults, had had direct personal experience of the Great Depression and the Second World War began to reach the age of retirement. The younger members of the profession who replaced them had had a different life perspective. Their formative years had been shaped by the Cold War, the conflict in Vietnam, and the rise of Martin Luther King and the black Civil Rights Movement within the United States.

The labour historian Bruce Nelson thus recalled that for him 'a product of suburbia, elite schooling, and conservative parents, the sixties represented a bracing challenge to the assumptions and mores that had shaped my parochial world'. The Civil Rights Movement 'was the crucible in which I came of age politically'.[1]

In many instances these new scholars were not just witnesses to the historic events of the 1950s and 1960s but in their own way made modest but useful contributions to them. 'I was not a full-time activist in the South', Nelson noted, but in common with 'many young people of my generation, I marched and picketed for civil rights, and in March 1965 I even had a brief but unforgettable moment on the front lines of battle in Selma'. Moreover, he reflected that what 'was true for me must have been true in equal or greater measure' for many new scholars 'who were students and political activists in the 1960s'.[2]

For a number of later scholars in African American history, like Leon Litwack, Staughton Lynd and Howard Zinn, their first involvement with the subject came not as academic researchers but as participants in civil rights demonstrations. In this vein historian Harvard Sitkoff recalled that his initial interest in the field 'came during my brief sojourn in the Southern black freedom struggle of the early 1960s', when alongside 'other Northern white college students I had gone to march, to picket, to sit-in. I did a bit.'[3] When students like Sitkoff later achieved academic tenure as historians their research interests were shaped by their earlier experiences. Encapsulating the feelings of many scholars of his generation, Sitkoff reflected that he considered himself to be 'part of a phalanx of young historians determined to expose the vicious continuity of racism in American life and thought'.[4]

Understandably, many of these rising academics concentrated their research on the civil rights revolution of the 1950s and 1960s, through which they had recently lived and in which they had participated. There was a tendency in early studies of this period to view it as a self-contained subject area that could be researched without detailed study of the civil rights struggles of earlier decades. This view was reinforced by a 'leader-oriented' perception of the black protests of the 1950s and 1960s that placed a disproportionate emphasis on the inspirational leadership of key individuals, most notably Martin Luther King, in explaining the achievements of the modern freedom struggle. King's assassination in Memphis, Tennessee, on 4 April 1968, only confirmed his hallowed status within the Civil Rights Movement. In common with other assassinated leaders of the 1960s, President John F. Kennedy, Robert Kennedy and Malcolm X, he became enveloped in a halo of martyrdom that precluded an objective historical understanding of his life and career.

By the 1980s distance began to remove enchantment from the view. Scholars became more critical in their portrayals of King and the two Kennedys, recognizing that the need to provide a fair and balanced analysis at times imposed a duty on historians to speak ill of the dead. This de-mythologizing in turn led to a deeper understanding of the racial conflicts of the period. Historians increasingly appreciated that the Civil Rights Movement was not just the achievement of a small number of courageous, charismatic individuals. The Movement was rather owned by countless grassroots activists whose efforts had been afforded too little recognition. It was also the culmination of profound changes in American society that had taken place over several decades.

This fresh insight prompted greater interest in the previously under-researched civil rights struggles of the 1930s and the 1940s. Other historians came to share the view of Harvard Sitkoff, an early researcher of the period, that it was an era in which the 'seeds that would later bear fruit had been planted'. These were 'nurtured by the legal and political developments, the ideas articulated, the alliances formed, and the expectations raised during the New Deal years. The sprouts of hopes prepared the ground for the struggles to follow. Harvest time would come for the next generation.' Sitkoff also identified a second, perhaps less uplifting, reason for his interest in the 1930s: 'Immersion in research and the retrogression in race relations during the Nixon years changed my focus', he reflected. The 'diminution of the campaign for black rights heightened my concern about its origins and the preconditions for its success'.[5]

Other factors may also have contributed to the greater interest of historians in the period. Growing awareness of the acute economic problems suffered by many African American communities during the 1980s and the 1990s perhaps drew some scholars to the 1930s, a decade when economic deprivation was also one of the most pressing problems experienced by black Americans. Similarly, it is significant that many scholars researching the years 1930–45, such as Eric Arneson, Melinda Chateauvert, Olen Cole and Neil McMillen, have incorporated oral testimony of surviving individuals from the period into their work. The passage of the years has meant that the number of such potential interviewees is now, in the words of McMillen, a 'thinning population'. This consideration may have acted as a catalyst to historians to document and record such recollections and life experiences before the opportunity to do so was lost forever.[6]

One consequence of the new interest in the 1930s has been a growing awareness of the efforts of civil rights activists of the period, both white and black, whose work had previously gone largely unrecognized by historians. In 1979 Jacquelyn Dowd Hall chronicled the life of the white anti-lynching campaigner Jessie Daniel Ames and the Association of Southern Women for the Prevention of Lynching (ASWPL) founded and headed by her in 1930. Similarly, in 1983 Raymond Gavins provided a scholarly biography of the African American Virginia educator and civil rights spokesperson Gordon Blaine Hancock. In a groundbreaking 1991 study of southern white liberalism, historian Linda Reed's *Simple Decency and Common Sense: The Southern Conference Movement, 1938–1963* provided a detailed account of the contributions of both the Southern Conference for Human Welfare (SCHW) and its educational offshoot the Southern Conference Educational Fund (SCEF) in breaking down racial barriers in the region. [7]

A bi-racial organization led predominantly by southern white liberals, the SCHW was founded in Birmingham, Alabama in 1938 to facilitate better racial understanding and promote black education and scholarly studies on race relations. The Conference Movement was intended to be a more dynamic alternative to its conservative predecessor the Commission on Inter-racial Cooperation (CIC). Created in 1919 in Atlanta, Georgia the biracial CIC was similarly supported by southern white liberals like Ames, and a few African American spokespersons, such as Hancock. Unfortunately there is no still detailed full-length scholarly study available on the work of the Commission.

Such omission is no accident. CIC backers like Ames and Hancock were committed to the concept of 'racial uplift', working to improve the lives of African Americans within the confines of a segregated society. For the generation of historians who reached adult maturity during the heady years of 1960s this philosophy had limited appeal. Spokespersons like Ames and Hancock appeared timid and conservative in comparison to the more heroic leadership of Martin Luther King and other icons of the Civil Rights Movement. Moreover, as British historian Adam Fairclough has pointed out, the concept of 'racial uplift' is easy to deride. 'It reeks of the condescension and snobbery with which middle-class reformers so often treat the objects of their charity, the great unwashed. It conjures up images of bustling busybodies scolding the poor for intemperance, lecturing them on thrift, and teaching them domestic arts such as needlework and the correct placement of the doily.'[8]

Even if this characterization contained more than an element of truth, by the 1980s and the 1990s historians began to acknowledge that it was unduly harsh and over-simplified. Under the cover of racial uplift, as Fairclough himself noted, African Americans won over white support for improvements in areas like health and education that significantly improved the lives of poor blacks.[9] Conversely, the continuing problems suffered by African Americans in the 1980s and 1990s, most notably social and material hardship in the inner cities, suggested that racial uplift could be as important an objective as desegregation. Similarly, black ghetto deprivation in cities across the nation highlighted the limitations of the seemingly more courageous campaigns of the later Civil Rights Movement in addressing the social and economic problems experienced by many black communities.

In another notable development, the charismatic African American religious visionary, Father Divine, became the subject of three full-length academic studies by Kenneth Burnham, Robert Weisbrot and Jill Watts.[10] Claiming to be the physical incarnation of God, Divine rejected traditional racial and gender classifications and exhorted his followers to rely on positive thinking to achieve personal fulfilment. On a practical level his community 'Peace Missions' established business co-operatives and restaurants to provide employment and cheap wholesome food for converts to his teachings. Reaching a peak of popularity during the Great Depression, the movement, with its headquarters in Harlem, briefly attained worldwide recognition with a following of up to two million supporters in the United States, as well as missions in Europe, Australia, Canada and the West Indies. Moreover, converts to the movement numbered not just African Americans but also wealthy and well-connected whites, including the niece of President Herbert Hoover and the Californian millionaire John Hunt.

Despite this success, earlier studies of Father Divine had been more salacious than scholarly. This tendency was manifested in its most extreme form in John Hosher's 1936 account *God in a Rolls-Royce: The Rise of Father Divine, Madman, Menace, or Messiah*. A white journalist, Hosher also personified the common racial prejudices of his day that contributed to the limited interest in serious study of African American life and culture by white historians of that era. Unabashed, he indulged in sweeping caricatured observations about African Americans, presenting bigoted assertions almost as if they were scientifically proven facts. He thus casually informed his readers that 'nothing else tastes as good to the negro' as fried chicken and that 'unlike most blacks' Father Divine 'was not lazy'. In short, as historian Robert Weisbrot has observed, Hosher seemed 'to find blacks fit subjects for ridicule, not simply as part of a wider human comedy but because they are black'.[11]

Robert Allerton Parker's *The Incredible Messiah* constitutes perhaps the most reputable of the 1930s studies of Father Divine. Thankfully lacking Hosher's overt racial prejudice, Parker attempted to engage in a serious analysis of the reasons for the appeal of the Peace Mission movement, concluding that the racism and oppression suffered by blacks in Harlem created a yearning for a messianic cult leader. At the same time Parker focused more on the 'emotional and cult features' of the movement rather than the philosophy and ideals behind it. Sara Harris's 1953 and 1971 biographies suffered from similar shortcomings. Harris's professional training and experience as a white social worker helped her to demonstrate genuine insight in her two works but they were still sensationalist in tone, with lurid emphasis on the alleged sexual peculiarities and excesses of Divine and his followers. Significantly, both at the start and the end of a scholarly preface written for Harris's second work, historian John Henrik Clarke felt the need to remind readers that it was 'a serious book about a serious subject'.[12]

African American commentators, although generally more favourable in assessing the Divine movement than their white counterparts, also tended to stress its sensationalist aspects rather than explore the social values that underpinned it. In *Harlem: Negro Metropolis*, the writer and novelist Claude McKay thus examined the 'cult features of the Peace Mission movement' and seemed 'to view Divine's ministry as a series of tactical coups without a unifying philosophy'. Similarly, in *'New World A-Coming'* author and journalist Roi Ottley concluded that the movement had 'no body of dogma to be explained to the multitude' and was 'chiefly significant as a social manifestation – that is, an acceleration of the search for the better way of life in a period of economic crisis'.[13]

In contrast to the growing body of work on Father Divine, the work of the National Association for the Advancement of Colored People (NAACP) in the 1930s has received comparatively limited coverage from historians. Robert Zangrando's *The NAACP Crusade Against Lynching, 1909–1950* (1980) examined one of the Association's leading campaigns of the decade. Historian Mark Tushnet focused on the NAACP's legal strategy against segregation and also provided a biographical account of the career of the NAACP's special legal counsel Thurgood Marshall. These works reflected the increasing significance of the NAACP's courtroom struggle against segregation from the mid-1930s onwards and also the growing importance of its legal wing. In 1939 the NAACP and the NAACP Legal Defense and Educational Fund Inc. were formally split into two separate organizations. Tax considerations were the specific catalyst for this change, as the NAACP's continued lobbying for a federal anti-lynching law meant that it was not eligible for tax-exempt status. At the same time the division also reflected the increasing significance and independence of the Legal Defense Fund.[14]

Since the 1970s B. Joyce Ross, Genna Rae McNeil and Carolyn Wedin have also provided biographical studies of three leading members of the Association, Joel Spingarn, Charles Hamilton Houston and Mary White Ovington respectively. However, this hardly constitutes saturation coverage given that the NAACP was the best-known and most influential national organization representing the interests of African Americans in the period. Most notable of all, until historian Kenneth Janken filled the void in 2003, there was no satisfactory full-length academic work on the life and career of Walter White, the Association's Executive Secretary from 1930 to 1955. Similarly, the only detailed biographical account of White's deputy, and the man who succeeded him as the Association's chief executive, Assistant Secretary Roy Wilkins, is that provided by Wilkins himself.[15]

This relative neglect of the NAACP can be attributed to a number of factors. White and Wilkins, like the organization they represented, acquired a reputation for being conservative and bureaucratic in outlook. Such characteristics have not endeared the two men or the NAACP to historians. Moreover, in common with many national and local NAACP activists, White and Wilkins were part of the professional, well-educated sections of African American society. In contrast the developments in African American historiography since the 1980s have tended to shift attention away from formal civil rights organizations and black leadership elites. Historians investigating the Civil Rights Movement of the 1950s and the 1960s increasingly recognized that existing studies had paid too much attention to such groups. Seeking to redress this imbalance, a growing number of scholars aimed their research at grassroots civil rights protest and the hitherto undervalued contribution of working-class black communities. Many of the scholars engaged in new research on the antecedents of the Civil Rights Movements in the 1930s and 1940s had a similar perspective. They shared a determination to avoid the mistake of seeing formal civil rights organizations and black elites as representing the views and aspirations of African American society as a whole.

Scholars who did choose to focus on the NAACP were no less informed by this viewpoint. Some of the most significant studies published during the late 1990s on the work of the Association thus concentrated on its organization at local level. In an influential journal article, 'A New Crowd Challenges the Agenda of the Old Guard in the NAACP, 1933–1941', Beth Tompkins Bates studied the tensions between the philosophy of the Association's hierarchical leadership and the desire of grassroots activists for the organization to develop a more coherent programme to address the economic problems faced by African Americans during the Great Depression.[16]

More generally, scholars researching African American life in the 1930s and 1940s avoided an examination of the NAACP altogether, because of its stereotyped image of being elitist and middle class. Instead, a growing number of historians developed an interest in studying the lives and experiences of working-class black communities. A significant development in this respect was the publication of an important 1993 article, '"We Are Not What We Seem": Rethinking Black Working Class Opposition in the Jim Crow South', by Robin D. G. Kelley. A rising young African American historian, Kelley called for a major reappraisal of the concept of black opposition and resistance to racial segregation and discrimination. He implicitly argued that historians had devoted too much attention to formal civil rights protest organizations and 'talented tenth' black spokespersons. Instead, Kelley looked at the day-to-day spontaneous actions of ordinary African Americans as a mode of resistance.[17] Drawing upon the ideas of the anthropologist James Scott, he argued that 'oppressed groups challenge those in power by constructing a "hidden transcript" of dissident political culture manifested in daily conversations, folklore, jokes, songs and other cultural practices'. Concentrating on the 'seemingly mundane', Kelley uncovered, as historian Eric Arnesen observed, ' a world of opposition that calls into question many southern historians' assertions of black acquiescence, resignation, and passivity, and promises to open up dramatic new areas of investigation to southern black and labor historians'.[18]

Although a necessary corrective to the work of earlier historians who had 'limited their scope to public action and formal organization', Kelley's line of investigation was not without problems of its own. It risked overstating the case by seeing almost every action by working-class African Americans as a covert form of resistance, whether it be attendance at blues clubs, employees leaving work early, or house servants burning the Sunday roast of white employers. Interpreting such incidents as quiet but heroic acts of defiance risked, as Arnesen also pointed out, 'creating a romanticized view of the black working class' in the same way that some labour historians have been accused of presenting an overly romantic image of the white working class.[19]

Kelley's call for more research on the lives of working-class blacks was reinforced by parallel developments in other areas of historical scholarship. During the 1980s and the 1990s historians recognized that studies on the American labour movement had paid too little attention to the experiences of black workers. This omission was the result of a number of factors. Traditional or 'old' labour histories written from around 1900 to the early 1960s had focused largely on the records of trade unions and the actions and structures of labour organizations. The views and experiences of workers themselves, whether black or white, were all but ignored.[20] In the late 1960s a fresh generation of rising young historians, like Herbert Gutman and David Montgomery, cast aside this conservative approach. Instead they argued for works that concentrated more on the lives of ordinary people. This development coincided with some of the most high profile years of the Civil Rights Movement. It would thus seem reasonable to suppose that these 'new' labour historians, many of whom had been profoundly influenced in their own lives by the black freedom struggle, would be particularly zealous in their research on African American workers. Surprisingly, with a few exceptions such as Gutman himself, this was not generally the case. In fact so little attention was paid to black workers that, as a number of historians have noted, the 'new' labour history had 'a race problem'. African American employees continued to be largely excluded from labour history narratives, 'entering the picture only as strikebreakers or as a "problem" that white labor had to confront'.[21]

In the late 1980s and early 1990s Herbert Hill, a black NAACP labour activist turned scholar, highlighted this neglect and advanced perhaps the most controversial explanation for it. He argued that 'new' labour historians had allowed themselves to become too preoccupied with Marxist social theory that required them 'either to ignore the racism of the white working class or to rationalize it by attributing it to manipulation by employers'.

Marxist ideology failed to 'recognize the primacy of race in the development of the American social order and, as a consequence, Marxists and those influenced by Marxist ideology' denied or minimized a force that had 'no place in their theory'. He could equally have added that exposing the racism of white employees would have tarnished the idealized construct of working-class life that some 'new' labour histories tended to evoke. Although Hill's causal analysis has not gone unchallenged, his charge that, for whatever reasons, African Americans were neglected in labour histories of the 1960s and 1970s has gained more general acceptance. In 2001 the labour historian Bruce Nelson thus acknowledged that 'for at least a generation' there had been 'a widespread, and largely unconscious, tendency to portray the working class as white (and usually male) – either to minimize the importance of race in writing the history of American workers or to assign it a distinctly secondary role as an explanatory factor'.[22]

Works on African American history during the 1960s and 1970s also marginalized black workers by focusing on formal civil rights organizations and the predominantly middle-class and professional spokespersons who led them. Simply put, if labour history suffered from a race problem, African American history suffered from a class problem.[23] August Meier and Elliott Rudwick's 1979 study, *Black Detroit and the Rise of the UAW*, was an important early indication that this situation was about to change. Although addressing the experiences of black workers in the Union of Automobile Workers, Meier and Rudwick also tended to downplay the extent of racism among white workers. In particular they credited union leaders of the 1930s and 1940s with possessing the foresight to win over the allegiance of black workers and actively courting African American organizations in order to bring black employees into the union fold.[24]

Historians Robert Korstad and Nelson Lichtenstein developed this line of thinking in a broader context in a 1988 journal article, 'Opportunities Found and Lost: Labor, Radicals, and the Early Civil Rights Movement'. They argued that during the 1930s and 1940s there was evidence of increasing mutual understanding and co-operation between white-dominated trade unions and black civil rights advocates. Tragically however, the fruits of this emerging alliance were blighted on the vine during the

McCarthyite years of intolerance, repression and recrimination in the late 1940s and early 1950s.[25]

At first Korstad and Lichtenstein's research had a major impact in the development of African American historiography. Over time, though, a proliferation of new studies, in part inspired by their article, cast doubt on the validity of Korstad and Lichenstein's findings. By the mid-1980s and through the 1990s and beyond historians like Eric Arnesen, Beth Tompkins Bates, Michelle Brattain, Melinda Chateauvert, William Harris, Bruce Nelson, Ernest Obadele-Starks, Paula Pfeffer and David Roediger contributed to 'a veritable outpouring of new scholarship on trade union racial practices, black and white minority workers' experiences and activism, and a white working class identity'.[26] A number of researchers, most notably Nelson and Roediger, highlighted the entrenched racial prejudice of rank and file white workers. Although some trade union leaders were relatively more enlightened, such evidence of intractable grassroots bigotry cast doubt on the possibility of any meaningful and enduring alliance between white-dominated trade unions and black civil rights campaigners, irrespective of the corrosive impact of McCarthyism.

At the same time that studies of the relationship between race and organized labour were passing through a period of significant upheaval, the historiography on American Communism also experienced a process of major revisionism. From the 1950s through to the early 1980s, decades marked by Cold War hostility and superpower rivalry, works on the history of the Communist Party of the United States of America (CPUSA) were, predictably, largely negative in tone. Scholars like Wilson Record, Theodore Draper and Harvey Klehr labelled the party as 'secretive, devious, manipulative, authoritarian and fundamentally insincere'. Indeed, it was not even a 'legitimate political party because it had no commitment to democracy and no loyalty to the United States'.[27] In short it was that worst of all things, un-American.

Beginning in the mid-1980s, and more strongly in the early 1990s, a number of developments combined to undermine this overly harsh and simplistic judgement. The collapse of the Soviet Union and end of the Cold War fostered an academic climate conducive to a more balanced understanding of American Communism. There was also a greater awareness of the short-comings of the United States itself, whether in respect to the Vietnam War abroad, or the excesses of McCarthyism at home. Only the most extreme of American patriots could continue to view the Cold War as an apocalyptic struggle between the sons of light and the powers of darkness. By and large historians did not fall into this category.[28]

New research on the CPUSA portrayed American Communists of the 1930s and 1940s in a more sympathetic manner. They were viewed as essentially sincere campaigners for social and economic justice rather than slavish disciples of a foreign power. In particular, a number of studies highlighted the genuine and often courageous opposition of party members to racial prejudice. Perhaps the most influential of these was Robin D. J. Kelley's *Hammer and Hoe*. In this study of Alabama Communists during the Great Depression, Kelley documented the heroic efforts of Communists, radical trade unionists and working-class blacks to challenge the white power structure in the state, most notably in the city of Birmingham. Although ulti-mately unsuccessful, it was the efforts of these groups, largely ignored by earlier historians, that constituted the principal threat to the status quo. In contrast, Birmingham's small middle-class black community was weakly organized, conservative in outlook, and condescending in attitude towards rank and file black workers.[29]

Collectively, new studies during the 1980s and 1990s on the CPUSA, the American labour movement and working-class black communities brought about an overdue reappraisal of African American history in the 1930s and 1940s. Most historians would now accept that earlier accounts of the civil rights struggle in these years were generally too focused on black elites and formal organizations. At the same time it can be argued that such revi-sionism risks fresh, albeit different, distortions of the historical record, or at the very least leaves important questions unresolved.

In respect to the CPUSA it is arguable, as Eric Arnesen has observed, that new historians of the party have been insufficiently critical of its motivations and actions in their attempt to distance themselves from earlier Cold War stereotypes. In doing so 'they run the risk of creating their own overly romantic vision of the party, and in the process tend to forget that it was a political organization and that political organizations, of whatever political stripe, often subordinate ideology to self-interest and sacrifice principle to perceived pragmatism'. Although sincere and courageous in opposing racial bigotry, American communists were still willing to denounce the NAACP when the party ordered them to do so. Similarly, during the Second World War the party encouraged harmonious labour relations in order to maximize wartime production. This strategy was not necessarily in the best interests of African Americans who, as in Asa Philip Randolph's March on Washington Movement in 1941, might have hoped to use the wartime emergency to exact improved working conditions and opportunities from employers and federal and state governmental agencies.[30]

In respect to rank-and-file white workers it is important, if depressing, to note that they were more than capable of harbouring deep racial prejudices without any encouragement from cynical capitalist employers seeking to divide their employees along racial lines. At the same time white workforces clearly never had exclusive control over working conditions and practices. Too much emphasis on white working-class communities risks obscuring the contribution of employers and the state in perpetuating racial discrimination.[31] Indeed, during the 1930s Franklin Roosevelt's New Deal initiatives marked a hitherto unprecedented extension of the power of federal government into the lives of ordinary Americans.

Since the 1960s Revisionist historians have become increasingly critical of the New Deal and its failure to address fundamental social and economic problems.[32] This reflects the wider changes in American society during the same period. In the late 1940s and the 1950s still painful memories of the mass unemployment of the Great Depression created a broad consensus of support among both liberals and conservatives for the idea of a federal welfare state that had been established by Roosevelt. During the 1960s John F. Kennedy's New Frontier initiatives and Lyndon Johnson's Great Society programme were even more ambitious, aspiring to permanently eliminate poverty and large-scale unemployment through a far-reaching series of welfare measures building on earlier New Deal agencies and legislation.

Unfortunately, in the mid-1970s rising unemployment and evidence of persistent and widening social inequalities painfully highlighted the failed aspirations of the Kennedy and Johnson administrations. In the 1980s and 1990s the new conservatism of the Republican Reagan and Bush administrations led to the questioning of the very idea of federal and state welfare programmes. Instead, private sector initiatives and rugged self-help were increasingly advanced as the most effective remedy for social ills. Such thinking continued to gain ground even during the Democratic Clinton administrations of the 1990s and, more predictably, under Republican George W. Bush in the early years of the twenty-first century. Perceptions of the New Deal evolved in a way that corresponded with the changing times. The Rooseveltian welfare state became increasingly viewed as at best a holding measure during a period of extreme crisis, at worst the product of a misconceived philosophy that created an unhealthy culture of dependency in American society that was to persist for almost fifty years.

The first concerted, sustained efforts by historians to assess the impact of the New Deal on US race relations can be traced back to the late 1960s and the 1970s, followed by a steadily growing body of work from the 1980s onwards. In short, the most important modern studies on the impact of the policies of the Roosevelt administration on African Americans appeared at a time when the image that both the historical profession and ordinary Americans held of the New Deal as a whole was becoming less positive. Predictably, the new studies of Roosevelt's record on race relations both reflected and reinforced this changing perception.

In the late 1960s historian John Salmond highlighted the endemic racial segregation and discrimination in the Civilian Conservation Corps (CCC), despite a provision in the legislation creating the Corps that 'in employing citizens for the purposes of this Act, no discrimination shall be made on account of race, color, or creed'.[33] In a more wide-ranging 1970 study Raymond Wolters documented the failure of two flagship New Deal agencies, the Agricultural Adjustment Act (AAA) and the National Recovery Administration (NRA), to address the needs of black workers and farmers in a non-discriminatory way. This was because the reality of the New Deal was that it was dominated by power politics. The strongest and most influential special interest groups commanded the greatest attention and made the most gains. African Americans were weak and badly organized, and consequently fared badly. This tendency was reinforced by the fact that New Deal agencies were operating in a segregated and racially discriminatory society. Inevitably, they manifested these same characteristics, particularly in the South, where much of the administration of the agencies was devolved down to teams of local officials comprised almost exclusively of racially conservative whites.[34]

In *Farewell to the Party of Lincoln: Black Politics in the Age of FDR*, Nancy Weiss attempted to explain why, from 1936 onwards, African American voters gave such strong support to the Roosevelt administration. Given the manifest shortcomings of New Deal initiatives already highlighted, it is perhaps not surprising that Weiss struggled to find a convincing answer to her own question. She was thus forced to conclude that, however limited the gains African Americans experienced as a result of the New Deal, they were still grateful to Roosevelt for them because it represented an advance on what had gone before.[35]

Historians seeking to advance a more positive image of the Rooseveltian state, such as Kevin J. McMahon, Harvard Sitkoff and Patricia Sullivan, tended to favour this comparative perspective. Moreover, they argued that there was a need to recognize the constraints under which Roosevelt was forced to operate, a consideration emphasized by the President himself. 'I did not choose the tools with which I must work. Had I been permitted to choose them I would have selected quite different ones', Roosevelt candidly explained to NAACP Executive Secretary Walter White at the height of the Great Depression. He thus felt unable to give public backing to the NAACP's campaign for a federal anti-lynching law, as 'I've got to get legislation passed by Congress to save America' and 'Southerners by reason of the seniority rule in Congress are chairman or occupy strategic places on most of the Senate and House Committees'. If he came out in favour of the anti-lynching bill, they could 'block every bill I ask Congress to pass to keep America from collapsing. I just can't take the risk.'[36]

Sitkoff and Sullivan sought to differentiate between racially conservative New Deal agencies, like the NRA and AAA, and more enlightened bodies like the Farm Security Administration (FSA), Works Progress Administration (WPA), and Public Works Administration (PWA), and the racially liberal officials like Clark Foreman, Harry Hopkins and Harold Ickes, who administered them. If the gains made by even the best agencies during the 1930s were still only limited, they nonetheless laid important foundations for the future, and took on greater significance over time. In particular, the New Deal marked a major growth in the power of federal government in impacting on the lives of ordinary Americans and a comparative diminution in the authority of state administrations. Focusing on the judiciary, McMahon argued that Roosevelt's troubled relationship with the United States Supreme Court served as a catalyst for the emergence of a new liberal consensus on the Court. Similarly, the Roosevelt years marked the start of a process of fundamental realignment within the Democratic party in its thinking on economic, social and racial issues.

This line of reasoning has not convinced all researchers. Under-whelmed by such argumentation, historian Nancy Grant's 1990 study *TVA and Black Americans: Planning for the Status Quo* criticized the Tennessee Valley Authority (TVA), traditionally seen as one of the New Deal's most innovative and liberal initiatives, for the shortcomings in its racial philosophy. Specifically, the TVA provided blacks with limited job opportunities that were predominantly unskilled in nature. The agency was marred by institutionalized racism and envisaged a future in which, although the Tennessee Valley would be economically revitalized, the fate of blacks in the region was to be confined to the subordinate roles that had been traditionally allocated to them. Similarly, in 1995 Kenneth O'Reilly penned a damning reappraisal of the limitations in President Roosevelt's own racial thinking.[37]

Gunnar Myrdal's *An American Dilemma: The Negro Problem and Modern Democracy* is the inevitable starting point for any historiographical understanding of the African American experience during the Second World War. During the 1930s and early 1940s the Swedish economist Myrdal engaged in a massive collaborative study of black living conditions in the United States. The resulting publication, two volumes totalling more than 1,500 pages, remains one of the most detailed and scholarly investigations on the subject.[38]

At times it also made uncomfortable reading. In depressing detail Myrdal highlighted the deprivations experienced by African Americans during the Great Depression. Moreover, he convincingly demonstrated that the efforts of some New Deal agencies, most notably the AAA, exacerbated, rather than alleviated, such suffering. Such analysis seemed to confirm the accuracy of historian Thomas Carlyle's perception of economics as the 'Dismal Science'. Myrdal himself, however, was no dismal scientist. His predictions for the future development of American race relations were optimistic. The unequal treatment afforded African Americans represented a painful contradiction between the nation's core values and the realities of everyday life. Dating back to the American Revolution, the Declaration of Independence and the Federal Constitution of 1787, the United States had been founded with a creed that stressed democratic egalitarianism and the basic right to life, liberty and the pursuit of happiness for all. Most white Americans sincerely believed in these high-minded principles yet failed to apply them when it came to their dealings with their black fellow citizens. This was the 'dilemma' referred to by Myrdal in the title of his study.

It was also a situation that was no longer sustainable. The enormous demands that resulted from the national war effort made such ambivalence an unaffordable luxury. This was particularly the case in a conflict that was supposedly being fought to uphold democratic freedoms and demonstrate the falseness of Nazi racial theories. Moreover, within the United States African Americans were displaying a new militancy in their struggle for more equal treatment, abandoning their former patience, submission and deference, the traits that conservative whites relied upon to perpetuate the racial status quo.

Instantly acclaimed as a classic by scholars and liberal political thinkers Myrdal's work became highly influential in US intellectual circles. Moreover, like great claret, its appeal only increased with the passing of the years, reaching a peak of popularity during the heady days of the Civil Rights Movement in the mid-1950s and early 1960s. Even the finest of wines, however, still have a finite shelf life. By the early 1970s it became clear that Myrdal's 1944 vintage was beginning to decline. When 'the Civil Rights Movement fell on hard times', as historian David Southern observed, 'it became fashionable to sneer at Myrdal's optimistic formulations'.[39]

In the grim racial climate of the 1980s and 1990s his belief that whites could be willingly co-opted into the civil rights struggle appeared more naive than prophetic, and the strategies he endorsed for racial uplift overly cautious and conservative. Myrdal's study had 'judged the NAACP the most effective of all black protest groups, celebrated the success of its legal campaign, and presented a moderate agenda for action almost identical to the NAACP's', Harvard Sitkoff critically observed in 1997. *An American Dilemma* had 'warned against the folly of black militancy in the South, accentuated the role of white liberal allies in the campaign for racial equality, and insisted that the key struggle was the moral one within the white conscience – and not a struggle for power between the races'. This 'placid prognosis' became so influential because it fitted 'the needs of a moderate African American leadership dreading racial conflict, or challenges to its own hegemony within black America and set the tone and the premises of action by the Civil Rights Movement in the postwar decade'.[40]

Myrdal's study also benefited from a lack of competition. During the late 1940s and the early 1950s the African American experience was still regarded as an academic backwater by most mainstream historians. Moreover, the Second World War was remembered as a time when all Americans had come together to face a common danger. Admittedly, this was not a viewpoint shared by all. The eminent African American historian John Hope Franklin recalled how, as a twenty-six-year-old scholar, he had responded to a call by the United States Navy for experienced administrators. Despite an already impressive curriculum vitae he was rejected for a post because, as his recruitment interviewer candidly acknowledged, he was still lacking one essential qualification, that of colour. After further similar experiences Franklin concluded that 'the United States, however much it was devoted to protecting the freedoms and rights of Europeans, had no respect for me, no interest in my well-being, and not even a desire to utilize my services'. He reflected that America 'did not need me and did not deserve me', and in consequence 'I spent the remainder of the war years successfully and with malice afore-thought outwitting my draft board and the entire Selective Service establishment'.[41] It was only in 1990, however, that Franklin publicly expressed his thoughts in print. In the early decades after the war it was all too apparent that the vast majority of Americans were not yet ready to heed the expression of such resentments. In keeping with the national mood, other scholars also lacked the inclination to focus on the injustices experienced by African Americans during the war years.

By the mid-1960s times had changed. Internal divisions within the United States were all too apparent and high profile civil rights protests by black demonstrators led to unprecedented interest in African American history by white scholars. In this climate historians understandably began to consider the black experience during the Second World War in an attempt to detect the early signs of the later civil rights confrontations of their own era. In an influential article the historian Richard Dalfiume hailed the War as the 'the forgotten years of the Negro revolution'.[42] He argued that the period had marked the growth of a new militancy in African American communities. Black Americans were no longer willing to submit passively to racial discrimination and segregation. This new mood of assertiveness was demonstrated by events like Asa Philip Randolph's threatened March on Washington Movement in 1941 to protest the lack of employment opportunities for blacks in defence industries, and the 'Double V' campaign of the black newspaper the *Pittsburgh Courier*, urging African Americans to fight racial injustice at home with the same vigour required in the struggle against totalitarianism abroad. Significantly, the NAACP also experienced a massive increase in support during the war years, growing from 50,000 members in 1940 to 500,000 members by 1945. In the light of later events it seemed clear that such developments were the first signs of a new momentum in the black freedom struggle that would culminate in the mass campaigns of the 1950s and 1960s.

Instantly appealing, the most obvious attraction of this line of argument, its simplicity, was also its greatest weakness. The

course of human events is invariably complex and often contradictory. By the mid-1970s there were signs that historians were
beginning to question the validity of such a straightforward interpretation of the changing pattern of race relations. Lee Finkle was
one of the first to sound a note of caution. He argued that, rather
than being an indication of increased militancy, the 'Double V'
campaign was a sign of black conservatism. Unwilling to appear
unpatriotic, black newspaper proprietors seized on a seemingly
bold slogan with a hidden objective of uniting their recalcitrant
mass readership behind the war effort. In reality, the campaign
constituted a familiar call to 'close ranks' disguised by militant
posturing. Significantly, no black newspaper was suppressed by
the federal authorities during the war or any black journalist
arrested for sedition.[43]

In the 1980s Charles W. Eagles highlighted the inherent
conservatism of the Roosevelt administration's wartime racial
policies. Although the President employed a special advisor on
race relations, Jonathan Daniels, a southern white liberal, the role
of Daniels was essentially that of a racial troubleshooter. His task
was to identify potential sources of racial conflict in advance and
defuse them before they could develop to the point where they
might interfere with wartime production, as happened with the
Harlem and Detroit race riots of 1943. In consequence the
administration's policies on race relations were reactive and
piecemeal rather than the result of any coherent long-term
policy.[44]

Making use of newly available government documents,
Patrick Washburn identified another reason for the wartime
quiescence of the black press: massive federal government surveillance.[45] In 1990 Merl Reed also utilized previously untapped
sources to produce an authoritative study of the Fair Employment
Practices Committee (FEPC), the federal agency set up by
Roosevelt under pressure from Randolph's March on Washington
Movement in 1941 to investigate racial discrimination in the
defence industries. Although Reed concluded that agency staff
were generally sincere in their efforts, his work did not counter
the consensus among historians that the influence of the FEPC
was undermined by higher level officials in the administration,
including the President, who declined to enforce its recommenda-

tions lest this interfere with the war effort. It was also possible to argue that improved employment opportunities for African Americans during the war were more a result of labour shortages than the good offices of the agency.[46]

In a more wide-ranging study published at the turn of the millennium, political scientist Daniel Kryder confirmed the generally negative views of earlier scholars on the wartime record of Roosevelt on racial issues. He concluded that the administration, like any central government in time of war, had two primary objectives, maximizing the war effort and surviving in office. The administration was prepared to endorse limited racial reforms in the interests of these larger concerns but such advances were not an objective in their own right.[47]

Kryder's study reflected the fact that by the end of the 1990s the process of revisionism was well under way. Harvard Sitkoff, who had previously championed the view of the Second World War as a watershed in the development of black militancy, now qualified his earlier findings. He argued that although there was evidence of greater assertiveness in the early years of the war, this largely disappeared after the Japanese attack on Pearl Harbor on 7 December 1941. This was because the entry of the United States into the conflict as a full combatant made it considerably more difficult for African Americans to protest racial injustice without seeming to be unpatriotic.[48]

In another revealing 1990s essay Neil R. McMillen highlighted the changes in thinking within the historical profession that had taken place since the 1960s. The 'reductionism of the "Double-V" argument may well have led historians to overstate the case for an unconditional black two-front war for freedom abroad and freedom at home', he reflected. Scholars 'should be wary of a determinism that reads every squall on the wartime color front as a storm of racial militancy'. It was arguable that historians, 'by and large as committed a group of "continuitarians" as can be found anywhere', had 'been led into teleological error and, by reading history backwards, could have found more continuity between wartime yearning and post-war confrontation than there may in fact be'.[49] The challenge facing historians in the early twenty-first century would seem to be to apply this necessary corrective to earlier studies without tilting the balance too far in the opposite direction. 'You might as well fall flat on your face', the humorist James Thurber once observed, 'as lean over too far backwards.'[50] If overstated, the revisionist case contains potentially fresh hazards of its own. Instead of searching for black militancy during the Second World War to account for the growth of later civil rights protest, historians could end up arguing the case for why the Civil Rights Movement should not have developed at all.

Notes

1 Bruce Nelson, *Divided We Stand: American Workers and the Struggle for Black Equality* (Princeton, New Jersey, 2001), p. xxi.

2 Nelson, *Divided We Stand*, p. xxi.

3 Harvard Sitkoff, *A New Deal for Blacks: The Emergence of Civil Rights as a National Issue. Volume I: The Depression Decade* (New York, 1978), p. vii.

4 Sitkoff, *A New Deal for Blacks*, p. viii.

5 Sitkoff, *A New Deal for Blacks*, pp. viii, 335.

6 Neil McMillen, 'Fighting for What We Didn't Have: How Mississippi's Black Veterans Remember World War II', in Neil R. McMillen (ed.), *Remaking Dixie: The Impact of World War II on the American South* (Jackson, Mississippi, 1997), p. 93.

7 Jacqueline Dowd Hall, *Revolt Against Chivalry: Jessie Daniel Ames and the Women's Campaign Against Lynching* (New York, 1979); Raymond Gavins, *The Perils and Prospects of Southern Black Leadership: Gordon Blaine Hancock, 1884–1970* (Durham, North Carolina, 1993); Linda Reed, *Simple Decency and Common Sense: The Southern Conference Movement, 1938–1963* (Bloomington, Indiana, 1991).

8 Adam Fairclough, *Better Day Coming, Blacks and Equality, 1890–2000* (New York, 2001), p. 163.

9 Fairclough, *Better Day Coming*, pp. 162–3.

10 Kenneth E. Burnham, *God Comes to America: Father Divine and the Peace Mission Movement* (Boston, 1979); Robert Weisbrot, *Father Divine and the Struggle for Racial Equality* (Urbana, Illinois, 1983); Jill Watts, *God, Harlem, USA: The Father Divine Story* (Berkeley, California, 1992).

11 Weisbrot, *Father Divine*, p. 226.

12 Robert Allerton Parker, *The Incredible Messiah: The Deification of Father Divine* (Boston, 1937); Sara Harris, *Father Divine* (New York, 1953); Sara Harris, *Father Divine*, revised enlarged edition (New York, 1971), pp. ix, xvi; Weisbrot, *Father Divine*, pp. 226–7.

13 Claude McKay, *Harlem: Negro Metropolis* (New York, 1940), pp. 32–72; Roi Ottley, *'New World A-Coming': Inside Black America* (Boston, 1943), p. 99; Weisbrot, *Father Divine*, pp. 228–9.

14 Robert L. Zangrando, *The NAACP Crusade Against Lynching, 1909–1950* (Philadelphia, 1980); Mark V. Tushnet, *The NAACP's Legal Strategy Against Segregated Education, 1925–1950* (Chapel Hill, North Carolina, 1987);

Mark V. Tushnet, *Making Civil Rights Law: Thurgood Marshall and the Supreme Court, 1936–1961* (New York, 1994).

15 B. Joyce Ross, *J. E. Spingarn and the Rise of the NAACP, 1911–1939* (New York, 1972); Genna Rae McNeil, *Groundwork: Charles Hamilton Houston and the Struggle for Civil Rights* (Philadelphia, 1983); Carolyn Wedin, *Inheritors of the Spirit: Mary White Ovington and the Founding of the NAACP* (New York, 1998); Kenneth Robert Janken, *White: The Biography of Walter White, Mr. NAACP* (New York, 2003); Roy Wilkins with Tom Mathews, *Standing Fast: The Autobiography of Roy Wilkins* (New York, 1982).

16 Merline Pitre, *In Struggle Against Jim Crow: Lulu B. White and the NAACP, 1900–1957* (College Station, Texas, 1999); Christopher Robert Reed, *The Chicago NAACP and the Rise of Black Professional Leadership, 1910–1966* (Bloomington, Indiana, 1997); Beth Tompkins Bates, 'A New Crowd Challenges the Agenda of the Old Guard in the NAACP, 1933–1941', *American Historical Review* (102, 1997), pp. 340–77.

17 Robin D. G. Kelley, '"We Are Not What We Seem": Rethinking Black Working Class Opposition in the Jim Crow South', *Journal of American History* (80, 1993), pp. 75–112.

18 Kelley, '"We Are Not What We Seem"', p. 77; Eric Arnesen, 'Up From Exclusion: Black and White Workers, Race, and the State of Labor History', *Reviews in American History* (26, 1998), p. 160.

19 Kelley, '"We Are Not What We Seem"', p. 83; Arnesen, 'Up From Exclusion', p. 160.

20 Arnesen, 'Up From Exclusion', p. 146; Herbert Hill, 'The Problem of Race in American Labor History', *Reviews in American History* (24, 1996), p. 189.

21 Nell Irvin Painter, 'The New Labor History and the Historical Moment', *International Journal of Politics, Culture and Society* (2, 1989), pp. 369–70; Hill, 'The Problem of Race', p. 190; Arnesen, 'Up From Exclusion', p. 146.

22 Hill, 'The Problem of Race', p. 192; Nelson, *Divided We Stand*, p. xxii.

23 Arnesen, 'Up From Exclusion', pp. 146, 158.

24 August Meier and Elliott Rudwick, *Black Detroit and the Rise of the UAW* (New York, 1979); Arnesen, 'Up From Exclusion', pp. 152–3.

25 Robert Korstad and Nelson Lichtenstein, 'Opportunities Found and Lost: Labor, Radicals, and the Early Civil Rights Movement', *Journal of American History* (75, 1988), pp. 786–811.

26 Eric Arnesen, *Brotherhoods of Color: Black Railroad Workers and the Struggle for Equality* (Cambridge, Massachusetts, 2001); Beth Tompkins Bates, *Pullman Porters and the Rise of Protest Politics in Black America, 1925–1945* (Chapel Hill, North Carolina, 2001); Michelle Brattain, *The Politics of Whiteness: Race, Workers and Culture in the Modern South* (Princeton, New Jersey, 2001); Melinda Chateauvert, *Marching Together: Women of the Brotherhood of Sleeping Car Porters* (Urbana, Illinois, 1998); William H. Harris, *Keeping the Faith: A. Philip Randolph, Milton P. Webster, and the Brotherhood of Sleeping Car Porters, 1925–37* (Urbana, Illinois, 1977); William H. Harris, *The Harder We Run: Black Workers Since the Civil War* (New York, 1982); Nelson, *Divided We Stand*; Ernest Obadele-Starks, *Black Unionism in the Industrial South* (College Station, Texas, 2000); Paula F.

Pfeffer, *A. Philip Randolph: Pioneer of the Civil Rights Movement* (Baton Rouge, Louisiana, 1990); David Roediger, *The Wages of Whiteness: Race and the Making of the American Working Class* (New York, 1991).

27 Wilson Record, *The Negro and the American Communist Party* (Chapel Hill, North Carolina, 1951); Wilson Record, *Race and Radicalism* (Ithaca, New York, 1964); Theodore Draper, *American Communism and Soviet Russia* (New York, 1960); Harvey Klehr, *The Heyday of American Communism: The Depression Decade* (New York, 1984); Fairclough, *Better Day Coming*, p. 142.

28 Fairclough, *Better Day Coming*, p. 142.

29 Mark Naison, *Communists in Harlem During the Depression* (Urbana, Illinois, 1983); Fraser Ottanelli, *The Communist Party of the United States: From the Depression Decade to World War II* (New Brunswick, New Jersey, 1991); Mark Solomon, *The Cry Was Unity: Communists and African Americans, 1917–1936* (Jackson, Mississippi, 1998); Robin D. G. Kelley, *Hammer and Hoe: Alabama Communists During the Great Depression* (Chapel Hill, North Carolina, 1990); Arnesen, 'Up From Exclusion', pp. 158–9.

30 Arnesen, 'Up From Exclusion', pp. 154–5.

31 Arnesen, 'Up From Exclusion', p. 166.

32 Nancy L. Grant, *TVA and Black Americans: Planning for the Status Quo* (Philadelphia, 1990).

33 John A. Salmond, 'The Civilian Conservation Corps and the Negro', *Journal of American History*, (52, 1965), pp. 73–88; John A. Salmond, *The Civilian Conservation Corps, 1933–1942: A New Deal Case Study* (Durham, North Carolina, 1967); John A. Salmond, 'The Civilian Conservation Corps and the Negro', in Bernard Sternsher (ed.), *The Negro in Depression and War: Prelude to Revolution, 1930–1945* (Chicago, 1969), p. 79.

34 Raymond Wolters, *Negroes and the Great Depression: The Problem of Economic Recovery* (Westport, Connecticut, 1970).

35 Nancy J. Weiss, *Farewell to the Party of Lincoln: Black Politics in the Age of FDR* (Princeton, New Jersey, 1983).

36 Sitkoff, *A New Deal for Blacks*; Harvard Sitkoff, 'The New Deal and Race Relations', in Harvard Sitkoff (ed.), *Fifty Years Later: The New Deal Evaluated* (New York, 1985), pp. 93–112; Patricia Sullivan, *Days of Hope: Race and Democracy in the New Deal Era* (Chapel Hill, North Carolina, 1996); Kevin J. McMahon, *Reconsidering Roosevelt on Race: How the Presidency Paved the Road to Brown* (Chicago, 2003); Franklin D. Roosevelt quoted in Roger Biles, *A New Deal for the American People* (DeKalb, Illinois, 1991), p. 180.

37 Grant, *TVA and Black Americans*; Kenneth O'Reilly, *Nixon's Piano: Presidents and Racial Politics from Washington to Clinton* (New York, 1995), pp. 109–44.

38 Gunnar Myrdal, *An American Dilemma: The Negro Problem and Modern Democracy*, 2 vols (New York, 1944).

39 David W. Southern, *Gunnar Myrdal and Black–White Relations: The Use and Abuse of An American Dilemma, 1944–1969* (Baton Rouge, Louisiana, 1987), p. xiv. See also Walter A. Jackson, *Gunnar Myrdal and America's*

Conscience (Chapel Hill, North Carolina, 1994) for a thoughtful and detailed assessment of Myrdal's work.

40 Harvard Sitkoff, 'African American Militancy in the World War II South: Another Perspective', in McMillen (ed.), *Remaking Dixie*, p. 89.

41 John Hope Franklin, 'Their War and Mine', *Journal of American History*, (77, 1990), pp. 576–8.

42 Richard M. Dalfiume, 'The Forgotten Years of the Negro Revolution', *Journal of American History*, (55, 1968). See also Richard M. Dalfiume, *Desegregation of the U.S. Armed Forces: Fighting on Two Fronts, 1939–1953* (Columbia, Missouri, 1969).

43 Lee Finkle, 'The Conservative Aims of Militant Rhetoric: Black Protest During World War II', *Journal of American History* (60, 1973); Lee Finkle, *Forum For Protest: The Black Press During World War II* (London, 1975); Patrick S. Washburn, *A Question of Sedition: The Federal Government's Investigation of the Black Press During World War II* (New York, 1986).

44 Charles W. Eagles, 'Two "Double Vs": Jonathan Daniels, FDR and Race Relations During World War II', *North Carolina Historical Review* (Summer 1982); Charles W. Eagles, *Jonathan Daniels and Race Relations: The Evolution of a Southern Liberal* (Knoxville, Tennessee, 1982).

45 Washburn, *A Question of Sedition*.

46 Merl E. Reed, *Seedtime for the Modern Civil Rights Movement: The President's Committee on Fair Employment Practice, 1941–1946* (Baton Rouge, Louisiana, 1991); Neil A. Wynn, *The Afro-American and the Second World War* (London, 1993), p. 55.

47 Daniel Kryder, *Divided Arsenal: Race and the American State During World War II* (Cambridge, 2000).

48 Harvard Sitkoff, 'Racial Militancy and Interracial Violence in the Second World War', *Journal of American History* (58, 1971); Sitkoff, 'African American Militancy in the World War II South'.

49 McMillen, 'Fighting for What We Didn't Have', p. 95.

50 James Thurber, 'The Bear Who Let It Alone', *New Yorker*, 29 April 1939.

4

The post-war Civil Rights Movement, 1945–1968

It is likely that most, if not all, history teachers and lecturers have at one time or another warned their students against the pitfalls of the 'great man' theory of history, seeking to explain the past as the result of the actions and ideas of a few famous, dynamic, individuals at the expense of paying too little attention to the abstract, but wider and more powerful, processes of political, social and economic change that invariably shape the course of human events. In short, as the British scholar Peter Ling has observed, historians mistrust a biography-centred approach to their subject and this is not just because 'skepticism is their preferred stance on everything'. Biographies, and even more so autobiographies, tend to 'inflate the role of' their subject 'and, by placing one person consistently in the foreground' they 'can overlook the contribution of less celebrated figures'. Moreover, they 'can also distort historical understanding by giving too little weight to structural forces that require less personal, even quantitative analysis'.[1]

The fact that Ling's reflections appear in the introduction to his biographical study of Martin Luther King highlights a paradox in the historiography of the post-war Civil Rights Movement, namely that historians working in this field have displayed a consistent tendency to focus their research on biographical studies of leading individuals. 'Biographical accounts', as the American historian Charles W. Eagles has noted, have 'from the beginning and throughout the 1990s' proved to be 'perhaps the most popular form of study of the Civil Rights Movement', both for 'scholars and other writers'.[2] This was especially the case in respect to the first studies of the Movement that appeared in the late 1960s and throughout the 1970s. Moreover, early accounts concentrated predominantly on the life of one individual in particular, Martin Luther King, resulting in a 'King-centric' approach to the subject.[3] Admittedly, even in these first studies, no serious historian was naive enough to explain the rise of mass black civil rights protests solely with reference to King, but he invariably occupied a centre stage position, seeming to dominate the individuals and events around him through his determination and vision like a historical colossus.

This perception was apparent in August Meier's thoughtful, and still valuable, 1965 essay 'On the Role of Martin Luther King' for the journal *New Politics*. Meier's article constituted one of the first scholarly accounts of King's life. A distinguished historian with a career built on research and teaching in African American history, Meier typically demonstrated deep insights in his analysis and was by no means uncritical of what he perceived as his subject's shortcomings. Nonetheless, he concluded that King occupied the 'vital center' of the Civil Rights Movement and was unique in his ability to articulate the grievances of diverse groups of black protesters to white audiences in a way that elicited sympathy rather than fear.[4]

The preoccupation with, and veneration of, Martin Luther King in early studies on the Civil Rights Movement can be explained by a number of factors. The distinctive and mesmerizing cadences of King's public addresses, accessible to American audiences through the still new mass medium of television, make him one of the most memorable public orators of the twentieth century. His intelligent and articulate responses in media interviews contrasted painfully with the uncouth and intemperate outbursts of some of his best-known segregationist opponents. In print he lucidly and persuasively explained the intellectual basis of his beliefs and showed these were rooted in the core values of western philosophy, demonstrating both his own erudition and the moral justification of the civil rights cause.[5]

The powerful public impact of King's many skills and abilities was enhanced still further by the tragic manner of his death. His assassination in Memphis, Tennessee on 4 April 1968 enveloped King's historical reputation in a halo of martyrdom and provided confirmation, if such were necessary, of his status as one of the icons of modern American life. His enduring impact on the public mind in the decades after his death is demonstrated by the fact that in 1983 Martin Luther King was given the accolade of an annual US public holiday named in his honour. No other figure in American history, including even the founder of the nation George Washington, has had this unique distinction conferred upon them in their own homeland.

In the first decade after his death the hallowed image of King in the public mind created a set of circumstances where it was near to impossible for historians to engage in objective critical appraisals of him. This situation was reinforced by the fact that many historians of the Civil Rights Movement were writing not as detached observers but were deeply committed to its aims and, in a number of cases, active participants in the black freedom struggle.

In the late 1940s August Meier had taught at Tougaloo College in Mississippi, an educational institution with an all-black student body. In the 1950s he joined the NAACP as a graduate student at Columbia University. In 1960, as a teacher at Morgan State College in Maryland, he took part in student-led protests to desegregate lunch counters in Baltimore. He attended meetings of the Student Nonviolent Coordinating Committee (SNCC) and the Congress of Racial Equality (CORE). In his own words, up to the mid-1960s Meier was a 'participant-observer' in the movement.[6]

During the late 1950s and early 1960s Howard Zinn taught at Spelman, the leading black women's college in Atlanta, Georgia, and lived in the local black community. He took part in protests to integrate the city's public facilities. In his role as a scholar Zinn then went on to write one of the earliest academic studies of the SNCC. Harvard Sitkoff, who authored one of the earliest scholarly accounts of the role of blacks in the New Deal, joined the NAACP and briefly participated in civil rights protests in the South. In 1965 more than forty historians demonstrated their support for the Civil Rights Movement by joining the Selma to Montgomery March in Alabama led by Martin Luther King. Moreover, this contingent included some of the most distinguished and influential members of the historical profession in the United States, including Richard Hofstadter, C. Vann

Woodward, John Hope Franklin and Kenneth Stampp.[7]

When such considerations are taken into account it is not surprising that early studies of King's life generally extolled his virtues and achievements, rather than lingering on his shortcomings and failures. In 1969 *My Life With Martin Luther King, Jr*, by King's widow Coretta Scott, was predictably uplifting. Similarly, the title of historian David Levering Lewis's 1970 work, *King: A Critical Biography*, is best understood as meaning sympathetically critical rather than having any negative connotations.[8] It was unthinkable for any scholar to write a work that sought to question the limitations of King's accomplishments or highlight his human weaknesses. Such an account would at best have appeared to be an exercise in bad taste for commercial gain, at worst a betrayal of the cause for which King had made the ultimate personal sacrifice. The changed climate brought about by King's assassination can be most clearly appreciated by a reading of August Meier's earlier *New Politics* article. Writing in 1965, Meier had mildly rebuked King for the fact that in 'a movement in which successful leaders are those who share in the hardships of their followers, in the risks that they take, in the beatings they receive, in the length of time that they spend in jail', King himself tended 'to leave prison for other important engagements, rather than remaining there and suffering with his followers'. Three years later, the expression of such sentiments was inconceivable.[9]

When eschewing a biographical approach, early historians of the Civil Rights Movement typically sought to achieve insights into their subject through traditional political and institutional studies. William C. Berman, Donald R. McCoy and Richard T. Reutten examined the civil rights record of the two administrations of Democratic President Harry S. Truman, 1945–53. Robert F. Burk provided a study on the administrations of Republican President Dwight D. Eisenhower, 1953–61, whilst Carl Brauer sought to shed light on the civil rights record of Eisenhower's Democratic successor, John F. Kennedy during his term in office from 1961–63. In another important study Steven Lawson concentrated on the struggle for black voting rights in the American South from the end of the Second World War through to the mid-1960s.[10]

Although such works marked important contributions in

terms of the development of knowledge and understanding, viewed from another perspective early studies of the civil rights struggle were as notable for the topics that were neglected as for those that were addressed. In many areas of historical scholarship the most striking feature of the mid-1960s through to the mid-1970s was the emergence of what became known as the 'new social history'. Transcending national, geographical and chronological boundaries, the diverse proponents of this genre shared a common goal of seeking to examine history 'from the bottom up'. Instead of looking at the lives of powerful individuals and the workings of governmental institutions they sought to direct their research at the lives of ordinary people in local communities, groups and individuals whose thoughts and experiences had previously gone unrecorded in traditional historical narratives.

In the field of English history this approach was typified in groundbreaking works such as E. P. Thomson's *The Making of the English Working Class* (1963) and Christopher Hill's *The World Turned Upside Down* (1972). In the study of American history Eugene Genovese's *Roll, Jordan, Roll* (1974) was typical of the prevailing trend of examining nineteenth-century slavery from the perspective of black slaves rather than through the political careers and social and economic life of their white masters.[11]

It would seem reasonable to expect that early historians of the post-war Civil Rights Movement would have embraced the 'new social history' with even greater enthusiasm than other members of the historical profession. After all, the very subject matter of their research was the struggle of an oppressed minority to achieve full democratic rights within American society. Moreover, the lives of African American communities had been largely ignored by earlier generations of mainstream scholars. The fact that most studies of the Civil Rights Movement published in the late 1960s and the 1970s did not incorporate this new approach thus requires some explanation.

One consideration was the spate of high profile political assassinations in the 1960s. Martin Luther King was only one of a number of prominent individuals linked with the civil rights struggle to meet a tragic and violent end. President John F. Kennedy was assassinated in 1963. His brother Robert, Attorney General during the Kennedy administration, shared a similar fate in 1968, as did the charismatic black radical Malcolm X in 1965. In death these 1960s icons, like Martin Luther King, were enveloped by the hallowed status of martyrdom. This veneration of fallen heroes encouraged a leader-centred approach to the study of the historical events in which they had been involved.

Another factor was that the Civil Rights Movement was a newly emerging topic for scholarly investigation. In other subject areas, with a long established historiography, the new social histories offered a fresh and innovative alternative to often tired and well-worn debates. Civil rights historians did not experience the same pressure to demonstrate originality, as they were the trailblazers in their field. At the same time this experience, albeit liberating, also had drawbacks. The new pioneers did not have a large, established body of archive resources at their disposal. Instead, they had to discover relevant primary source materials for themselves. Unsurprisingly, scholars confronted with this task initially focused their attention on traditional kinds of evidence with which they were familiar, such as political archives and the records of leading civil rights pressure groups. This reinforced the tendency to understand events through the policies of presidential administrations and the actions of nationally known civil rights leaders and the organizations they headed.[12]

In addition to the obvious biographies, Howard Zinn's 1964 study *SNCC: The New Abolitionists* thus provided an early account of the Student Nonviolent Coordinating Committee. In 1973 August Meier and Elliott Rudwick provided the first scholarly history of the Congress of Racial Equality. In 1981 Clayborne Carson published a more detailed and considered study of the SNCC, and in 1987 Adam Fairclough's *To Redeem the Soul of America* provided an authoritative history of Martin Luther King's Southern Christian Leadership Conference (SCLC). Jesse Thomas Moore, Nancy J. Weiss and most recently Dennis C. Dickerson contributed works on the National Urban League and Whitney M. Young, the League's Executive Director from 1961 to 1971. Predictably, the only one of the 'big five' civil rights groups not to benefit from an authoritative organizational history was the National Association for the Advancement of Colored People (NAACP). Conservative in image, and labyrinthine and bureaucratic in the nature and extent of its archives, the Association lacked the appeal of the more radical civil rights organizations in attracting chroniclers of its work.[13]

By the early 1980s civil rights historians had in any case begun to adopt new lines of enquiry in their research. 'Influenced by larger trends in the historical profession', in particular the now not so new social history, with 'its emphasis on women, minorities, the "inarticulate", and others whose presence was usually omitted from traditional histories', researchers, as historian Charles Eagles has observed, 'widened their view and dropped their gaze to see many previously overlooked stories'.[14]

An early indication of this change was Sara Evans's 1979 study *Personal Politics: The Roots of Women's Liberation in the Civil Rights Movement and the New Left*. In this important turning point in marking the recognition of the role of women in the movement, Evans argued that the involvement of women in civil rights protest was a prelude to their later participation in the women's liberation movement. A different, but related, development came in the proliferation of local and regional studies. In 1980 William Chafe's *Civilities and Civil Rights* recounted the history of civil rights protest in Greensboro, North Carolina, birthplace of the student 'sit-in' movement of the 1960s. In a leading article published the same year, J. Mills Thornton III looked at the Montgomery Bus Boycott. These accounts were followed by widely acclaimed local studies on Tuskegee, Alabama, by Robert J. Norrell and St Augustine, Florida, by David R. Colburn.[15]

Sociologist Aldon Morris's 1984 study, *The Origins of the Civil Rights Movement* was also influential, stressing the importance of social and economic change at grassroots level in the emergence of organized civil rights protest. Morris was one of the first scholars to challenge the traditional 'Montgomery to Memphis' chronology of the civil rights struggle adopted by earlier scholars, who had portrayed the emergence of Martin Luther King in the 1955 Montgomery Bus Boycott as marking the birth of the Civil Rights Movement and his death in Memphis thirteen years later as heralding its final demise. Instead, Morris drew attention to earlier protest activity, most notably the 1953 Bus Boycott in Baton Rouge, Louisiana. His work complemented the earlier work of fellow sociologist Doug McAdam, which questioned the idea of elite leadership of civil rights protest and instead highlighted broader long-term historical processes as the key catalyst for the emergence of the post-war Civil Rights Movement.[16]

At the same time Martin Luther King himself remained a major focus of attention for researchers during the 1980s and 1990s, but new accounts of his life began to reflect the wider developments in the study of the Civil Rights Movement. There were also indications that, with the passage of the years, biographers were becoming more objective in their portrayals of King, highlighting his weaknesses as well as his strengths. Although this trend was not as pronounced as in the case of critical revisionist accounts of other 1960s icons, most notably President John F. Kennedy, it was still a significant departure.

This was borne out in David Garrow's *Bearing the Cross: Martin Luther King, Jr., and the Southern Christian Leadership Conference*. A political scientist, Garrow's 1986 study was justly acclaimed as the most authoritative biography of King, a status that it has retained into the early years of the twenty-first century, despite much competition. The author of numerous works on King, Garrow demonstrated both encyclopaedic knowledge and an impeccable standard of academic scholarship in his writings.[17] In the words of one reviewer, Garrow simply appeared 'to have read everything by and about his subject'. Moreover, he was able to gain fresh insights by utilizing the extensive Federal Bureau of Investigation (FBI) surveillance records on King released under the Freedom of Information Act.[18]

In general historical biographers have a tendency to empathize with their chosen subject. To devote several years, in some cases decades, to researching the life of a historical figure represents a daunting commitment of time and effort. The sustained motivation needed for such a task is often derived from the fact that it constitutes a labour of love, namely that the scholar in question has a profound admiration for, or is at least strongly sympathetic to, his/her chosen subject. Admittedly, some researchers appear to relish the opportunity for character assassination, especially if the individual that they have opted to write about is in some way notorious, but such accounts constitute the minority. Unsurprisingly, *Bearing the Cross* was a biographical study of the sympathetic variety. At the same time Garrow's in-depth knowledge and understanding of his subject enabled him to appreciate more fully than some earlier biographers King's human frailties. King was a 'saint with feet of clay', prone to agonizing self-doubt and serial extra-marital infidelities.[19]

King's fallibility was further emphasized with the appearance of *The Papers of Martin Luther King* from the early 1990s onwards. A major academic project, edited by a team of eminent scholars led by historian Clayborne Carson, this ambitious undertaking saw the publication of King's private papers and other primary source materials that had previously been accessible only to dedicated researchers.[20] In compiling the early volumes for this series it became apparent that in preparing his PhD thesis in Philosophy at Boston University in the early 1950s, King had extensively plagiarized the work of another student. The shock of this revelation prompted a period of angst and heartfelt debate in the academic community. In the eyes of historians, committed to upholding scholarly ethics, plagiarism could be viewed as a far more serious offence than adultery. In the event, King's historical reputation suffered little direct harm. Some scholars sought to find mitigation for King's actions. His plagiarism was thus defended as the innocent 'borrowing' of ideas rather than an act of conscious misconduct. More sensibly, others noted that King's student indiscretions should not be allowed to detract from the scope and courage of his achievements in later life. Indeed the realization that King was not some divine being, but vulnerable to the same weaknesses to which all human flesh is heir, arguably made his accomplishments all the more impressive.[21]

The evidence of plagiarism did, however, influence the course of historiographical debate in more subtle ways. It cast doubt on the idea, consciously fostered by King himself in his public writings and speeches, that his commitment and vision as a race leader were rooted in an unshakeable belief in the moral rightness of his cause derived from his study of the core values of western philosophy. Instead, it seemed more convincing to argue, as Garrow had done earlier in *Bearing the Cross*, that King derived his inner strength from his religious faith and community values instilled by his Baptist upbringing. The 1990s thus saw the publication of important new studies on King that considered his role as a church leader. In *Voice of Deliverance* (1992) professor of English Keith Miller examined how King pieced together his sermons and his use of language in them. In 1998 theology professor Richard Lischer studied King as a preacher and orator, both as a church minister and a wider public moralist, highlighting King's inspirational qualities as a speaker.[22]

At the same time, the wider public recognition of King's human failings underlined the fact that the Civil Rights Movement was not brought into being by one superhuman being but was rather the collective achievement of countless lesser-known individuals at grassroots level. This realization reinforced the already prevailing trend towards more local and regional studies of the movement. Typifying this mood, Clayborne Carson, the leading editor of *The Papers of Martin Luther King*, thus reflected that, 'If King had never lived, the black freedom struggle would have followed a course of development similar to the one it did.' Elaborating further, he noted:

> The Montgomery bus boycott would have occurred, because King did not initiate it. Black students probably would have rebelled – even without King as a role model – for they had sources of tactical and ideological inspiration besides King. Mass activism in southern cities and voting rights efforts in the Deep South were outgrowths of large-scale social and political forces, rather than simply consequences of the actions of a single leader. Though perhaps not as quickly and certainly not as peacefully nor with as universal a significance, the black movement would probably have achieved its major legislative victories without King's leadership, for the southern Jim Crow system was a regional anachronism, and the forces that undermined it were inexorable.[23]

Interestingly, when in 1993 the University of Newcastle upon Tyne organized a 'Martin Luther King Memorial Conference on Civil Rights and Race Relations', to commemorate the twenty-fifth anniversary of King's death, there were more papers on the work of the Civil Rights Movement at regional and local level than on the martyred leader himself.[24] Similarly, after working for five years as one of the editors for *Birth of a New Age*, the third volume of *The Martin Luther King Papers*, covering King's life and leadership during the period of the Montgomery Bus Boycott 1955–6, the first reaction of historian Stewart Burns was not to be inspired to undertake further study of King. Instead he concluded 'that "King-related" documents' revealed 'only part of the epic story of the Montgomery movement, presenting a particular and incomplete perspective on events'. Seeking to remedy this imbalance, in 1996 he went on to publish *Daybreak of Freedom: The Montgomery Bus Boycott*, a collection of primary source materials highlighting the involvement of less well-known individuals and ordinary black citizens in Montgomery to the Boycott campaign.[25]

The Newcastle upon Tyne conference and *Daybreak of Freedom* reflected the fact that by the late 1980s and throughout the 1990s there was a consolidation of earlier trends. A number of important new local and regional studies appeared. In *Righteous Lives* Kim Lacy Rogers examined the Civil Rights Movement in New Orleans. British historian Adam Fairclough opted for a broader canvas, providing a detailed and authoritative account of the black freedom struggle in twentieth-century Louisiana, whilst John Dittmer and Charles Payne contributed important studies on the neighbouring state of Mississippi.[26]

Broadly speaking, the local and regional studies published in the 1980s and 1990s can be subdivided into two categories: those that looked at states or regions over a number of decades, and works that focused on brief periods, specific issues and particular communities.[27] The late 1980s onwards was marked by a growing number of studies of the latter sort. Scholars Howard Smead and Stephen J. Whitfield published accounts on the 1950s lynchings of Mack Charles Parker and Emmett Till in Mississippi. In 1988 journalists Seth Cagin and Philip Dray examined the infamous murders of three civil rights workers, Andrew Goodman, Michael Schwerner and James Chaney in the Magnolia state during the 1964 Mississippi Summer Project civil rights campaign.[28]

In the 1990s Glenn T. Eskew and Glenda Alice Rabby looked at the Civil Rights Movement in Birmingham, Alabama, and Tallahassee, Florida, respectively, while Richard A. Couto analysed the impact of the Movement in four rural southern communities. In the early years of the new millennium the interest of scholars in local and regional studies of both the broad and narrow varieties seemed undiminished, with the publication of

Beyond Atlanta: The Struggle for Racial Equality in Georgia, 1940–1980 by British historian Stephen G. N. Tuck in 2001, followed in 2002 by *Redefining the Color Line*, a study of black activism in Little Rock, Arkansas by fellow British scholar John A. Kirk, and *Dividing Lines*, a detailed account of the civil rights campaigns in Montgomery, Birmingham, and Selma, Alabama, by American historian J. Mills Thornton III.[29]

Work on the role of women in the civil rights struggle also gathered momentum. The year 1987 saw the publication of two important autobiographical accounts by civil rights activists Mary King and Jo Ann Gibson Robinson. The title of Robinson's work, *The Montgomery Bus Boycott and the Women Who Started It*, reflected the growing recognition of the pivotal role of women in the civil rights struggle. In 1990 *Trailblazers and Torchbearers*, edited by Vicki L. Crawford, Jacqueline A. Rouse and Barbara Woods, provided biographical portraits of women civil rights campaigners from the 1940s through to the mid-1960s. In the years that followed full-length biographical studies appeared on a number of female activists, most notably Ella Baker, Fannie Lou Hamer, Ruby Doris Smith Robinson and Rosa Parks. Belinda Robnett's *How Long? How Long? African American Women and the Struggle for Civil Rights* (1997) examined the contribution of women from a broader perspective. In 1999 British scholars Peter Ling and Sharon Montieth edited a valuable collection of essays on *Gender in the Civil Rights Movement*. The following year *Deep in Our Hearts* made available the reminiscences and reflections of nine white women who had been civil rights campaigners during the 1950s and the 1960s. Conversely, *Sisters in the Struggle* (2001) a collection of essays edited by Bettye Collier-Thomas and V. P. Franklin, focused on the contribution of black women to the civil rights struggle. [30]

In addition to building on existing foundations, scholars of the late 1980s and 1990s also began to explore hitherto neglected areas. Despite the obvious importance of Christian teachings to the Civil Rights Movement, researchers in the 1970s and 1980s had shown comparatively little interest in a concerted study of the role of the churches and religious leaders in the freedom struggle. This began to change with the publication of *Southern Civil Religions in Conflict* (1987), in which historian Andrew M.

Manis examined the reactions of white and black southern Baptists to civil rights issues from the late 1940s through to the late 1950s. In the early 1990s historian James F. Findlay went on to look at the involvement of the National Council of Churches in the Civil Rights Movement during the 1950s and 1960s. In 1997 theology professor Charles Marsh looked at the religious and racial beliefs of participants on both sides of the civil rights conflict in Mississippi, and in a 1998 journal article 'Religious Ideas of the Segregationists', historian David L. Chappell argued that southern white opponents of the Civil Rights Movement were handicapped by self-doubts about the moral basis of their cause. Jane Dailey took a different view, concluding in a later 2004 essay that segregationist resistance was reinforced by traditional church teachings against miscegenation. In 2001 historian S. Jonathan Bass examined Martin Luther King's 1963 'Letter from Birmingham Jail' and profiled the eight southern white religious leaders to whom it was addressed.[31]

A clear trend from the mid-1990s onwards was for scholars to study the response of particular religious denominations to the civil rights struggle. In *Religion and Race*, Joel L. Alvis Jr examined the dilemmas faced by southern Presbyterians from the mid-1940s through to the early 1980s, while Gardiner H. Shattuck Jr appraised the response of Episcopalians to civil rights issues from the 1860s to the 1970s. In a prize-winning 2001 study, *Getting Right With God*, British scholar Mark Newman focused on Southern Baptists. In line with David Chappell's earlier essay, Newman found that white Baptists in the South were divided in their views on civil rights. A hard-line segregationist minority argued that segregation was justified in scripture, but the progressive wing of the church increasingly viewed segregation and discrimination as contrary to biblical teachings. Over time the arguments of this group gradually won over the majority of moderate segregationists within the church, and ultimately even the hard-line opponents of integration.[32]

The Civil Rights Movement of the 1950s and 1960s raised difficult ethical issues for religious leaders of all faiths, but the moral challenge was perhaps most painful of all for southern Jewish communities. Members of a long persecuted minority it was easy for Jews in the region to empathize with the experiences of African Americans. At the same time active support for the civil rights campaign carried the risk of provoking anti-Semitic violence and retaliation by segregationist groups. In *The Quiet Voices* (1997), a collection of biographical essays, Mark K. Bauman and Berkeley Kalin examined how southern Rabbis confronted this dilemma. The following year British historian Clive Webb looked at the response of the Jewish community in Montgomery, Alabama to the civil rights conflicts in the city between 1954 and 1960. In a subsequent, more wide-ranging, study Webb analysed the ambivalent historical relationship between Jewish and African American communities from slavery through to the early 1970s. In keeping with the growing emphasis given by historians to the role of women in the Civil Rights Movement this latter work also included a chapter on the contribution of Jewish women in the struggle for school desegregation, an issue that was explored in more detail in Debra Schultz's later work, *Going South: Jewish Women in the Civil Rights Movement*.[33]

The relationship between black civil rights and US foreign policy was another little-explored area that attracted the attention of scholars in the 1990s. The last years of the twentieth century saw a proliferation of studies on the international dimensions of the black freedom struggle by a range of scholars, including general overviews by Brenda Gayle Plummer, Penny M. Von Eschen and Michael L. Krenn.[34] Other researchers chose to address more specific issues. Carol Anderson examined the dilemmas posed for the United Nations by the black freedom struggle. In *Fighting on Two Fronts* (1997) historian James E. Westheider focused on the experiences of African American servicemen in the Vietnam War, while Jonathan Zimmerman looked at black Peace Corps volunteers in Africa in an article for the *Journal of American History*. In *Toward the Beloved Community* (1995) religious studies scholar Lewis V. Baldwin studied Martin Luther King's response to the anti-apartheid struggle in South Africa, whilst in *Proudly We Can Be Africans* James Meriwether assessed the special relationship between African Americans and Africa from the 1930s to the early 1960s. Conversely, Renee Romano examined the reactions of African Diplomats in the United States to the civil rights campaigns of black Americans.[35]

The first years of the new millennium were notable for an upsurge of academic interest in the complicated relationship between black civil rights and the Cold War, prompted in part by the collapse of communism in Eastern Europe during the 1990s and a desire to evaluate the Cold War in historical perspective as a period of international rivalry that now clearly belonged to the past. Interestingly, scholars have been divided in their assessment of the impact of East–West tensions on US race relations. Researchers such as Thomas Borstelmann, Mary L. Dudziak and Azza Salama Layton, writing after the fall of the Soviet Union in the early 1990s, generally supported the optimistic interpretation first advanced by C. Vann Woodward some four decades earlier, namely that the Cold War hastened the move towards desegregation. This was because racial injustice at home was a major embarrassment for successive US presidential administrations and an equally valuable propaganda issue for the Soviet Union when the two superpowers competed for moral supremacy on a global stage, particularly in their efforts to win over the hearts and minds of predominantly non-white nations in the Third World.[36]

Others such as American scholar Manning Marable, and more recently British historian Adam Fairclough, were less sanguine. Although fully aware of the beneficial aspects of the Cold War for the civil rights struggle, they concluded that these were more than outweighed by its more negative connotations.[37] Researchers working prior to the final end of the Cold War were particularly inclined to support this interpretation. In an influential 1988 article, 'Opportunities Found and Lost: Labor, Radicals, and the Early Civil Rights Movement', Robert Korstad and Nelson Lichtenstein argued that tentative links developing between civil rights groups and organized labour during the New Deal and the Second World War withered away in the repressive post-war climate of anti-communism.[38] Left-wing groups and individuals sympathetic to black civil rights were forced to devote all their energies towards self-preservation as they were subjected to the McCarthyite witch-hunts of the late 1940s and early 1950s, during which almost any liberal spokesperson risked accusations of being a Soviet Fifth Columnist, seeking to undermine the moral fibre of the United States from within. The issue of black civil rights itself became perceived as somehow suspect or subversive and in the southern states, the region of the nation where McCarthyism was arguably most virulent and persisted longest, even mainstream organizations like the NAACP became a target for persecution by state and local authorities.

African Americans like W. E. B. Du Bois, Paul Robeson and Josephine Baker who used the mass media to speak out against racial injustice in the United States were labelled unpatriotic and subjected to harassment by federal government agencies and the courts. Conversely, white segregationists angrily portrayed themselves as loyal American citizens under siege. Although all too often synthetic and self-seeking, it is possible that such arguments also reflected sincere emotion, as was highlighted by historian David A. Horowitz. In another thoughtful 1988 journal article, he suggested that white southerners genuinely viewed the efforts of civil rights campaigners and northern liberals to enforce desegregation as an attempt to interfere with their right to freedom of association and to destroy the distinctive regional identity of the South. In short, civil rights initiatives represented an attempt to replace individualism with centrally enforced conformity as prevailed in the communist societies of Eastern Europe. Whether cynical or genuine, the considerable efforts made by southern segregationists to take advantage of the domestic Cold War climate to elicit support for their cause were further highlighted in two full-length 2004 studies by George Lewis and Jeff Woods.[39]

The famous school desegregation decision of the US Supreme Court in the 1954 *Brown* ruling was another issue that engaged the minds of historians in the 1990s, but for different reasons. If the Cold War attracted interest as a period of history that had clearly drawn to a close, *Brown* merited attention because of the ongoing legacy of desegregation and the continuing involvement of the Supreme Court in civil rights issues, most notably ruling on the constitutionality of affirmative action or positive discrimination programmes designed to benefit historically disadvantaged minorities, most particularly African Americans.

Building on earlier important studies by Richard Kluger and Raymond Wolters in the 1970s and 1980s, scholars of the 1990s and early years of the twenty-first century scrutinized the *Brown* decision from almost every conceivable angle. Robert A. Pratt,

Davison M. Douglas, David S. Cecelski, Robyn Duff Ladino and William Henry Kellar examined the impact of school desegregation on individual southern communities. Adopting a different approach, Mark Tushnet published two studies on the life and career of Thurgood Marshall, the NAACP's lead-lawyer in *Brown*, whilst *Crusaders in the Courts* by Jack Greenberg made available the thoughts of another member of the NAACP legal team.[40]

In an influential 1994 journal article, University of Virginia law professor Michael Klarman questioned the accepted wisdom that *Brown* was a major catalyst in the emergence of the Civil Rights Movement. Reflecting new thinking among civil rights historians, he argued that civil rights protests had already gained considerable momentum before the court's ruling and were the culmination of long-term political, social and economic developments rather than any short-term factor. The principal importance of *Brown* was not the impact of the ruling on the morale of civil rights campaigners but its effect on the minds of white southerners. The decision prompted a violent racial 'backlash' by segregationists against civil rights protesters. In a further 'ripple effect', previously apathetic northern whites were shocked at the regular scenes of racial brutality on network television news broadcasts and began demanding federal government intervention in support of civil rights campaigners.[41]

Klarman's provocative and original thesis prompted heated academic discussion and acted as a catalyst for further scholarly debate on the merits of the *Brown* ruling and its wider long-term consequences. In *Race, Law and Culture* (1997) professor of jurisprudence and political science Austin Sarat edited an important new collection of essays by scholars from a range of academic disciplines. In 2001 historian James T. Patterson published a new full-length study on the *Brown* decision and its ongoing legacy almost fifty years later. An essay collection, *What Brown v. Board of Education Should Have Said: The Nation's Top Legal Experts Rewrite America's Landmark Civil Rights Decision* (2001) offered another perspective, as did Peter Irons's *Jim Crow's Children: The Broken Promise of the Brown Decision* the following year. In 2004, special editions of both the *Journal of Southern History* and *Journal of American History* largely devoted to *Brown*, on the fiftieth anniversary of the Supreme Court's famous ruling, appeared to provide final proof of the seemingly inexhaustible enthusiasm of scholars for rearguing the rights and wrongs of the case.[42]

Klarman's 1994 article was significant not just because of the debate it provoked on the Supreme Court. It was equally important as an early example of a growing awareness by historians of the need to study not just the thoughts and actions of civil rights campaigners but also their segregationist opponents. Early scholars of the civil rights struggle, as has already been indicated, firmly endorsed the aims and objectives of the black protest movement. Admittedly, not all researchers were committed grassroots activists like Howard Zinn and Leon Litwack but, almost without exception, they still supported civil rights campaigns in their hearts and minds.[43]

Though commendable as an indication of the generally liberal values of the academic community, such partisanship had certain disadvantages from a historiographical point of view. With a few exceptions, most notably Numan Bartley's *The Rise of Massive Resistance: Race and Politics in the South During the 1950s* (1969) and Neil R. McMillen's *The Citizens' Council: Organized Resistance to the Second Reconstruction, 1954–64* (1971), early historians of the Civil Rights Movement concentrated their research on the protesters, with whom they empathized, rather than the southern segregationists who sought to preserve the racial status quo.[44] This imbalance persisted throughout the 1980s and for much of the 1990s, constituting what historian Charles W. Eagles has described as an 'asymmetrical approach' to the study of the past. The end product of this was 'an abnormal way of writing history', with scholars neglecting their professional duty to understand the proponents of segregation because they 'seem to have assumed that little remains to be learned about the segregationists or that they are simply too unattractive or unimportant to warrant examination'.[45]

Justified and perceptive as they may have been, there were indications that even as Eagles penned such thoughts scholars were seeking to achieve greater balance. In 1995 historian Dan T. Carter published a prize-winning study of Alabama's segregationist leader George Wallace and in 1997 journalist Roy Reed produced an authoritative biography of Arkansas segregationist Orval Faubus. The subjects of both works were revealed to be more complex and enigmatic than their public image as unsophisticated reactionary bigots. Conservative on black civil rights, Faubus was a liberal reformer when it came to public expenditure on education and welfare benefits for the elderly. In the mid-1970s Wallace met with civil rights leaders to seek forgiveness for his earlier segregationist stance in seeming acts of contrition that in some respects foreshadowed the later restorative justice commissions of post-apartheid South Africa.[46] In *Restructured Resistance* (1998) Jeff Roche examined the segregationist cause in Georgia, and in 1999 Numan V. Bartley published a new edition of *The Rise of Massive Resistance*, reflecting, as the author himself noted, 'a renewed interest' by scholars 'in the conservative defenders of the status quo'. The aforementioned works of David L. Chapell and Mark Newman provided new insights on the religious ideas of southern segregationists.[47]

Viewed collectively the new works on the segregationists highlighted a further limitation in earlier civil rights histories, namely a tendency to view the movement as a bi-polar struggle between two monolithic coalitions. From this perspective the civil rights battles of the 1950s and 1960s were commonly portrayed as an apocalyptic conflict between the powers of good and the forces of evil, in which the armies of the latter displayed an unquestioning loyalty to their cause and a willingness to resort to any extremes of violence and depravity to achieve final victory. By the early years of the twenty-first century it became clear to scholars that such imagery was overly melodramatic. White segregationist groups suffered from inconsistencies, divisions and self-doubt. Moreover, segregationist violence if often shocking was less extensive and extreme than it appeared in traditional histories of the Civil Rights Movement. The injury or martyrdom of any civil rights campaigner constituted both a morally unacceptable act of aggression and a personal tragedy, but the actual number of fatalities was limited, and far fewer than the number of lives lost in the anti-apartheid struggle in South Africa. For all 'the jailings, the beatings, and the deaths', as British historian Adam Fairclough observed in 2001, 'the Civil Rights Movement succeeded in transforming Southern race relations with remarkably few casualties.' The great strength of non-violent civil rights protest 'was its ability to expose and discredit the South's racism while inhibiting the white propensity to violence'.[48]

By the same token, by the late 1990s historians began to appreciate that not just southern segregationists but also civil rights organizations suffered from internal weaknesses. The Civil Rights Movement was a coalition of diverse and at times competing groups and interests rather than a monolithic vehicle for black protest.[49] Historians had long since recognized the potential for conflict between young, secular-minded activists in the SNCC and CORE and the more conservative NAACP and church-oriented SCLC. Equally, there was the risk of tensions between male and female campaigners and black and white protesters, while large numbers of African Americans took no active part in civil rights campaigns at all. In their influential new studies on Birmingham, Alabama, Glenn Eskew and Andrew Manis highlighted another fault-line: class. In particular, Manis noted the success of local civil rights activist the Reverend Fred Shuttlesworth in winning a large following among working-class black communities, in contrast to the less enthusiastic reception he was afforded by 'the silk-stocking, middle class black churches' in the city. The growing scholarly awareness of the contribution of both black and white working-class groups to the civil rights struggle was also reflected in Timothy Minchin's *Hiring the Black Worker* (1999) and *The Color of Work* (2001), which provided detailed accounts of the struggle for integration in the southern textile and paper industries respectively.[50]

Scholars also continued to redefine the traditional chronology of the Civil Rights Movement, acknowledging the importance of the years prior to 1954 as providing the foundations for later more publicly recognized protest campaigns. Although reflecting a more comprehensive understanding of the Civil Rights Movement, this approach, as in similar studies of the 1930s and early 1940s, was not without pitfalls in its own right. In attempting to redress the comparative lack of research on civil rights issues before *Brown*, historians potentially run the risk of erring too much in the opposite direction, seeing every development as a precursor to the campaigns of 1954–68. Michael R. Gardner's 2002 study, *Harry Truman and Civil Rights: Moral*

Courage and Political Risks was thus criticized by one reviewer for over-emphasizing the commitment and idealism of America's first post-war president in advancing the cause of black civil rights. The civil rights advances initiated during his terms in office could arguably be more convincingly attributed to hard-headed short-term political and electoral calculation, rather than principled concern for the plight of African Americans.

Conversely, David Niven's *The Politics of Injustice* (2003), a study of the civil rights record of the Kennedy administration, was vulnerable to attack from the opposite direction. Critical of Kennedy's cautious stance on the issue, Niven argued that more vigorous support for civil rights would have been not only morally right but politically circumspect, taking advantage of growing public support for the Civil Rights Movement and the increasing electoral importance of African American voters. This optimistic assessment is at the very least debatable. In particular it can be seen as underestimating the still considerable public and congressional opposition to civil rights in the early 1960s and overly influenced by the more radical advances achieved by the Lyndon Johnson administrations, 1963–69, operating in very different political and racial conditions. [51]

Within the 'Montgomery to Memphis' timeframe it had been customary for historians of the 1970s and 1980s to view the years 1963–65 as marking the zenith of the Civil Rights Movement. This value judgement can be traced back to the first studies on the civil rights campaigns of 1954–68. Focusing their research on traditional governmental and legislative primary source materials, it was natural for early civil rights scholars to view the 1964 Civil Rights Act and 1965 Voting Rights Act as constituting the high-point in civil rights gains.[52]

In contrast, the years 1966–68 saw little in the way of further legislative advances. The most notable exception, the 1968 Civil Rights Act, was less far-reaching than the two earlier pieces of legislation and its unexpected passage could be attributed to the outpouring of public and Congressional sympathy for civil rights in the immediate aftermath of the assassination of Martin Luther King. This posthumous achievement notwithstanding, King's civil rights leadership during the last three years of his life was in a state of crisis. Confronted with growing divisions within the Civil

Rights Movement, urban race riots in cities of the North, and criticized by establishment figures for his public opposition to the Vietnam War, his final years appeared to be ones of disillusionment and failure. For this reason early civil rights scholars tended to concentrate their research on the seemingly halcyon period of the Movement between 1954 and 1965.

During the 1990s this situation began to change. In *Northern Protest: Martin Luther King, Jr., Chicago, and the Civil Rights Movement* and *The Last Crusade: Martin Luther King, Jr., the FBI, and the Poor People's Campaign,* James R. Ralph and Gerald B. McKnight respectively provided full-length studies of two of King's last major initiatives. In a 2002 biography British historian Peter Ling challenged conventional wisdom more overtly, concluding that King's greatest achievements came not in the period 1955–65 but during his turbulent final years. It was the King of these 'later struggles' who emerged as 'the more heroic figure, as a leader striving to develop his ability to address injustice and as someone prepared to face the price of unpopularity and isolation'.[53]

By its very nature the process of historiographical revisionism can never reach any final or definitive conclusion but is always ongoing. At the same time, after a prolonged period of intensive study it is common for the academic debate on any given topic to experience a temporary lull, a time of reflection and consolidation rather than innovation, before later research, with fresh perspectives, revives the discussion and takes it in new directions. After more than three decades of detailed examination it might be supposed that the historiography of the post-war Civil Rights Movement was on the point of entering such a hiatus. The continuing ability of scholars in the early twenty-first century to discover new areas of research for investigation and engage in original thinking suggests, however, that this moment, although possibly impending, has not yet arrived.

Notes

1 Peter J. Ling, *Martin Luther King, Jr.* (London, 2002), p. 1.
2 Charles W. Eagles, 'Toward New Histories of the Civil Rights Era', *Journal of Southern History* (66, 2000), p. 825.
3 Ling, *Martin Luther King, Jr.* p. 1.

4 August Meier, 'On the Role of Martin Luther King', *New Politics* (4, 1965), pp. 1–8. Reprinted in August Meier, *A White Scholar and the Black Community, 1945–1965: Essays and Reflections* (Amherst, Massachusetts, 1992), pp. 212–22.

5 For example, Martin Luther King Jr, *Stride Toward Freedom: The Montgomery Story* (New York, 1958); Martin Luther King Jr, *Why We Can't Wait* (New York, 1964); Martin Luther King Jr, *Where Do We Go From Here? Chaos or Community?* (New York, 1967).

6 Eagles, 'Toward New Histories of the Civil Rights Era', p. 819; Meier, *A White Scholar and the Black Community*, pp. 3–38.

7 Eagles, 'Toward New Histories of the Civil Rights Era', pp. 819–21.

8 Coretta Scott King, *My Life With Martin Luther King, Jr.* (New York, 1969); David Levering Lewis, *King: A Critical Biography* (New York, 1970).

9 Meier, *A White Scholar and the Black Community*, p. 213.

10 William C. Berman, *The Politics of Civil Rights in the Truman Administration* (Columbus, Ohio, 1970); Donald R. McCoy and Richard T. Reutten, *Quest and Response: Minority Rights and the Truman Administration* (Lawrence, Kansas, 1973); Robert F. Burk, *The Eisenhower Administration and Black Civil Rights* (Knoxville, Tennessee, 1984); Carl M. Brauer, *John F. Kennedy and the Second Reconstruction* (New York, 1977); Steven F. Lawson, *Black Ballots: Voting Rights in the South, 1944–1969* (New York, 1976).

11 E. P. Thompson, *The Making of the English Working Class* (London, 1963); Christopher Hill, *The World Turned Upside Down: Radical Ideas During the English Revolution* (London, 1972); Eugene D. Genovese, *Roll, Jordan, Roll: The World the Slaves Made* (New York, 1974).

12 Steven F. Lawson, 'Freedom Then, Freedom Now: The Historiography of the Civil Rights Movement', *American Historical Review* (96, 1991), pp. 456–7; Eagles, 'Toward New Histories of the Civil Rights Era', p. 822.

13 Howard Zinn, *SNCC: The New Abolitionists* (Boston, 1965); August Meier and Elliott Rudwick, *CORE: A Study in the Civil Rights Movement, 1942–1968* (Urbana, Illinois, 1973); Clayborne Carson, *In Struggle: SNCC and the Black Awakening of the 1960s* (Cambridge, Massachusetts, 1981); Adam Fairclough, *To Redeem the Soul of America: The Southern Christian Leadership Conference and Martin Luther King, Jr.* (Athens, Georgia, 1987); Jesse Thomas Moore, *Search for Equality: The National Urban League, 1910–61* (Philadelphia, 1982); Nancy J. Weiss, *Whitney M. Young, Jr., and the Struggle for Civil Rights* (Princeton, New Jersey, 1989); Dennis C. Dickerson, *Militant Mediator: Whitney M. Young Jr.* (Lexington, Kentucky, 1998).

14 Eagles, 'Toward New Histories of the Civil Rights Era', p. 826.

15 Sara Evans, *Personal Politics: The Roots of Women's Liberation in the Civil Rights Movement and the New Left* (New York, 1980); William H. Chafe, *Civilities and Civil Rights: Greensboro, North Carolina, and the Black Struggle For Freedom* (Oxford, 1981); J. Mills Thornton III, 'Challenge and Response in the Montgomery Bus Boycott of 1955–1956', *Alabama Review* (33, 1980), pp. 163–235; Robert J. Norrell, *Reaping the Whirlwind: The Civil Rights Movement in Tuskegee* (New York, 1986); David R. Colburn, *Racial Change and Community Crisis: St Augustine, Florida, 1877–1980*

(Gainesville, Florida, 1991).

16 Aldon Morris, *The Origins of the Civil Rights Movement: Black Communities Organizing for Change* (New York, 1984); Doug McAdam, *Political Process and the Development of Black Insurgency, 1930–1970* (Chicago, 1982).

17 David J. Garrow, *Bearing the Cross: Martin Luther King, Jr., and the Southern Christian Leadership Conference* (New York, 1986).

18 Steven F. Lawson, 'Review Essay: Martin Luther King, Jr., and the Civil Rights Movement', *Georgia Historical Quarterly* (71, 1987), p. 251.

19 Garrow, *Bearing the Cross*, p. 587; Lawson, 'Martin Luther King, Jr., and the Civil Rights Movement', p. 254.

20 Clayborne Carson et al. (eds), *The Papers of Martin Luther King, Jr.: Volume I: Called To Serve, January 1929–June 1951; Volume II: Rediscovering Precious Values, July 1951–November 1955; Volume III: Birth of a New Age, December 1955–December 1956; Volume IV: Symbol of the Movement, January 1957–December 1958; Volume V: Threshold of a New Decade, January 1959–December 1960* (Berkeley, California, 1992, 1994, 1996, 2000 and 2005).

21 David Thelen (ed.), 'Becoming Martin Luther King, Jr., – Plagiarism and Originality: A Round Table', *Journal of American History* (78, 1991).

22 Keith D. Miller, *Voice of Deliverance: The Language of Martin Luther King, Jr., and Its Sources* (New York, 1992); Richard Lischer, *The Preacher King: Martin Luther King Jr. and the Word that Moved America* (New York, 1995).

23 Clayborne Carson, 'Martin Luther King, Jr.: Charismatic Leadership in a Mass Struggle', in David Thelen (ed.), 'A Round Table: Martin Luther King, Jr.', *Journal of American History* (74, 1987), pp. 451–2.

24 Brian Ward and Tony Badger (eds), *The Making of Martin Luther King and the Civil Rights Movement* (London, 1996).

25 Stewart Burns (ed.), *Daybreak of Freedom: The Montgomery Bus Boycott* (Chapel Hill, North Carolina, 1997), p. xv.

26 Kim Lacy Rogers, *Righteous Lives: Narratives of the New Orleans Civil Rights Movement* (New York, 1993); Adam Fairclough, *Race and Democracy: The Civil Rights Struggle in Louisiana, 1915–1972* (Athens, Georgia, 1995); John Dittmar, *Local People: The Struggle for Civil Rights in Mississippi* (Urbana, Illinois, 1994); Charles Payne, *I've Got the Light of Freedom: The Organizing Tradition and the Mississippi Freedom Struggle* (Berkeley, California, 1995).

27 Adam Fairclough, 'State of the Art: Historians and the Civil Rights Movement', *Journal of American Studies* (24, 1990), pp. 392–3.

28 Howard Smead, *Blood Justice: The Lynching of Charles Mack Parker* (New York, 1986); Stephen J. Whitfield, *A Death in the Delta: The Story of Emmett Till* (New York, 1988); Seth Cagin and Philip Dray, *We Are Not Afraid: The Story of Goodman, Schwerner and Chaney and the Civil Rights Campaign in Mississippi* (London, 1988).

29 Glenn T. Eskew, *But For Birmingham: The Local and National Movements in the Civil Rights Struggle* (Chapel Hill, North Carolina, 1997); Glenda Alice Rabby, *The Pain and the Promise: The Struggle for Civil Rights in Tallahassee, Florida* (Athens, Georgia, 1999); Richard A. Couto, *Ain't Gonna Let Nobody Turn Me Around: The Pursuit of Racial Justice in the Rural South*

(Philadelphia, 1991); Stephen G. N. Tuck, *Beyond Atlanta: The Struggle for Racial Equality in Georgia, 1940–1980* (Athens, Georgia, 2001); John A. Kirk, *Redefining the Color Line: Black Activism in Little Rock, Arkansas, 1940–1970* (Gainesville, Florida, 2002); J. Mills Thornton III, *Dividing Lines: Municipal Politics and the Struggle for Civil Rights in Montgomery, Birmingham, and Selma* (Tuscaloosa, Alabama, 2002).

30 Mary King, *Freedom Song: A Personal Story of the 1960s Civil Rights Movement* (New York, 1987); David J. Garrow (ed.), *The Montgomery Bus Boycott and the Women Who Started It: The Memoir of Jo Ann Gibson Robinson* (Knoxville, Tennessee, 1987); Vicki L. Crawford, Jacqueline A. Rouse and Barbara Woods (eds), *Women in the Civil Rights Movement: Trailblazers and Torchbearers, 1941–1965* (Bloomington, Indiana, 1993); Joanne Grant, *Ella Baker: Freedom Bound* (New York, 1998); Barbara Ransby, *Ella Baker and the Black Freedom Movement: A Radical Democratic Vision* (Chapel Hill, North Carolina, 2002); Kay Mills, *This Little Light of Mine: The Life of Fannie Lou Hamer* (New York, 1994); Chana Kai Lee, *For Freedom's Sake: The Life of Fannie Lou Hamer* (Urbana, Illinois, 1999); Cynthia Griggs Fleming, *Soon We Will Not Cry: The Liberation of Ruby Doris Smith Robinson* (Lanham, Maryland, 1998); Douglas Brinkley, *Rosa Parks* (New York: Viking, 2000); Belinda Robnett, *How Long? How Long? African American Women in the Struggle for Civil Rights* (New York, 1997); Peter J. Ling and Sharon Montieth (eds), *Gender in the Civil Rights Movement* (New York, 1999); Constance Curry et al., *Deep in Our Hearts: Nine White Women in the Freedom Struggle* (Athens, Georgia, 2000); Bettye Collier-Thomas and V. P. Franklin (eds), *Sisters in the Struggle: African-American Women in the Civil Rights and Black Power Movements* (New York, 2001).

31 Andrew M. Manis, *Southern Civil Religions in Conflict: Black and White Baptists and Civil Rights, 1947–1957* (Athens, Georgia, 1987); James F. Findlay, *Church People in the Struggle: The National Council of Churches and the Black Freedom Movement* (New York, 1993); Charles Marsh, *God's Long Summer: Stories of Faith and Civil Rights* (Princeton, New Jersey, 1997); David L. Chappell, 'Religious Ideas of the Segregationists', *Journal of American Studies* (32, 1998); Jane Dailey, 'Sex, Segregation, and the Sacred after *Brown*', *Journal of American History* (91, 2004); S. Jonathan Bass, *Blessed Are The Peacemakers: Martin Luther King Jr., Right White Religious Leaders, and the 'Letter From Birmingham Jail'* (Baton Rouge, Louisiana, 2001).

32 Joel L. Alvis, *Religion and Race: Southern Presbyterians, 1946–1983* (Tuscaloosa, Alabama, 1994); Gardiner H. Shattuck Jr, *Episcopalians and Race: Civil War to Civil Rights* (Lexington, Kentucky, 2000); Mark Newman, *Getting Right With God: Southern Baptists and Desegregation, 1945–1995* (Tuscaloosa, Alabama, 2001).

33 Mark K. Bauman and Berkley Kalin (eds), *The Quiet Voices: Southern Rabbis and Black Civil Rights, 1880s to 1990s* (Tuscaloosa, Alabama, 1997); Clive Webb, 'Closing Ranks: Montgomery Jews and Civil Rights, 1954–60', *Journal of American Studies* (32, 1998); Clive Webb, *Fight Against Fear: Southern Jews and Black Civil Rights* (Athens, Georgia, 2001); Debra L.

Schultz, *Going South: Jewish Women in the Civil Rights Movement* (New York, 2001).

34 Brenda Gayle Plummer, *Rising Wind: Black Americans and U.S. Foreign Affairs, 1935–1960* (Chapel Hill, North Carolina, 1996); Penny M. Von Eschen, *Race Against Empire: Black Americans and Anticolonialism, 1937–1957* (Ithaca, New York, 1997); Michael L. Krenn, *Black Diplomacy: African Americans and the State Department, 1945–1969* (Armonk, New York, 1999); Michael L. Krenn (ed.), *The African-American Voice in U.S. Foreign Policy Since World War II* (New York, 1998).

35 Carol Anderson, *Eyes Off the Prize: The United Nations and the African American Struggle for Human Rights, 1944–1955* (Cambridge, 2003); James E. Westheider, *Fighting On Two Fronts: African Americans and the Vietnam War* (New York, 1997); Jonathan Zimmerman, 'Beyond Double Consciousness: Black Peace Corps Volunteers in Africa, 1961–1971', *Journal of American History* (82, 1995): Lewis V. Baldwin, *Toward The Beloved Community: Martin Luther King Jr. and South Africa* (Cleveland, Ohio, 1995); James H. Meriwether, *Proudly We Can Be Africans: Black Americans and Africa, 1935–1961* (Chapel Hill, North Carolina, 2002); Renee Romano, 'No Diplomatic Immunity: African Diplomats, the State Department, and Civil Rights, 1961–1964', *Journal of American History* (87, 2000).

36 Mary L. Dudziak, *Cold War, Civil Rights: Race and the Image of American Democracy* (Princeton, New Jersey, 2000); Azza Salama Layton, *International Politics and Civil Rights Policies in the United States, 1941–1960* (Cambridge, 2000); Thomas Borstelmann, *The Cold War and the Color Line: American Race Relations in the Global Arena* (Cambridge, Massachusetts, 2001); C. Vann Woodward, *The Strange Career of Jim Crow*, revised 2nd edn (New York, 1966), pp. 130–4.

37 Manning Marable, *Race, Reform and Rebellion: The Second Reconstruction in Black America, 1945–1990*, revised 2nd edn (London, 1991), pp. 13–39; Fairclough, 'State of the Art', pp. 389–90; Adam Fairclough, *Better Day Coming: Blacks and Equality, 1890–2000* (New York, 2001), pp. 211–18.

38 Robert Korstad and Nelson Lichtenstein, 'Opportunities Found and Lost: Labor, Radicals, and the Early Civil Rights Movement', *Journal of American History* (75, 1988).

39 Gerald Horne, *Black and Red: W. E. B. Du Bois and the Afro-American Response to the Cold War, 1944–1963* (New York, 1985); Gerald Horne, *Communist Front: The Civil Rights Congress, 1946–56* (New York, 1988); Gerald Horne, *Black Liberation/Red Scare: Ben Davis and the Communist Party* (Delaware, 1994); David Levering Lewis, *W. E. B. Du Bois: The Fight for Equality and the American Century, 1919–1963* (New York, 2000), pp. 548–53; Mary L. Dudziak, 'Josephine Baker, Racial Protest, and the Cold War', *Journal of American History* (81, 1994); David A. Horowitz, 'White Southerners' Alienation and Civil Rights: The Response to Corporate Liberalism, 1956–1965', *Journal of Southern History* (54, 1988); George Lewis, *The White South and the Red Menace: Segregationists, Anticommunism, and Massive Resistance, 1945–1965* (Gainesville, Florida, 2004); Jeff Woods, *Black Struggle, Red Scare: Segregation and Anti-*

Communism in the South, 1948–1968 (Baton Rouge, Louisiana, 2004).

40 Richard Kluger, *Simple Justice: The History of Brown v. Board of Education and Black America's Struggle for Equality* (New York, 1975); Raymond Wolters, *The Burden of Brown: Thirty Years of School Desegregation* (Knoxville, Tennessee, 1984); Robert A. Pratt, *The Color of Their Skin: Education and Race in Richmond, Virginia, 1954–1969* (Charlottesville, Virginia, 1992); Davison M. Douglas, *Reading, Writing, and Race: The Desegregation of the Charlotte Schools* (Chapel Hill, North Carolina, 1995); David S. Cecelski, *Along Freedom Road: Hyde County, North Carolina, and the Fate of Black Schools in the South* (Chapel Hill, North Carolina, 1994); Robyn Duff Ladino, *Desegregating Texas Schools: Eisenhower, Shivers, and the Crisis at Mansfield High* (Austin, Texas, 1996); William Henry Kellar, *Make Haste Slowly: Moderates, Conservatives, and School Desegregation in Houston* (College Station, Texas, 1999); Mark V. Tushnet, *Making Civil Rights Law: Thurgood Marshall and the Supreme Court, 1936–1961* (New York, 1994); Mark V. Tushnet, *Making Constitutional Law: Thurgood Marshall and the Supreme Court, 1961–1991* (New York, 1997); Jack Greenberg, *Crusaders in the Courts: How a Dedicated Band of Lawyers Fought for the Civil Rights Revolution* (New York, 1994).

41 Michael J. Klarman, 'How Brown Changed Race Relations: The Backlash Thesis', *Journal of American History* (81, 1994).

42 Austin Sarat (ed.), *Race, Law, and Culture: Reflections on Brown v. Board of Education* (New York, 1997); James T. Patterson, *Brown v. Board of Education: A Civil Rights Milestone and Its Troubled Legacy* (New York, 2001); Jack M. Balkin (ed.), *What Brown v. Board of Education Should Have Said: The Nation's Top Legal Experts Rewrite America's Landmark Civil Rights Decision* (New York, 2001); Peter Irons, *Jim Crow's Children: The Broken Promise of the Brown Decision* (New York, 2002); 'Forum: Reflections on the Brown Decision After Fifty Years', *Journal of Southern History* (90, 2004); 'Round Table: Brown v. Board of Education Fifty Years After', *Journal of American History* (91, 2004).

43 Eagles, 'Toward New Histories of the Civil Rights Era', pp. 039 11.

44 Numan V. Bartley, *The Rise of Massive Resistance: Race and Politics in the South During the 1950s* (Baton Rouge, Louisiana, 1969); Neil R. McMillen, *The Citizens' Council: Organized Resistance to the Second Reconstruction, 1954–64* (Urbana, Illinois, 1971).

45 Eagles, 'Toward New Histories of the Civil Rights Era', pp. 815, 842–3.

46 Dan T. Carter, *The Politics of Rage: George Wallace, The Origins of the New Conservatism, and the Transformation of American Politics* (New York, 1995), pp. 460–1; Roy Reed, *Faubus: The Life and Times of an American Prodigal* (Fayetteville, Arkansas, 1997).

47 Jeff Roche, *Restructured Resistance: The Silbey Commission and the Politics of Desegregation in Georgia* (Athens, Georgia, 1998); Bartley, *The Rise of Massive Resistance* (1997 edn), p. viii; Chapell, 'Religious Ideas of the Segregationists'; Newman, *Getting Right With God*.

48 Fairclough, *Better Day Coming*, pp. 292–3.

49 Fairclough, 'State of the Art', p. 393.

50 Eskew, *But For Birmingham*, pp. 259–97; Andrew M. Manis, *A Fire You*

Can't Put Out: The Civil Rights Life of Birmingham's Reverend Fred Shuttlesworth (Tuscaloosa, Alabama, 1999), p. 4; Glenn T. Eskew, '"The Classes and the Masses": Fred Shuttlesworth's Movement and Birmingham's Black Middle Class', in Marjorie L. White and Andrew M. Manis (eds), *Birmingham Revolutionaries: The Reverend Fred Shuttlesworth and the Alabama Christian Movement for Human Rights* (Macon, Georgia, 2000), pp. 31–48; Timothy J. Minchin, *Hiring the Black Worker: The Racial Integration of the Southern Textile Industry, 1960–1980* (Chapel Hill, North Carolina, 1999); Timothy J. Minchin, *The Color of Work: The Struggle for Civil Rights in the Southern Paper Industry, 1945–1980* (Chapel Hill, North Carolina, 2001).

51 Michael R. Gardner, *Harry Truman and Civil Rights: Moral Courage and Political Risks* (Carbondale, Illinois, 2002); John White, *The Times Higher Education Supplement*, 12 September 2003, p. 27; David Niven, *The Politics of Injustice: The Kennedys, the Freedom Rides, and the Electoral Consequences of a Moral Compromise* (Knoxville, Tennessee, 2003).

52 Lawson, 'Freedom Then, Freedom Now', pp. 456–7; Ling, *Martin Luther King, Jr.*, p. 5.

53 James R. Ralph, *Northern Protest: Martin Luther King, Jr., Chicago, and the Civil Rights Movement* (Cambridge, Massachusetts, 1993); Gerald B. McKnight, *The Last Crusade: Martin Luther King, Jr., the FBI, and the Poor People's Campaign* (Oxford, 1998); Ling, *Martin Luther King, Jr.*, p. 5. The trend to focus more on the late 1960s would appear to be maintained in Simon Hall's *Peace and Freedom: The Civil Rights and Antiwar Movements of the 1960s* (Philadelphia, 2004). The most up-to-date scholarship on King himself is provided by British historian John A. Kirk, *Martin Luther King* (London, 2004), now available in a new 2005 paperback edition.

5

Malcolm X and Black Power, 1960–1980

The historiography of the Civil Rights Movement of 1955–68 is both rich and extensive. Expressed in terms of the language and imagery of the natural world, the diversity, fecundity and quality of the scholarship is akin to the luxuriant growth of a tropical rain forest. Sadly, this pleasing vista is not an appropriate description for the body of published research by historians on Black Nationalist groups of the period or the Black Power Movement of the late 1960s and 1970s. The scholarly output on these subject areas has, by comparison, been sparse, stunted, and more reminiscent of the spartan slopes of an exposed Alpine mountainside.

This stark contrast is the result of a number of factors. Primary source material is less readily available for Black Nationalist groups and spokespersons than for mainstream civil rights organizations. In part this is because they simply tended to be less meticulous in keeping regular, detailed administrative records. When archive material is preserved there is the added difficulty that the guardians of such documents may well be reluctant to share this information with outsiders, particularly when they are educated, predominantly middle-class, white historians. When undertaking research for a biography of Malcolm X in the early 1970s, white journalist Peter Goldman was thus disappointed by the fact that the martyred race leader's half-sister, Ella Collins, and his widow, Betty Shabazz, both declined to be interviewed. On a personal level Goldman liked Shabazz 'and in fact rather sympathized with her suspicions', but 'in the end' he 'could not overcome them'.[1]

The Black Muslims, or Nation of Islam (NOI), presented

especial problems for scholars. During the 1960s and early 1970s the theology of the Nation instructed followers that all whites were blue-eyed devils. Clearly, they could not be trusted to present an accurate and impartial account of the Nation's aims and objectives. Indeed, they could be relied upon to do exactly the opposite. It is no coincidence that a black African born in Nigeria, political scientist E. U. Essien-Udom, penned one of the few detailed and insightful studies on the organization. As well as having his racial ancestry on his side, Essien-Udom won over the confidence of members of the Nation by participating 'continuously in the religious, social, and to a limited extent, business activities of the Muslims in Chicago' over a two-year period. He also 'learned the "ways" of the Negro lower class in Chicago's Black Belt' and 'spent considerable time at many Negro civic, social, and religious activities' in the city.

Even then he was not always able to overcome innate distrust. A carefully prepared written survey 'aimed at securing personal data on members' of the Nation amounted to nothing because Chicago 'Muslims, apparently directed by the officers of the Temple, failed to respond' and in consequence 'five hundred copies of a twelve-page questionnaire prepared at considerable expense were utterly wasted', because just 'four Muslims returned them'. 'The difficulty of studying the group', Essien-Udom concluded, lay 'partly in its lack of appreciation of the "scientific" value of the information they would provide'. It could also be attributed to 'their deep-seated suspicion of the outsider'. Their 'sense of persecution and fear of the so-called "enemy"' made it difficult to secure their co-operation. At times they appeared unable to understand that the divulging of information was 'permissible from the point of view of those in authority. Suspicion, fear, and the apparent atmosphere of secrecy which surrounds the movement made it difficult for the writer to secure exact data on its membership and its finances.'[2]

In fairness, it should be said that it is not just that Black Nationalist groups and individuals associated with them have been unwilling to confide in scholars. Historians have also been inclined to avoid researching such subject areas for reasons of their own. Early academic studies on the black freedom struggle in the 1950s and 1960s, as has already been noted, concentrated on traditional primary source materials, such as legal and political records and the files of civil rights organizations. Evidence of this sort encouraged scholars to measure the success or failure of black protest in conventional terms, for example in the number of favourable decisions handed down by the United States Supreme Court, the passage of new legislation or other tangible political initiatives. Even when applied to mainstream civil rights organizations, the use of such criteria suffered from a number of limitations, but they were particularly unhelpful when it came to evaluating the achievements of Black Power spokespersons and the groups they represented. The achievements of race leaders like Malcolm X and Stokely Carmichael generally took more subtle, less tangible, forms. These included community empowerment, heightened racial pride and consciousness, and a decolonization of the black ghetto mind, rather than specific political initiatives to address the physical problems of the inner cities. It was thus easy for scholars in the 1960s and 1970s to conclude that the Black Power Movement was lacking in any true substance, meaning or accomplishments, and was therefore not worthy of serious study.

This negative perception was reinforced by the fact that more conservative civil rights leaders were often vehement in their denunciations of black radicals, blaming them, to some extent justifiably, for the declining levels of white support for black civil rights in the late 1960s and the growing internal divisions within the Civil Rights Movement. In a 1965 article for the journal *Dissent*, Tom Kahn and Bayard Rustin accused Malcolm X of engaging in loud-sounding but empty rhetoric that was 'not essentially different from what one hears in Harlem bars after midnight'. Roy Wilkins, Executive Secretary of the NAACP, denounced Black Power as 'anti-white power'. It was a 'reverse Mississippi, a reverse Hitler, a reverse Ku Klux Klan'. It was 'the father of hatred and the mother of violence', driven by 'the wicked fanaticism which has swelled our tears, broken our bodies, squeezed our hearts, and taken the blood of our black and white loved ones. It shall not poison our forward march.' In similar, if less melodramatic, vein Rustin condemned Black Power for diverting the Civil Rights Movement from a meaningful debate over strategy and tactics, isolating the black community and encouraging anti-black forces. It was an ideology of despair that abandoned the idea of integration in the pessimistic belief that the ghetto must last forever.[3]

The first time that many white Americans realized there was a radical black alternative to the Civil Rights Movement was in 1959 with the broadcast of *The Hate That Hate Produced*, a television documentary by white journalist Mike Wallace and his black colleague Louis Lomax on the Nation of Islam. The programme highlighted the controversial religious teachings of the Nation and showed scenes from a play written by minister Louis X, or Louis Farrakhan, as he was later to become better known, in which the white man was put on trial for his crimes against the black race. The charismatic Malcolm X, who also featured prominently in the documentary, became a nationally known figure overnight and subsequently became both a regular contributor in television debates on racial issues and a sought after speaker on the college lecture circuit.

In the wake of the programme, scholars, in common with ordinary members of the general public, developed a sudden interest in the Nation. Hitherto the academic community had shown singularly little interest in the NOI. 'Prior to 1960', as historian Claude Andrew Clegg III has noted, 'an article and a master's thesis, both from a sociological perspective, were the main scholarly accounts of the Nation of Islam.' The article, 'The Voodoo Cult Among Negro Migrants in Detroit', by Erdmann D. Beynon, was published in *The American Journal of Sociology* in 1938 and examined the origins of the organization, its broad ideology and the social and economic background of its followers. It was, however, 'short on historical antecedents' and failed 'to situate the organization within the history of black nationalism or Islam in the United States'. The thesis, a 1951 MA dissertation in sociology at the University of Chicago by Hatim A. Sahib, was entitled simply 'The Nation of Islam' and studied the development of the movement in the years immediately after the Second World War. Sahib conducted detailed interviews with NOI head Elijah Muhammad and critically assessed the reasons for the popularity of the movement among ghetto black communities, in particular the psychological needs that it met. At the same time his analysis was 'strictly rooted in the sociological theories of the period' and barely looked at 'the historical and ideological environment that sired the Nation'. The work of Beynon and Sahib combined did little more than provide readers with 'a snapshot of the movement and its leaders at selected times in its history' and failed to 'construct spatial or historical contexts necessary for fully understanding Muhammad or the Muslims'.[4]

In the early 1960s scholars, albeit from disciplines other than history, began to make up for lost time. Setting a high standard C. Eric Lincoln's 1961 publication *The Black Muslims in America* provided a thoughtful, though depressingly negative, appraisal that concluded that the NOI was 'extremist, escapist and dysfunctional' and 'a mere deviant reaction to the racism and segregation that prevailed in American society'. Focusing on the 1950s and the early 1960s, his study was also sociological in perspective, paying only limited attention to the earlier history of the movement.

In another intelligent and well-researched work the following year, E. U. Essien-Udom's *Black Nationalism* added the perspective of a political scientist. More sympathetic to the NOI than Lincoln, Essien-Udom was inclined to stress the positive aspects of the movement. He noted the success of the Nation in redeeming drug addicts, alcoholics and criminals. Moreover, he argued that the inner cities of the North, where the Nation recruited most strongly, suffered from a black equivalent of the 'American Dilemma' famously highlighted by Swedish sociologist Gunnar Myrdal in the 1940s. Living in a culture and society that attached enormous importance to career advancement and material success, black ghetto residents experienced poor self-esteem because of their poverty and low social standing. At the same time, their position as a permanent underclass made it impossible for them to fulfil the aspirations of middle-class white society which they were everywhere encouraged to emulate. In these dispiriting circumstances the NOI provided black ghetto populations with a positive alternative to despair and self-loathing. Although still poor in economic terms, converts to the Nation took a pride in themselves and their community. They dressed smartly and their homes, if modestly furnished, were clean and well maintained. Their high self-esteem and commitment to hard work and family values made Muslims more attractive to potential white employers and thus helped them to achieve better employment opportunities than other black ghetto residents.[5]

Forsaking television for the printed word, Louis Lomax's *When the Word is Given* (1963) constituted another solid contribution to the growing literature on the Nation. While less scholarly than the works by Lincoln and Essien-Udom, for example forsaking footnotes, Lomax's study was also journalistic in the positive sense of the word, embodying the active investigative research associated with a reporter, but without the sensationalist approach that often accompanies it. Examining Malcolm X as much as the Nation itself, Lomax also unwittingly highlighted a key factor behind the growing body of literature on the organization. In short, the NOI benefited from its close association in the public mind with its best-known and most charismatic member. The unfortunate corollary of this was that when Malcolm X parted company with the Nation in the final months of 1963, both scholars and the general public lost interest in it, and serious published research on the NOI effectively came to a halt.[6]

In contrast, the cult of celebrity and mystique surrounding Malcolm X continued to grow. Indeed, this was taken to new levels as a result of two specific developments. In February 1965 NOI members assassinated Malcolm X to silence him as an alternative, dissident voice to the Nation. Ironically, this murderous act had exactly the opposite effect. In death Malcolm X, like Martin Luther King three years later, attained the status of martyrdom, ensuring that he would continue to be an iconic figure for generations of African Americans to come. His place in history was further reaffirmed by the publication of his autobiography only a few months after his life was so cruelly cut short. Transcribed and edited with the assistance of African American journalist Alex Haley, *The Autobiography of Malcolm X* quickly became regarded as the authoritative account of his life and became an inspirational text for Black Power leaders of the late 1960s and early 1970s. In the absence of a more conventional legacy in the form of legislative and organizational achievements, it was regarded both by scholars and the wider public as one, if not the greatest, of his accomplishments.[7]

The Autobiography also set a precedent in other ways. It

reflected the fact that most of the important accounts on black radicalism in the late 1960s and early 1970s were written by active participants in the black freedom struggle rather than members of the academic community. Some of these were written by figures associated with the mainstream Civil Rights Movement, like Bayard Rustin, who were sharply critical of black militants for being divisive and impractical. More widespread, however, were works written by radicals themselves.[8]

A prime example of this was the 1967 publication of *Black Power: The Politics of Liberation in America* by Stokely Carmichael and Charles Hamilton, which became a standard text on the Black Power Movement. Drawing on the ideas of Malcolm X and Martinique born Algerian nationalist Frantz Fanon in his seminal study *The Wretched of the Earth*, Carmichael and Hamilton sought to place the struggle for black civil rights in America in the wider context of the global liberation struggle by non-white peoples against western imperialism. In this context they argued that African Americans in the United States suffered from a form of 'internal colonialism' from city, state and federal governmental agencies in the same way that black Africans were the victims of 'external colonialism' imposed by the European powers that occupied and administered their homelands.

Although cleverly constructed, the difficulty with this analytical framework was that, in common with many of the ideas and values associated with the Black Power Movement, it was not particularly helpful in identifying practical solutions for the problems experienced by African Americans. A small minority of all Americans, they could hardly hope to rise up in armed rebellion and expel the white population of the United States in a way that was possible for black liberation movements in the Third World. Carmichael and Hamilton implicitly acknowledged this dilemma in their observation that they had 'no pat formulas' for countering racism. They could not 'offer a blueprint' or 'set any timetable for freedom'. In short, their study was 'not a handbook for the working organizer'.[9]

Many first-hand accounts, as might be expected, took the form of autobiographical reminiscences by leading or well-known individuals recounting their personal experiences of the black freedom struggle. Studies in this category included works by

James Forman and Henry Rap Brown of the SNCC and the writings of Black Panther activists Eldridge Cleaver, George Jackson, Huey Newton and Bobby Seale.[10] Publications by scholars continued to be limited in number, and even then often took the form of edited collections of writings, speeches, and reminiscences by or about leading radicals.[11]

The cumulative effect of such works was to encourage an unbalanced and distorted image of the past. The testimony of those actually involved in the events about which they were writing obviously constituted a valuable contribution in understanding the history of the Black Power Movement. At the same time over-dependence on memoirs brings problems of its own. Historians, as has already been indicated, are generally distrustful of a biography-centred approach to the study of the past. Biographies, by their nature, focus on the life of prominent individuals rather than organizations or the experiences of local communities. Autobiographies not only share this tendency but suffer from additional drawbacks as well. They are 'filtered through the perceptions of the writer', and consequently, as African American scholar Charles E. Jones has observed, 'they sometimes become a forum for pursuing personal grudges and vendettas, which is less likely to occur in systematic, scholarly studies'.[12] When the author is more charitable than vindictive in disposition the reverse problem applies, that important information may be omitted to avoid embarrassment for friends and associates. In particular writers are prone to be over-generous and forgiving when it comes to appraising their own past conduct. Both intentionally and unconsciously they are likely to magnify their own role in events and suffer from selective memory loss when it comes to recalling their mistakes and shortcomings.

Many accounts by Black Power advocates went out of their way to emphasize the extent to which the author, or his or her organization, had been influenced by the ideas of Malcolm X and viewed him as a role model. Black Panther founder Bobby Seale thus recalled that on hearing of Malcolm X's assassination he was so distraught that he 'cried like a baby', and to vent his anger and frustration threw half bricks at cars and smashed his fist through a window.[13] In part the honest acknowledgement of a key source of inspiration, such admissions also had a more subtle purpose. They enabled writers to portray themselves as the true heir to the martyred icon, continuing to spread his message and ideas. A diverse, and often conflicting, range of groups and individuals were able to appropriate Malcolm X's memory in this way. This was because in the last year of his life, as was made clear in his autobiography, Malcolm X was undergoing a process of transition in his philosophy and this period of growth and development was still incomplete at the time of his death. The various attempts to secure status and recognition by association with him had the result of further enhancing the mythology that surrounded Malcolm X. In 'the renaissance of black nationalism in the late 1960s' as African American scholar Manning Marable has observed, 'Malcolm X was elevated to the position of cultural and political icon, as various ideological tendencies contested for his mantle of uncompromising leadership.'[14]

This growth in stature was reflected in the expanding literature on him. African American scholar John Henrik Clarke and Marxist thinker George Breitman both published edited collections of primary source materials on Malcolm X. The Socialist Workers Party also produced brief but useful compilations of his maxims and speeches.[15] This was not simply to make Malcolm X's thoughts and ideas available to a wider audience but was also a means of supporting the thesis advanced by Breitman and fellow Marxist intellectuals that in the last months of his life Malcolm X was in the process of becoming a revolutionary socialist. This controversial theory was most clearly outlined by Breitman in his 1967 study *The Last Year of Malcolm X: The Evolution of a Revolutionary*. Although Breitman ably demonstrated that there was at least some justification for this point of view, the weakness in his case was that it clearly relied on a selective reading of Malcolm X's writings and speeches. His claims were also firmly denied by Malcolm X's widow, Betty Shabbazz. In a less provocative, but arguably more convincing, 1973 study white journalist Peter Goldman portrayed Malcolm X as a public moralist who acted as a voice of conscience highlighting the nation's wrongs and injustices.[16]

By the 1970s and 1980s academics were beginning to make a welcome, if overdue, contribution to the understanding of Black Nationalism of the 1960s. In organizational histories of the

Congress of Racial Equality (CORE) and the Student Nonviolent Coordinating Committee (SNCC) historians August Meier, Elliott Rudwick and Clayborne Carson demonstrated the deeply divisive and destructive impact of Black Power philosophy on the Civil Rights Movement. In a later study British historian Adam Fairclough examined the response of Martin Luther King and the Southern Christian Leadership Conference (SCLC) to the emergence of Black Power. At the same time the main focus of all these works was the mainstream Civil Rights Movement rather than black radicalism.[17]

Another important development came in 1981 with the publication of Eugene Victor Wolfenstein's *The Victims of Democracy: Malcolm X and the Black Revolution*. A professor of political science and practising psychoanalyst, Wolfenstein brought a new dimension to the historiography on Malcolm X. Adopting a psycho-biographical approach, he depicted Malcolm X's life as a struggle to find psychic release as a member of an oppressed racial minority group.[18]

It required the passage of a decade before the next full-length scholarly study on Malcolm X was published. In *Malcolm: The Life of a Man Who Changed Black America*, a second groundbreaking psychological study, political scientist Bruce Perry offered a different interpretation. Already the editor of an earlier collection of Malcolm X's speeches, Perry was no stranger to his subject. In his new work he argued that Malcolm X's adult life could best be understood as an attempt by Malcolm X as an individual to escape the mental trauma and suffering inflicted by a deeply disturbed, dysfunctional childhood and equally troubled adolescence. Informed by painstaking and meticulous research that included literally hundreds of interviews with family, friends and acquaintances of Malcolm X, Perry questioned the accepted version of the race leader's life derived from Malcolm X's 1965 autobiography. He pointed to revealing omissions and distortions in *The Autobiography of Malcolm X* and substantiated these claims by evidence obtained from his research findings. Surprisingly, earlier biographers had generally accepted *The Autobiography* as an accurate account of Malcolm X's life without seeking to systematically verify its accuracy, reflecting the increasingly revered and hallowed image of him in the years after his death. Respected for his commitment and dedication as a researcher, Perry's conclusions reached as a result of his findings were more controversial. At worst, his study could be seen as portraying Malcolm X as less an inspirational race leader than a kind of psychological basket case seeking to compensate for a loveless childhood.[19]

Historian Clayborne Carson's 1991 publication *Malcolm X: The FBI File* indicated not just growing scholarly interest in Malcolm X but also a historiographical trend of a different sort. By the 1980s the release of FBI files kept on both mainstream civil rights leaders like Martin Luther King and black radicals like Malcolm X provided a wealth of new primary source materials for historians. More depressingly, as was highlighted in a number of studies, it demonstrated the disturbing extent of the Bureau's surveillance of individuals associated with the black freedom struggle.[20] Perhaps most pointed of all was the observation of African American filmmaker Spike Lee who, on being made aware of the more than 3,600 pages of FBI papers released on Malcolm X, reflected if that was what the Bureau was prepared to admit to, what did that suggest about what was not released, what files were destroyed and which 'documents will we never know about?'[21]

Malcolm X continued to fascinate researchers throughout the 1990s. In 1995 cultural historian and Baptist minister Michael Eric Dyson reflected on the differing interpretations of Malcolm X's legacy and the meaning of the martyred race leader in his own life and work.[22] In *Martin and Malcolm and America: A Dream or a Nightmare*, published in 1996, theology professor James Cone argued that the two dominant figures of black America in the 1960s were beginning to 'appreciate each other's views about America' in the last years of their lives. Following his break with the Nation of Islam in 1963, Malcolm X 'began to acknowledge the value of Martin Luther King's contribution to the black freedom movement' and 'began to advocate "hope", that is, the participation of African-Americans in the American political process'. Conversely, in the years 1965–8 the dreams of Martin Luther King were shattered as 'he observed the nightmare in American cities and on the battlefields of Vietnam' and he 'began to talk like Malcolm X'.[23]

Although vulnerable to the criticism of being an overly romantic attempt to reconcile the views of the two men, Cone's study also provided insight as to why Malcolm X continued to remain such an influential figure in the minds of both scholars and the wider public more than thirty years after his death. Cone, by his own acknowledgement, was 'an African American theologian whose perspective on the Christian religion was shaped by Martin Luther King and whose black consciousness was defined by Malcolm X'. In over 'twenty years of writing and teaching black liberation theology' he had sought to 'relate Malcolm X and Martin King to Christian living in America, seeking to show that *justice* and *blackness* are essential ingredients in the identity of the Christian faith for African-Americans'.[24]

Put another way, the two men had an enduring and deeply personal significance for the generation of Americans who had reached intellectual maturity in the 1960s and early 1970s. Moreover, the issues of racism, war and inner city deprivation that they had sought to address continued to be intractable contemporary problems in the United States of the 1990s. In the case of Malcolm X his public profile was further enhanced by his iconic status in American popular culture of the 1990s, most notably in the lyrics of Rap artists and Spike Lee's acclaimed 1992 cinematic biography *Malcolm X*. Ironically, his memory was also kept alive by the high 1990s profile of Louis Farrakhan, the controversial leader of the NOI since the 1970s. Malcolm X's widow and children were known to hold Farrakhan responsible for masterminding his assassination and consequently media coverage of Farrakhan inevitably included frequent reminders of Malcolm X.

In the late 1990s another theologian, Louis A. DeCaro, analysed Malcolm X as a religious leader, concluding that in the last years of his life Malcolm X was moving away from the unconventional religious teachings of the NOI to embrace orthodox Islam.[25] Like Cone, DeCaro's personal background, as an African American and committed Christian, was a strong motivating factor in his research. At the same time his work can also be seen as part of a broader historiographical trend in the late 1990s that saw scholars showing particular interest in the importance of theology and religious leaders in the black freedom struggle of the 1960s, as has been noted earlier.[26] The 1990s revival of the Nation of Islam under Louis Farrakhan may also have encouraged greater academic interest in the NOI. In this vein historian Claude Andrew Clegg's 1997 study, *An Original Man: The Life and Times of Elijah Mohammad* provided a welcome, if overdue, scholarly biography of Farrakhan's mentor and predecessor as leader of the Nation.[27]

Perhaps the most radical of all Black Power organizations during the 1960s and 1970s, the Black Panther Party (BPP) also benefited from a resurgence of public interest from the early 1990s onwards. One indication of this was a series of new editions of existing works on the Panthers and writings by Panther leaders.[28] These were complemented by a spate of fresh, and hitherto unpublished, series of memoirs and reminiscences by former Panther activists.[29]

This renewed fascination with the Panthers warrants some explanation. In part it can be seen as depressing testimony to the fact that the racial problems in America's inner cities that had comprised the strongholds of the Panthers remained as intractable at the end of the twentieth century as they had been in the 1960s. Inspired by the social and community action programmes of the former BPP to alleviate ghetto poverty and deprivation, in 1991 African American talk-show host Aaron Michaels even formed his own organization, the New Black Panther Party, with the specific objective of trying to address these still unresolved issues.

Like Malcolm X, the BPP also benefited from sympathetic cinematic representation in the 1995 film *Panther*, by African American filmmaker Mario Van Peebles, a release that was accompanied by a book publication.[30] Even without such favourable publicity, the controversial image of the Panthers made the organization a natural focus for media interest. This was borne out in journalist Hugh Pearson's 1994 study, *The Shadow of the Panther*, a controversial narrative history of the BPP that highlighted the drug addiction problems of Panther founder Huey Newton and depicted the Party as 'essentially an organization of street thugs'.[31] Pearson's lurid style did little to dispel the most common misgiving of historians about journalistic accounts, namely that inspired by the lure of commercial gain, rather than scholarly curiosity, they all too often abandon objectivity in favour of sensationalism.

Regardless of media hype, a series of events ensured that the Panthers continued to feature regularly in news broadcasts even after the final demise of the organization in 1982. On August 12 1989 Huey Newton was dramatically killed in a drugs related shooting in West Oakland, California. There were also regular and disturbing reports of miscarriages of justice involving still incarcerated Panthers convicted of offences in the late 1960s and early 1970s when the Party was made a systematic target of police and FBI oppression.[32]

Unfortunately, the high public profile of the Panthers notwithstanding, published academic studies on the Party remained relatively few and far between, with accounts of the Panthers still dominated by the autobiographies of former members and journalists. By the end of the decade, however, there were at least some tentative indications that this imbalance might be rectified with the publication of two important essay collections, *The Black Panther Party Reconsidered*, edited by historian Charles Jones, and *Liberation, Imagination, and the Black Panther Party*, edited by former Panther Kathleen Cleaver and journalist George Katsiaficas. Both of these anthologies included numerous contributions by scholars as well as the reminiscences of Panther activists.[33]

The nature and importance of African American cultural achievement in the Black Power Movement was a topic that was given rather more attention by scholars of the 1990s. In 1992 historian William L. Van Deburg published *New Day in Babylon*, a study of the Black Power Movement and American culture between the mid-1960s and the mid-1970s. Five years later, in *Black Camelot*, he followed this up with an analysis of African American cultural icons of the 1960s and 1970s. In 1999 Komozi Woodard contributed a study on Black Power cultural nationalist Amiri Baraka (Le Roi Jones). Julius E. Thompson examined the work of Dudley Randall and the Black Arts Movement, and in 2003 Scot Brown provided a much needed full-length study of Maulenga Karenga and his nationalist-cultural 'US' organization.[34]

In part these works reflected the growing interest of scholars in cultural history at this time. In fairness, it was also the case that the significance of the cultural dimensions of the Movement had long been recognized by scholars, even when they had chosen not to examine it in any detail. Admittedly, earlier historians of Black Power had generally been dismissive of the Movement, perceiving it as impractical and bringing little in the way of meaningful lasting gains. At the same time the heightened racial pride and consciousness associated with Black Power had often been acknowledged as an exception to the rule, marking one of the few positive developments, if not the only one, that could be attributed to it. Simply put, as British cultural historian Brian Ward has observed, there was 'a strong tendency' by scholars to depict 'important artistic movements and cultural innovations' as 'consolation prizes designed to make African Americans feel better when the "real" Movement for racial equality fractured and stalled in the second half of the 1960s'.[35]

In two other important works by historians in the 1990s Gerald Horne analysed the 1960s ghetto race riots in the Watts district of Los Angeles, California, and Timothy Tyson examined the life and career of the militant black activist Robert F. Williams.[36] Thoughtful and well researched, both studies filled important gaps in the existing literature, with Tyson's work in particular being credited for drawing the attention of scholars to a deep-rooted tradition of black radicalism that provided an important alternative to the values of the mainstream Civil Rights Movement during the 1950s and 1960s. Williams also represented a philosophy of armed self-defence within working-class African American communities that contrasted with the more middle-class non-violent protest associated with Martin Luther King. This under-researched aspect of the black freedom struggle was further explored by Lance Hill in *The Deacons for Defense* (2004). Formed in Jonesboro, Louisiana in 1964 the Deacons championed the cause of armed self-defence within the state. Offering a more radical alternative to King, the Deacons rapidly gained folk-hero status in the region and at their peak in the late 1960s attracted several hundred members in some twenty-one branches across the Deep South.[37]

Although a well-merited tribute to the quality of their scholarship, the plaudits afforded by scholars to the work of Tyson and

Hill can also be seen as depressing indications of the still under-developed historiography on Black Power. The fact that it took the publication of their studies to remind scholars that there was a black radical tradition was poignant testimony to the limited amount of research that had been undertaken by historians on the subject. Similarly, Horne's thorough investigation of rioting in Watts highlighted the lack of full-length studies by historians on the urban disorders in other US cities during the 1960s.

The lack of scholarly interest in the Black Power Movement was also reflected in a 2001 study of the civil rights policies of the Nixon administrations of 1969–74 by historian Dean J. Kotlowski. In a challenging revisionist account Kotlowski questioned the accuracy of the conventional negative interpretation attached to Nixon's record on civil rights by historians. He argued that Nixon's bigoted personal views on race were offset by the President's determination as a self-made man to promote equal opportunities for advancement for all Americans regardless of their ethnic background. In advancing this claim Kotlowski paid only scant attention to the wholesale persecution of Black Power radicals, most notably the Black Panthers, during the Nixon years, noting only that the President's vision of African American leadership 'did not include Black Power advocates'.[38]

In the late 1960s and early 1970s Black Power activists represented a stark alternative to the values of mainstream civil rights campaigners. A similar, and equally striking, contrast exists in respect to the historiography on the two movements. Civil rights campaigners and their organizations have benefited from extensive academic research, notable for its richness and diversity of scholarship in respect not just to national leaders but also to grassroots campaigners and women activists. This cannot be said of the literature on black radicalism of the period, where autobiographical reminiscences and accounts by journalists, rather than scholarly publications, have often predominated. In consequence, discussion has focused largely on the contributions of the best-known spokespersons, almost invariably male, with little attention paid to the work of local Black Power activists and women in the movement. Ironically, the aspect of Black Power that has perhaps received the most attention from historians, its cultural dimensions, is one of the areas that have been least well addressed in the many scholarly accounts of the Civil Rights Movement.[39]

Notes

1 Peter Goldman, *The Death and Life of Malcolm X* ([New York, 1973] 2nd edn, Urbana, Illinois, 1979), p. xviii.

2 E. U. Essien-Udom, *Black Nationalism: The Rise of the Black Muslims in the U.S.A.* ([Urbana, 1962] Harmonsdworth, 1966), pp. 11–13.

3 Tom Kahn and Bayard Rustin, 'The Ambiguous Legacy of Malcolm X', *Dissent* (12, 1965), p. 190; Roy Wilkins quoted in Adam Fairclough, *Better Day Coming: Blacks and Equality, 1890–2000* (New York, 2001), p. 314; Bayard Rustin, '"Black Power" and Coalition Politics', *Commentary*, (42, 1966).

4 Claude Andrew Clegg III, *An Original Man: The Life and Times of Elijah Muhammad* (New York, 1997), p. 345.

5 C. Eric Lincoln, *The Black Muslims in America* (Boston, 1961); Clegg, *An Original Man*, pp. 345–6; Essien-Udom, *Black Nationalism*, pp. 262–75.

6 Louis E. Lomax, *When the Word is Given* (Cleveland, Ohio, 1963); Clegg, *An Original Man*, p. 346.

7 Malcolm X with Alex Haley, *The Autobiography of Malcolm X* (New York, 1965).

8 Kahn and Rustin, 'The Ambiguous Legacy of Malcolm X'; Rustin, '"Black Power" and Coalition Politics'.

9 Stokely Carmichael and Charles Hamilton, *Black Power: The Politics of Liberation in America* (London, 1967), p. vii; Frantz Fanon, *The Wretched of the Earth* (New York, 1961).

10 Eldridge Cleaver, *Soul On Ice* (New York, 1968); Eldridge Cleaver, *Post-Prison Writings and Speeches* (New York, 1970); Bobby Seale, *Seize the Time: The Story of the Black Panther Party and Huey p. Newton* (New York, 1970); George Jackson, *Soledad Brother: The Prison Letters of George Jackson* (New York, 1970); George Jackson, *Blood in My Eye* (New York, 1972); Huey p. Newton, *The Genius of Huey p. Newton: Minister of Defense Black Panther Party* (San Francisco, 1970); James Forman, *The Making of Black Revolutionaries* (New York, 1972); Toni Morrison (ed.), *To Die for the People: The Writings of Huey p. Newton* (New York, 1972); Huey P. Newton, *Revolutionary Suicide* (New York, 1973); Henry Rap Brown, *Die, Nigger, Die* (New York, 1973); Bobby Seale, *A Lonely Rage: The Autobiography of Bobby Seale* (New York, 1978).

11 George Breitman (ed.), *Malcolm X Speaks* (New York, 1965); John Henrik Clarke (ed.), *Malcolm X: The Man and His Times* (New York, 1969); George Breitman (ed.), *By Any Means Necessary: Speeches, Interviews and a Letter by Malcolm X* (New York, 1970); Philip S. Foner (ed.), *The Black Panthers Speak* (New York, 1970).

12 Charles E. Jones (ed.), *The Black Panther Party Reconsidered* (Baltimore, Maryland, 1998), pp. 10–11.

13 Seale, *Seize the Time*, p. 1.

14 Manning Marable, *Race, Reform and Rebellion: The Second Reconstruction in Black America, 1945–1990,* revised 2nd edn (London, 1991), p. 254.

15 Clarke (ed.), *Malcolm X: The Man and His Times*; Breitman (ed.) *Malcolm X Speaks*; Breitman (ed.), *By Any Means Necessary*; Malcolm X, *Malcolm X Talks to Young People* (New York, 1969); Malcolm X, *Malcolm X on Afro-American History* (New York, 1970).

16 George Breitman, *The Last Year of Malcolm X: The Evolution of a Revolutionary* (New York, 1967); Goldman, *The Death and Life of Malcolm X.*

17 August Meier and Elliott Rudwick, *CORE: A Study in the Civil Rights Movement, 1942–68* (Urbana, Illinois, 1973); Clayborne Carson, *In Struggle: SNCC and the Black Awakening of the 1960s* (Cambridge, Massachusetts, 1981); Adam Fairclough, *To Redeem the Soul of America: The Southern Christian Leadership Conference and Martin Luther King, Jr.* (Athens, Georgia, 1987).

18 Eugene Victor Wolfenstein, *The Victims of Democracy: Malcolm X and the Black Revolution* (Berkeley, California, 1981).

19 Bruce Perry (ed.), *Malcolm X: The Last Speeches* (New York, 1989); Bruce Perry, *Malcolm: The Life of a Man Who Changed Black America* (New York, 1991).

20 Clayborne Carson (ed.), *Malcolm X: The FBI File* (New York, 1991); David J. Garrow, *The FBI and Martin Luther King, Jr.: From 'Solo' to Memphis* (New York, 1981); Kenneth O'Reilly, 'The FBI and the Civil Rights Movement During the Kennedy Years: From the Freedom Rides to Albany', *Journal of Southern History* (54, 1988); Kenneth O'Reilly, 'The FBI and the Politics of the Riots, 1964–1968', *Journal of American History* (75, 1988); Kenneth O'Reilly, *'Racial Matters': The FBI's Secret File on Black America, 1960–1972* (New York, 1989); Huey P. Newton, *War Against the Panthers: A Study of Repression in America* (New York, 1996).

21 Introduction by Spike Lee in Carson (ed.), *Malcolm X: The FBI File,* p. 14.

22 Michael Eric Dyson, *Making Malcolm: The Myth and Meaning of Malcolm X* (New York, 1995).

23 James H. Cone, *Martin and Malcolm and America: A Dream or a Nightmare* (New York, 1996).

24 Cone, *Martin and Malcolm and America,* p. x.

25 Louis A. DeCaro, *On the Side of My People: A Religious Life of Malcolm X* (New York, 1996); Louis A. DeCaro, *Malcolm and the Cross: The Nation of Islam, Malcolm X, and Christianity* (New York, 1998).

26 See chapter 4, pp. 92–100.

27 Clegg, *An Original Man.*

28 Bobby Seale, *Seize the Time: The Story of the Black Panther Party and Huey P. Newton* (Baltimore, Maryland, 1991); Eldridge Cleaver, *Soul on Ice* (New York, 1992); Philip S. Foner (ed.), *The Black Panthers Speak* (New York, 1995); Huey P. Newton, *Revolutionary Suicide* (New York, 1995); Toni Morrison (ed.) *To Die For The People* (New York, 1995); Newton, *War Against the Panthers*; David Hilliard and Donald Wise (eds), *The Huey P. Newton Reader* (New York, 2002).

29 Elaine Brown, *A Taste of Power: A Black Woman's Story* (New York, 1992);

David Hilliard and Lewis Cole, *This Side of Glory: The Autobiography of David Hilliard and the Story of the Black Panther Party* (Boston, 1993); William Lee Brent, *Long Time Gone: A Black Panther's True-Life Story of His Hijacking and Twenty-Five Years in Cuba* (New York, 1996).

30 Mario Van Peebles, Ula Y. Taylor and J. Tarika Lewis, *Panther: A Pictorial History of the Black Panthers and the Story Behind the Film* (New York, 1995).

31 Hugh Pearson, *The Shadow of the Panther: Huey P. Newton and the Price of Black Power in America* (Reading, Massachusetts, 1994); Jones (ed.), *The Black Panther Party Reconsidered*.

32 Jones (ed.), *The Black Panther Party Reconsidered*, pp. 363–89, 417–41; Kathleen Cleaver and George Katsiaficas (eds), *Liberation, Imagination, and the Black Panther Party: A New Look at the Panthers and Their Legacy* (New York, 2001), pp. 212–36.

33 Jones (ed.), *The Black Panther Party Reconsidered*; Cleaver and Katsiaficas (eds), *Liberation, Imagination, and the Black Panther Party*.

34 William L. Van Deburg, *New Day in Babylon: The Black Power Movement and American Culture, 1965–1975* (Chicago, 1992); William L. Van Deburg, *Black Camelot: African-American Culture Heroes in Their Times* (Chicago, 1997); Komozi Woodard, *A Nation Within a Nation: Amiri Baraka (Le Roi Jones) and Black Power Politics* (Chapel Hill, North Carolina, 1999); Julius E. Thompson, *Dudley Randall and the Black Arts Movement* (New York, 1997); Scot Brown, *Fighting for US: Maulenga Karenga, the US Organization, and Black Cultural Nationalism* (New York, 2003).

35 Brian Ward (ed.), *Media, Culture, and the Modern African American Freedom Struggle* (Gainesville, Florida, 2001), p. 2.

36 Gerald Horne, *Fire This Time: The Watts Uprising and the 1960s* (Charlottesville, Virginia, 1995); Timothy B. Tyson, *Radio Free Dixie: Robert F. Williams and the Roots of Black Power* (Chapel Hill, North Carolina, 1999).

37 Lance Hill, *The Deacons for Defense: Armed Resistance and the Civil Rights Movement* (Chapel Hill, North Carolina, 2004); Charles W. Eagles, 'Toward New Histories of the Civil Rights Era', *Journal of Southern History* (66, 2000), p. 839.

38 Dean J. Kotlowski, *Nixon's Civil Rights: Politics, Principle and Policy* (Cambridge, Massachusetts, 2001), pp. 2, 179.

39 Ward (ed.), *Media, Culture, and the Modern African American Freedom Struggle*, p. 13, n. 5.

6

The new conservatism: black civil rights since 1980

The historiography of the African American experience since 1980 is, for obvious reasons, less expansive than for earlier decades. Evaluating this period also poses special challenges for scholars, since it involves making assessments of trends and developments that are not yet fully complete. Normally historical researchers benefit from the advantage of perspective, writing about affairs that, if often controversial, have clearly run their course, and individuals whose careers belong to the past rather than the present. Simply put, historians usually enjoy the prerogative of being wise after the event.

Admittedly, the fact that race relations remains a serious and high profile unresolved issue in early twenty-first-century America can be said to influence the scholarly debate on almost *any* aspect of African American history. At the same time the early Civil Rights Movement of the 1930s and 1940s and the black freedom struggle of the 1950s and 1960s are distinct past periods that can be evaluated as a whole in their own right, even if from a wider perspective they can also be viewed as but the early completed acts in a still unfolding drama. This is clearly not the case in respect to more recent decades. Members of the historical profession have thus been understandably reticent in passing judgment on the 1980s and the 1990s.

Historians are inevitably the last members of the academic community to provide commentary or analysis on any given developments in the course of human events, but they are rarely the first. Instinctively reluctant to venture where angels fear to tread, they are more inclined to wait, and tread instead upon those that do. The early pioneers willing to risk such a fate are more usually journalists, economists, political scientists and sociologists, that is researchers from interest groups that typically aspire to have an active input into the public debate on events while they are still unfolding, rather than just analyse them in retrospect. This is not to say that historians do not also hope to have some influence on current affairs, but rather that they most commonly seek to do so by presenting past events in a new light that might influence contemporary thinking on related issues. The publication of C. Vann Woodward's seminal study on segregation, *The Strange Career of Jim Crow*, in 1955 was thus intended both to correct public misconceptions about the history of race relations in the American South since the Civil War and also to ease the region's move towards integration initiated by the US Supreme Court's ruling in the *Brown* v. *Board of Education* decision the previous year.[1]

The subject matter of the first studies of the African American experience in the last two decades of the twentieth century has been influenced by a number of factors. In common with early works on the Civil Rights Movement of the 1950s and 1960s there has been a tendency for researchers to concentrate primarily on nationally known leaders and major political and legislative developments. In part this is because primary source materials are most easily accessible for such individuals and initiatives. They are also a natural focus of attention for authors by virtue of their high media profile. This is particularly the case in respect to studies by journalists who, more so than most academics, write not just to expand the boundaries of existing knowledge, but also depend on the commercial viability of such publications for some of their annual income. Partly because of this, researchers have also been inclined to focus on developments perceived as having immediate relevance. The downside to this approach is that it risks overemphasizing the importance of events and individuals that command high levels of public attention in the short term, but, when viewed more dispassionately over a broader timescale, may be seen to have had only limited impact and significance.

The fact that many developments during the 1980s and 1990s are still too recent to be clearly viewed in retrospect has encouraged some commentators to seek an analytical perspective by relating the period to the events of the preceding decades. More specifically, the state of US race relations in the last years of the twentieth century has been used to measure the extent of the successes and failures of the black freedom struggle of the 1950s and 1960s. Just as many studies on the 1930s and 1940s have sought to examine the African American experience of these years to identify the *causes* of the post-war Civil Rights Movement, so works on the 1980s and 1990s have sought to highlight its principal *consequences*.

The influence of all of these factors can be identified in the early historiography on Jesse Jackson, arguably the best-known African American spokesperson of the 1980s and the 1990s. A rising young aide of Martin Luther King in the 1960s, the first serious biographical study of Jackson appeared as early as 1975.[2] However, it was not until his high profile presidential campaigns of 1984 and 1988 that he became a sustained focus of scholarly attention.

Reflecting the scepticism of many observers, African American scholar Adolph L. Reed's 1986 study, *The Jesse Jackson Phenomenon: The Crisis of Purpose in Afro-American Politics*, was deeply critical of Jackson's 1984 bid for the presidential nomination of the Democratic Party. Reed portrayed Jackson's campaign as empty symbolism irrelevant to the needs of the vast majority of African Americans. At no time did Jackson have any realistic chance of becoming his party's chosen candidate or having a substantive influence on the policies it adopted. His electioneering was thus little more than an act of self-promotion that risked drawing away support from other liberal-thinking candidates who were serious contenders for the nomination. Moreover, Jackson personified an anachronistic style of thinking in African American society. He represented an elitist and hierarchical form of church leadership associated with the civil rights struggles of the 1950s and 1960s. Although this may have been appropriate at that time, the sweeping advances in black voting rights achieved since meant that it was now black political candidates accountable through the ballot box, rather than unelected church ministers, who were the true representatives of African American communities.[3]

The perils of passing judgement so soon after the event were highlighted when in a second presidential campaign, two years after the publication of Reed's work, Jackson fared significantly better, at one point even seeming to have a real chance of being selected as the Democratic Party candidate. Although such heady expectations ultimately proved unrealizable, this impressive showing in 1988 undermined Reed's argument that Jackson was only running a token campaign and could not be regarded as a serious candidate.

Predictably, Jackson's two bids for the presidency prompted a number of scholarly studies, principally by political scientists.[4] If the collective implication of these works was that Jackson's campaigns had changed the political landscape of America, paving the way for the election of, if not himself, a future African American candidate for the presidency, the events of the 1990s demonstrated that such conclusions were at best premature, and at worst wildly optimistic. Jackson himself abandoned his quest for elective political office and no willing and able alternative African American candidate emerged to take his place as a presidential contender. Although Jackson remained a nationally known figure, as the result of his economic self-help initiatives, occasional diplomatic forays in world affairs, and regular appearances as a TV chat show host, the number of fresh publications on him noticeably declined. It also became hard to avoid the conclusion that earlier studies written on Jackson during the heady days of his 1980s campaigns had overestimated his long-term importance as a race leader.

Inevitably, there were some notable studies that constituted the exception to the rule. In 1996 journalist Marshall Frady published a new full-length biography of Jackson. The following year political scientist Karin L. Stanford published *Beyond the Boundaries: Reverend Jesse Jackson in International Affairs*, examining Jackson's career as a 'citizen diplomat'.[5] Although subsequent revelations of her extramarital affair with Jackson highlighted deeply personal reasons for Stanford's interest in her subject, her study was also prompted by sound academic rationale. Reminiscing about her early years in graduate school, Stanford recalled being struck by the fact that 'as a student of political science, I found that only a handful of scholars endeavoured to locate African Americans in international affairs'.[6]

Viewed in a wider context Stanford's work was notable in that it coincided with a series of new publications on the role of African Americans in world affairs in earlier decades.[7] One can only speculate as to why a once neglected topic should have suddenly benefited from so much scholarly attention. One factor was perhaps the high media profile of race relations in international affairs brought about as a result of the collapse of the apartheid regime in South Africa in the early 1990s, and the election of Nelson Mandela as the country's first black President in 1994. On a less dramatic note, it is often the case that the publication of just one or two pioneering works on any given subject can act as a catalyst for further studies by encouraging other researchers to investigate more fully the issues raised.

Reed's 1986 thesis that Jackson represented an anachronistic style of race leadership reflected not just his misgivings about Jackson as an individual but also the fact that by the mid-1980s increasing numbers of black candidates had successfully contested elections for political office at city, state and national level across America. This was most notably highlighted by the ever-increasing number of African American mayors in the nation's leading cities and the 1971 formation of the Congressional Black Caucus (CBC), a bi-partisan body of African American members of the United States Senate and House of Representatives. Reed concluded that it was this growing black political class that would provide the real solutions for the problems faced by African American communities.

By the mid-1990s the still all too obvious problems of ghetto poverty, race-related crime, and enduring racial tensions throughout the nation led scholars to adopt a gloomier prognosis. In a 1996 study, *We Have No Leaders*, political scientist Robert C. Smith concluded that since the 1970s the black Civil Rights Movement had 'been almost wholly encapsulated into mainstream institutions; co-opted and marginalized'. In consequence it had 'become largely irrelevant in terms of a politics and policies that would address the multi-faceted problems of race in the post-civil rights era'.[8]

Similarly in *African-American Mayors: Race, Politics and the American City*, a 2001 collection of essays edited by historians David R. Colburn and Jeffrey S. Adler, the various contributors celebrated the electoral success of African American mayors from the late 1960s through to the mid-1990s, but also highlighted the intractable nature of the problems in many of the nation's inner cities. The phenomenon of 'white flight', as white residents and businessmen abandoned metropolitan centres to relocate to the suburbs, deprived city administrations of vital tax revenues. At the same time rising levels of crime and urban decay necessitated increased expenditure on education, social services and welfare programmes, placing big city mayors in an impossible position.[9]

In a 1987 study, *The Truly Disadvantaged*, conservative black sociologist William Julius Wilson controversially argued that such inner city problems were actually evidence of the increasing irrelevance of race in American life. Building on the thesis first advanced in his earlier work, *The Declining Significance of Race*, he concluded that the major dilemma for American society at the end of the twentieth century was not race, but class. Thanks to the gains made as a result of the Civil Rights Movement of the 1950s and 1960s, by the 1980s growing numbers of African Americans had managed to achieve middle-class status and incomes. The main division in American life was thus not between blacks and whites, but between haves and have-nots.[10]

Wilson's thesis was in keeping with the right-wing political philosophy of the Republican administrations of Ronald Reagan, 1981–89, and George Bush, 1989–93, which opposed federal government and state affirmative action, or positive discrimination programmes on behalf of ethnic minorities, on the grounds that advances in race relations since the 1960s meant that there was no longer any justification for giving special consideration to African Americans and other historically persecuted racial groups. Within the academic community, however, his arguments were less enthusiastically received. The American Association of Black Sociologists issued a statement that accused Wilson of ignoring 'the problem of persistent oppression of blacks' and engaging in a 'misrepresentation of the black experience'.[11]

In *Behind the Mule: Race and Class in African-American Politics* (1994), political scientist Michael C. Dawson argued that newly affluent black Americans identified much more closely with other less fortunate African Americans than with middle-class whites. A minority oppressed for centuries would not exchange racial loyalties for class ones so easily. Liberal and radical African American scholars such as Gerald Horne and Manning Marable highlighted the extent to which African Americans, who comprised a disproportionately high percentage of inner city residents, experienced much higher levels of crime, poverty and deprivation than their white counterparts.[12] Other studies of the 1990s demonstrated the alarming extent of both individual and institutionalized racism in American law enforcement agencies, while the human cost of inner city decay was made clear in a series of revelations by journalists and street gang members, which showed the distrubing levels of alienation and violence in ghetto youth culture.[13]

A notable historiographical development of the late 1990s was a sudden proliferation of studies on Louis Farrakhan, leader of the black separatist organization the Nation of Islam (NOI). This interest in a person previously largely ignored by researchers can be attributed to a number of factors. The relative decline in the high media profile of Jesse Jackson encouraged commentators on race relations to look to alternative African American spokespersons. Farrakhan was a shrewd self-publicist with a talent for attracting press attention. Calculated outspoken statements on controversial issues, combined with periodic symbolic initiatives to promote racial pride and solidarity among African Americans, ensured that he featured regularly in the national news headlines. His celebrity status peaked with the successful organization of the 'Million Man March' on Washington DC in October 1995, an event in which at least 400,000 African American men took part, despite, or perhaps in part because of, the condemnations of national politicians and mainstream race leaders.

Predictably, a spate of publications on Farrakhan appeared in the months and years that followed. Journalists Arthur J. Magida, A. Marshall and Florence Hamlish Levinsohn responded to the public's desire to know more about the NOI leader. This curiosity was fuelled by the fact that, as civil rights leader and scholar Julian Bond observed in his foreword to Magida's biographical study, just the two words Louis Farrakhan immediately evoked 'fear and loathing in many minds' and 'devotion, admiration and respect' in others.[14]

Some commentators were spurred on by their concern at Farrakhan's provocative and at times morally repugnant teachings. In addition to being journalists, Levinsohn and Magida were also Jewish and in part impelled to understand the reasons for Farrakhan's apparent anti-Semitism. In *Ministry of Lies*, published three years earlier, Jewish Professor Harold Brackman provided a detailed scholarly rebuttal of an earlier NOI tract, *The Secret Relationship Between Blacks and Jews*, which had accused the Jewish race of 'monumental culpability' in slavery and the slave trade. In *The Trouble With Farrakhan and the Nation of Islam* (1997), committed Christian and social worker Elreta Dodds recorded 'Shouts of praise and a resounding "Thank You" to Jesus Christ, Lord and Saviour' for giving her 'the strength and fortitude to take on such an endeavor'. She then proceeded to 'expose Farrakhan' as 'an antichrist and a false prophet steered by racist views'.[15]

Demonstrating greater capacity for self-restraint, 'middle class, educated and Christian' journalist Amy Alexander edited a 1998 essay collection, *The Farrakhan Factor: African-American Writers on Leadership, Nationhood, and Minister Louis Farrakhan*. The varied selection of writings drew on contributions from 'academics, community activists, poets, journalists and historians from all across America', including two distinguished professors in African American studies, Henry Louis Gates Jr, and Michael Eric Dyson.[16] Full-length scholarly studies on Farrakhan also began to appear.[17] In perhaps the most perceptive of these, British political scientist Robert Singh drew inspiration from a renowned older thesis by American historian Richard Hofstadter, arguing that Farrakhan could be viewed as part of a deep-seated paranoid tradition in American political life.

This conclusion reflected the generally negative tone of most academic writings on Farrakhan. Whereas journalistic accounts tended to focus more on the sensationalist aspects of Farrakhan's career, a principal concern of scholars was that behind his bold rhetoric the NOI leader had no real solutions for the problems faced by African Americans at the end of the twentieth century. Farrakhan, as Henry Louis Gates succinctly observed, was a man of visions, but not of vision.[18] The years following the Million Man March appeared to bear out the validity of such reservations. Adept at staging a one-off event, Farrakhan proved unable to translate this success into any long-term programme for racial uplift. Distracted by health scares, he began to feature less prominently in national news headlines. Researchers also lost interest in Farrakhan and, viewed in retrospect, his earlier high profile appeared to have been as much the result of media hype as any substantive contribution he was able to offer as a race leader.

White supremacist organizations also featured prominently in national news stories during the 1990s. At times scarcely a month seemed to pass without either a fresh report of a shootout between some far-right militia group and law enforcement officers, or a news story of some racially or politically motivated crime. In this context it is interesting to note that these developments coincided with a sudden growth of interest by historians in far-right movements in earlier decades of the twentieth century, most notably the Ku Klux Klan of the 1920s and the Massive Resistance of the 1950s and 1960s.[19]

The worst outrage occurred in 1995 when hundreds of federal government employees in Oklahoma City were either killed or injured by a bomb planted by political extremist, Timothy McVeigh. One consequence of the tragedy was a sudden proliferation of studies, by both journalists and academics, of white supremacist networks and far-right organizations, highlighting the dangers posed by such groups to the nation's internal security and political stability.[20] This momentum was, however, short-lived. By the end of the decade the sense of crisis had subsided and in the early years of the twenty-first century the shocking events of 11 September 2001 focused the minds of Americans on terrorist threats of a different sort.

By the mid-1990s the first academic studies of the Republican administrations of Ronald Reagan, 1981–89, and George Bush, 1989–93, began to appear. In *A Kinder, Gentler Racism? The Reagan-Bush Civil Rights Legacy*, political scientist Steven A. Shull highlighted 'how two conservative presidents confronted and confounded a policy they opposed: the primacy of the national government in ensuring social and economic equity, particularly among minorities and women'.[21] In other critical works historians Dan T. Carter and Kenneth O'Reilly demonstrated the continuity between the political philosophy of the earlier

Alabama segregationist George Wallace and that of the Reagan and Bush administrations. Presenting Wallace's ideas in more palatable form, the two presidents targeted rising crime and welfare abuse as electoral issues to make coded appeals to the unspoken prejudices of white Americans who perceived African Americans and other ethnic minority groups as recidivist criminals and social security scroungers. In two studies on Louisiana's David Duke, author Michael Zatarain, political scientist Douglas Rose and others demonstrated how the former Klansman turned Republican made similar, if less subtle, appeals to take advantage of the growth of right-wing populism in mainstream US public opinion.[22]

Early studies of the Clinton administrations of the 1990s acknowledged the Democratic President's personally enlightened views on civil rights issues but also highlighted the extent to which he was forced to continue and even expand the policies of the Reagan-Bush era to appease right-wing Republican majorities in Congress and the increasingly conservative outlook of the electorate.[23] This uncompromising public mood was reflected in two new studies of the late 1990s that extolled the record of the Reagan administration in reversing affirmative action programmes as an enlightened colourblind policy that curtailed special privileges for minority groups and promoted equal opportunities for all. In time-honoured fashion, the writings of scholars began to reflect the social and political values of the era in which they themselves lived.[24]

Notes

1 C. Vann Woodward, *The Strange Career of Jim Crow* (New York, 1955). For a discussion of the impact and significance of this work see chapter 1, pp. 16–19.

2 Barbara A. Reynolds, *Jesse Jackson: The Man, the Movement, the Myth* (Chicago, 1975).

3 Adolph L. Reed, *The Jesse Jackson Phenomenon: The Crisis of Purpose in Afro-American Politics* (New Haven, Connecticut, 1986).

4 Thomas E. Cavanaugh and Lorn S. Foster, *Jesse Jackson's Campaign: The Primaries and Caucuses* (Washington DC, 1984); Thomas Landess and Richard Quinn, *Jesse Jackson and the Politics of Race* (Ottawa, 1985); Sheila D. Collins, *The Rainbow Challenge: The Jackson Campaign and the Future of U.S. Politics* (New York, 1986); Roger D. Hatch, *Beyond Opportunity: Jesse*

Jackson's Vision for America (Philadelphia, 1988); Ernest R. House, *Jesse Jackson and the Politics of Charisma* (Boulder, Colorado, 1988); Ronald W. Walters, *Black Presidential Politics in America: A Strategic Approach* (Albany, New York, 1988); Lucius J. Barker and Ronald W. Walters (eds), *Jesse Jackson's 1984 Presidential Campaign and Change in American Politics* (Urbana, Illinois, 1989); Frank Clemente and Frank Watkins (eds), *Keep Hope Alive: Jesse Jackson's 1988 Presidential Campaign* (Boston, 1989); Elizabeth O. Colton, *The Jackson Phenomenon: The Man, The Power, The Message* (New York, 1989); Lorenzo Morris (ed.), *The Social and Political Implications of the 1984 Jesse Jackson Presidential Campaign* (New York, 1990); Arnold Gibbons, *Race, Politics and the White Media: The Jesse Jackson Campaigns* (Lanham, Maryland, 1993).

5 Marshall Frady, *Jesse: The Life and Pilgrimage of Jesse Jackson* (New York, 1996); Karin L. Stanford, *Beyond the Boundaries: Reverend Jesse Jackson in International Affairs* (Albany, New York, 1997).

6 Stanford, *Beyond the Boundaries*, p. xv.

7 See chapter 4, pp. 100–1.

8 Robert C. Smith, *We Have No Leaders: African Americans in the Post-Civil Rights Era* (Albany, New York, 1996), p. xvi.

9 David R. Colburn and Jeffrey S. Adler (eds), *African-American Mayors: Race, Politics and the American City* (Urbana, Illinois, 2001).

10 William Julius Wilson, *The Declining Significance of Race* (Chicago, 1978); William Julius Wilson, *The Truly Disadvantaged: The Inner City, the Underclass, and Public Policy* (Chicago, 1987).

11 Quoted in Manning Marable, *Race, Reform and Rebellion: The Second Reconstruction in Black America, 1945–1990*, 2nd edn (London, 1991), pp. 158–9, 241 n. 9.

12 Michael C. Dawson, *Behind the Mule: Race and Class in African-American Politics* (Princeton, New Jersey, 1994); Gerald Horne, *Reversing Discrimination: The Case for Affirmative Action* (New York, 1992); Manning Marable, *Black Liberation in Conservative America* (Boston, 1997).

13 Robert Gooding-Williams (ed.), *Reading Rodney King: Reading Urban Uprising* (New York, 1993); Christian Parenti, *Lockdown America* (London, 1999); Leon Bing, *Do Or Die* (New York, 1991); S. Shakur, *Monster: The Autobiography of an LA Gang Member* (New York, 1993); Luis J. Rodriguez, *Always Running: LA Vida Loca, Gang Days in LA* (n.p., 1994); Yusuf Jah and Sister Shah' Keyah, *Uprising: Cripps and Bloods Tell the Story of America's Youth in the Crossfire* (New York, 1995); S. Beth Atkin, *Voices from the Streets: Young Former Gang Members Tell Their Stories* (Boston, 1996); Gina Sikes, *8 Ball Chicks: A Year in the Violent World of Girl Gangs* (New York, 1997); Joseph Rodriguez, Ruben Martinez and Luis Rodriguez, *East Side Stories: Gang Life in East LA* (New York, 1998).

14 Arthur J. Magida, *Prophet of Rage: A Life of Louis Farrakhan and his Nation* (New York, 1996), p. ix; A. Marshall, *Louis Farrakhan: Made in America* (n.p., 1996); Florence Hamlish Levinsohn, *Looking For Farrakhan* (Chicago, 1997).

15 Harold Brackman, *Ministry of Lies: The Truth Behind the Nation of Islam's 'The Secret Relationship Between Blacks and Jews'* (New York, 1994); Elreta

Dodds, *The Trouble With Farrakhan and the Nation of Islam: Another Message to the Black Man in America* (Detroit, 1997), pp. iv–v.

16 Amy Alexander (ed.), *The Farrakhan Factor: African-American Writers on Leadership, Nationhood, and Minister Louis Farrakhan* (New York, 1998), pp. 3, 17.

17 Mattias Gardel, *Countdown to Armageddon: Louis Farrakhan and the Nation of Islam* (London, 1996); Robert Singh, *The Farrakhan Phenomenon: Race, Reaction and the Paranoid Style in American Politics* (Washington DC, 1997).

18 Henry Louis Gates Jr, 'The Charmer', in Alexander, *The Farrakhan Factor*, p. 50.

19 See chapter 2, pp. 53–6, and chapter 4, pp. 104–6.

20 Raphael S. Ezekiel, *The Racist Mind: Portraits of American Neo-Nazis and Klansmen* (New York, 1995); James Ridgeway, *Blood in the Face: The Ku Klux Klan, Aryan Nations, Nazi Skinheads and the Rise of a New White Culture* (New York, 1995); Vincent Coppola, *Dragons of God: A Journey Through Far-Right America* (Atlanta, Georgia, 1996); Morris Dees with James Concoron, *Gathering Storm: America's Militia Threat* (New York, 1996); John George and Laird Wilcox, *American Extremists: Militias, Supremacists, Klansmen, Communists, and Others* (New York, 1996); Michael Barkun, *Religion and the Racist Right: The Origins of the Christian Identity Movement* (Chapel Hill, North Carolina, 1997); Jesse Daniels, *White Lies: Race, Class, Gender and Sexuality in White Supremacist Discourse* (New York, 1997); Betty A. Dobratz and Stephanie L. Shanks-Meile, *'White Power, White Pride!' The White Supremacist Movement in the United States* (New York, 1997); Kenneth S. Stern, *A Force Upon the Plain: The American Militia Movement and the Politics of Hate* (Norman, Oklahoma, 1997); Howard L. Bushart, John R. Craig and Myra Barnes, *Soldiers of God: White Supremacists and Their Holy War for America* (New York, 1998).

21 Steven A. Shull, *A Kinder, Gentler Racism? The Reagan–Bush Civil Rights Legacy* (New York, 1993).

22 Dan T. Carter, *From George Wallace to Newt Gingrich: Race in the Conservative Counterrevolution, 1963–1994* (Baton Rouge, Louisiana, 1996); Kenneth O'Reilly, *Nixon's Piano: Presidents and Racial Politics from Washington to Clinton* (New York, 1995), pp. 331–406; Michael Zatarain, *David Duke: Evolution of a Klansman* (Gretna, Louisiana, 1990); Douglas Rose (ed.), *The Emergence of David Duke and the Politics of Race* (Chapel Hill, North Carolina, 1992).

23 O'Reilly, *Nixon's Piano*, pp. 407–23; Dilys M. Hill and Paul S. Herrnson (eds), *The Clinton Presidency: The First Term, 1992–1996* (London, 1999), pp. 104–25.

24 Raymond Wolters, *Right Turn: William Bradford Reynolds, the Reagan Administration, and Black Civil Rights* (New Brunswick, New Jersey, 1996); Nicholas Laham, *The Reagan Presidency and the Politics of Race: In Pursuit of Colorblind Justice and Limited Government* (Westport, Connecticut, 1998).

7

African Americans and US popular culture since 1895

Many moons ago when the world was young, and the author of this book was an even younger undergraduate at the University of Cambridge, he was confronted by a question on an examination paper for Part I of the Historical Tripos that began with the statement 'Popular culture since 1945 has been an excellent way of killing time for those who like it dead.' Predictably, this assertion was followed by an invitation to 'discuss' and, in fairness to my former examiners, such a bold proposition was doubtless intended to prompt vigorous debate. At the same time the value judgement in the question can be seen as reflecting something of the attitudes of mainstream historians towards popular culture prior to the 1970s. In earlier decades standard historical texts often avoided any consideration of culture at all. Where such discussion was included it was commonly confined to a section that appeared to be uncomfortably bolted on to the main text and the culture in question was almost invariably of the 'highbrow' rather than the popular variety. In short, as cultural historian Michael Bertrand has noted, scholars 'recurrently treated popular culture as an unwelcome guest, to be looked upon with suspicion and doubt'.[1]

This inhospitable approach can be seen as the result of a number of factors. In the first instance, as has already been hinted, until the 1960s historians were inclined to view popular culture as 'vulgar and uncultured', and scholars instinctively avoided 'investigating the realm of the "low brow" to protect their own (or someone else's) notion of intellectual integrity'. Moreover, there was also the perception that popular culture did not afford genuine insights into attitudes and values of the general public but was rather the artificial creation of a culture industry that by clever merchandizing manipulated malleable consumers into buying its products, however trite and banal. In twentieth-century life, popular culture had supplanted religion as the opium of the people and the 'exertions and inclinations of consumers [were] as repetitive and meaningless as the pabulum they consume. Drugged or numbed into submission, individuals [were] no longer able to resist or evaluate critically what the media inflicts upon them'.[2]

These elitist attitudes were reinforced by more practical considerations. Writing as late as 1990 the eminent African American historian and civil rights activist Vincent Harding reflected on the reluctance of historians to examine the cultural dimensions of the civil rights struggle in the post-1945 era. He concluded that this was because historians were too inclined to view civil rights activity in terms of conventional initiatives, such as courtroom battles, non-violent protests, electoral campaigns and efforts to secure the passage of new legislation. This marginalized important developments in areas such as film, music, radio and television taking place at the same time. In consequence, as British cultural historian Brian Ward has observed, 'in most overviews and many monographs' on the post-war Civil Rights Movement the consideration of cultural issues was usually confined to 'little more than a cursory mention of the freedom songs', or the reflections on civil rights by renowned African American novelist James Baldwin in his much publicized 1962 essay 'The Fire Next Time', or the more racially and politically aware releases of leading black soul artists such as Aretha Franklin or James Brown. [3]

Although, as the observations of Harding and Ward indicate, there is still a need for more research on the relationship between civil rights and popular culture, there were also important advances in the subject area during the last three decades of the twentieth century, with both the volume and quality of published research gathering increasing pace over time. To some extent, as is often the case with historiographical developments, this can be attributed to the fact that a small number of studies on a hitherto neglected topic can act as a catalyst for further debate and fresh publications, ultimately reaching a point where research on a subject area acquires a self-sustaining momentum. Equally, it can be seen as part of a general and wider long-term trend in the historical profession towards a less elitist approach to the study of the past, first manifested in the 'new social history' of the 1960s and 1970s.

Generational change was another consideration. Just as American historians reaching academic maturity in the 1950s and 1960s were influenced by the dramatic developments in the black civil rights struggle of these decades, scholars born after the Second World War were the first historians to experience the daily impact of television from their earliest childhood years. Unquantifiable though it may be, it is at least conceivable that this fact contributed to scholars of this generation becoming less condescending in their attitudes towards popular culture and more appreciative of its significance and meaning. Whatever the explanation, it is undeniable that in the final quarter of the twentieth century the academic study of popular culture underwent something of a revolution, during which the subject area became a major focus for innovative and high quality scholarship. Given that research on African American history experienced similar developments in the same period it is not surprising that research on the relationship between popular culture and the black freedom struggle also began to flourish.

The first tentative indications that times were changing came in the 1960s and, more particularly, the 1970s. The sustained civil rights protests of these years contributed to growing interest by scholars in examining the strategies of protest and accommodation adopted by African Americans in earlier periods. During the Black Power era of the late 1960s and early 1970s this trend was reinforced by increasing demands by African American students for the introduction of college and university courses on black history and culture. Advances in scholarly research and teaching and learning, as is often the case, were linked.

The daily lives of black slaves in the antebellum South, 1790–1860, became an especial focus for academic study. Formerly studies on slavery, or the 'peculiar institution' as it was known, had concentrated predominantly on the experiences of white slaveholders.[4] This now changed. Instead, historians sought to understand the institution from the perspective of the oppressed rather than the oppressor. The fact that the vast majority of these black victims were illiterate, leaving behind little in the way of conventional written source materials, encouraged researchers to examine aspects of slave culture, such as music and folklore, to understand the thoughts and feelings of slaves. Moreover, scholars such as John Blassingame, Lawrence Levine, George Rawick, Albert Raboteau, and Marxist historian Eugene Genovese, argued that slaves used African American culture as a way of resisting the daily oppression of the peculiar institution and as a means of reaffirming their own identity and self-esteem.[5]

Focusing not just on slavery but also the period after its abolition, in 1865, African American historian Herbert Gutman examined black family life through to the mid-1920s.[6] Musicologists and cultural historians Robert M. W. Dixon and John Godrich, Dena Epstein, Tony Russell and Eileen Southern provided a series of influential and groundbreaking studies on the heritage of African American music.[7] In particular British academic Paul Oliver contributed revealing insights into the social and cultural meaning in the Blues, a subject of investigation prompted both by Oliver's scholarly desire for knowledge and his personal passion for the genre.[8]

Adopting a different line of enquiry, other researchers sought to identify the historical origins of common demeaning stereotypes of African Americans that had been used to help justify denying equal citizenship rights to them. Historians Winthrop Jordan and Gary Nash traced negative images of black Africans back to early colonial America and beyond.[9] Picking up where Jordan left off, George M. Frederickson looked at changing white perceptions of blacks during the course of the nineteenth century, while fellow historian I. A. Newby examined the often bizarre arguments advanced by racial conservatives to justify the spread of segregation in the early decades of the twentieth century.[10]

Literary scholar Donald G. Baker sourced racist images in early twentieth-century American popular novels, and in *Blacking Up* cultural historian Robert C. Toll traced the racial attitudes of modern white America back to minstrel shows of the 1830s. Although minstrel shows had long since lost their mass popular appeal by the early twentieth century, Toll argued that their significance lay in the fact that the racial prejudices they encouraged persisted in the American psyche. Like the Cheshire cat in *Alice Through the Looking Glass*, 'the minstrel show, long after it had disappeared, left its central image – the grinning black mask – lingering on, deeply embedded in the American consciousness'.[11]

Historian Daniel Leab also took up this theme in *From Sambo to Superspade*, a 1973 study on the portrayal of African Americans in Hollywood film. He argued that the images of blacks on the silver screen were strongly influenced by the nineteenth-century minstrel tradition. The result was the 'Sambo' stereotype, in which the 'movies presented blacks as subhuman, simpleminded, superstitious and submissive. They exhibited qualities of foolish exaggeration and an apparently hereditary clumsiness and ignorance as well as an addictive craving for fried chicken and watermelon.' Leab's work was notable as one of a number of studies in the early 1970s that provided the first detailed considerations of racial imagery in Hollywood film.[12]

Leab's line of enquiry also typified what by the 1980s had become a dominant trend in studies by cultural historians, namely to explore the origins, character and significance of stereotyped depictions of African Americans in US popular culture. In *Blacks and White TV* (1983) cultural historian J. Fred MacDonald thus examined the portrayal of African Americans on network television, first successfully introduced commercially to American audiences in 1948. Scholars Sam Dennison, William L. Van Deburg and Joseph Boskin took a broader perspective, tracing the development of stereotyped depictions of black Americans back to the nineteenth century and earlier.[13]

In marked contrast to the striking advances being made in respect to other areas of popular culture, the role of African Americans in sport had hitherto remained a topic largely ignored in scholarly studies. Inevitably, there were occasional worthy exceptions. In *The Revolt of the Black Athlete* (1969) black sociologist and protest activist Harry Edwards had chronicled the development of the campaign among African American athletes to boycott the 1968 Olympic Games in Mexico City. In *Bad Nigger!* (1975) Al-Tony Gilmore examined the public reaction of Americans to the highly publicized and controversial career of Jack Johnson, who in the early years of the twentieth century became the first African American to win the world heavyweight boxing championship.[14] More generally, however, the academic community, and historians in particular, had shown little interest in the relationship between race and sport.

This situation began to change in the mid-1980s with the publication of a number of biographies on African American sporting heroes of the past, a welcome development in part prompted by the global celebrity status of recently retired world heavyweight boxing champion Muhammad Ali. In 1985 Chris Mead provided a detailed account of the life and career of boxing legend Joe Louis. The following year sports historian William J. Baker published a study on another black sporting icon of the 1930s, Jesse Owens. In *Papa Jack* boxing historian Randy Roberts met the need for a full-length scholarly biography of Jack Johnson, identified by Ali himself as one of his sporting role models. In keeping with other scholarly studies of the decade these accounts highlighted the way in which media coverage of their subjects had both reflected and reinforced the negative racial stereotyping of African Americans.[15]

The 1990s saw both rapid and unprecedented developments in the academic study of popular culture. In part this interest can be seen as reflecting the cult of celebrity that enveloped the leading stars of sport, music, film and television entertainment at the close of the century. Equally, it was the result of a snowball effect as new researchers developed lines of enquiry first explored in the pioneering works of previous decades. Some publications consolidated earlier studies. Thomas Cripps's *Making Movies Black: The Hollywood Message Movie from World War II to the Civil Rights Era* provided a natural companion volume to his earlier work *Slow Fade to Black* that looked at African Americans in film between 1900 and 1940. In 1994 Donald Bogle's expanded and updated edition of his study *Toms, Coons, Mulattoes, Mammies and Bucks* became the standard account of racial stereotyping in film.[16]

In *Living Color*, associate professor of information and media studies Sasha Torres edited a collection of essays on race and television and another compilation of writings by varied authors, edited by cultural studies scholars L. Spigel and M. Curtin, addressed the wider issue of social conflict and television in the

1960s. In *Enlightened Racism: The Cosby Show* (1992) S. Jhally and J. Lewis provided a detailed study on the racial imagery in one of the most acclaimed and commercially successful television productions of the 1980s and early 1990s. At the end of the decade Krystal Zook examined the portrayal of race in the most recently created of the major American television networks in *Color By Fox*. Two years later Donald Bogle's *Prime-Time Blues* supplanted J. Fred MacDonald's 1983 work as the most authoritative one-volume study on the portrayal of African Americans on television.[17]

Sport also benefited from more attention. Journalist Thomas Hauser's 1991 work *Muhammad Ali: His Life and Times* became the authoritative biography of boxing's best-known and most admired black icon. In *Bad Intentions* and *A Savage Business* fellow sports columnists Peter Heller and Richard Hoffer respectively looked at the turbulent career of world heavyweight boxing champion Mike Tyson.[18] These works reflected the fact that up to the mid-1990s the literature on sport was provided largely by journalists, with comparatively few publications coming from scholarly researchers, an imbalance that if regrettable was also understandable. Works written to appeal to the large potential market comprised by sports fans were inevitably likely to have greater commercial appeal for publishing houses than more academic studies. It is also perhaps the case that, taken as a whole, the scholarly profession is not renowned as a section of the community that contains a large number of sports enthusiasts.

Fortunately, by the late 1990s there were signs that the level of research on sport by historians and academic cultural analysts was increasing, a development perhaps prompted in part by the intensive media coverage devoted to the troubles and misfortunes of some of the nation's best-known black sporting celebrities, such as Muhammad Ali, Mike Tyson, and most notably O. J. Simpson. Historian and passionate baseball devotee Jules Tygiel provided an overdue scholarly biography of Jackie Robinson, who in 1947 made history by becoming the first African American to play in major league baseball. Bruce Adelson addressed the significant, if less glamorous, breakthroughs achieved by African Americans in minor league baseball. Thomas R. Hietala and Andrew M. Kaye contributed important studies on three black sporting heroes of an earlier era, namely Jack Johnson, Joe Louis, and Theodore 'Tiger' Flowers, who in 1926 became the first African American to win the world middleweight boxing championship. Focusing on a later era, Amy Bass and Douglas Hartmann added fresh works on the Black Power protests by African American athletes at the 1968 Mexico Olympics. Patrick B. Miller, David K. Wiggins and Gary A. Sailes edited essay collections on African Americans in sport, and in a controversial 1997 publication John Hoberman examined racial stereotyping in sport. He concluded that the popular image of African Americans as natural athletes both reinforced negative white stereotypes of blacks, as physically aggressive and lacking in intellect, and also damaged the development of African American schoolchildren by encouraging them to neglect classroom study in favour of success on the sports field. In the wake of the media-fest surrounding his 1995 trial and acquittal for the murder of his wife Nicole, disgraced former American football star O. J. Simpson also became a focus for scholarly investigation.[19]

Cultural historians William Barlow and Reebee Garfalo contributed important essays on African Americans and popular music in the twentieth century in a valuable 1993 anthology of writings edited by Jannette L. Dates and Barlow that examined the role of black Americans across a broad range of cultural areas. In 1998 *Just My Soul Responding*, a monograph by British historian Brian Ward, came close to providing the definitive account of the complex relationship between the black freedom struggle and American popular music from the mid-1940s through to the mid-1970s.[20]

Whereas Ward's study concentrated on Rhythm and Blues, Rock 'n' Roll, and Soul and Disco, *Jazz: A History of America's Music* (2000) by historian Geoffrey C. Ward and historical documentary filmmaker Ken Burns, examined the impact on US race relations of a musical genre more commonly associated with an earlier age. The impact of the work was heightened by the fact that it was written to accompany a major television series directed by Burns on the subject. In an important 2001 essay collection *Media, Culture, and the Modern African American Freedom Struggle*, Brian Ward and historian Peter Townsend contributed further insights into the links between Jazz and the civil rights struggle of the 1950s and 1960s. Conversely, in *Race, Rock, and Elvis*, published the previous year, historian Michael T. Bertrand emphasized the importance of Rock 'n' Roll in breaking down racial barriers in the American South after the Second World War as young white southerners embraced black-inspired music.[21]

Black Hip Hop culture of the 1980s and 1990s, and the controversial musical genre of Rap that it embraced, also began to attract the attention of cultural scholars by the mid-1990s, most notably in Tricia Rose's insightful study *Black Noise* (1994) and Todd Boyd's equally perceptive *Am I Black Enough For You?* (1997). At the same time Rose's work, written before the emergence of West Coast Gangsta Rap, demonstrated the pitfalls of writing about contemporary areas of popular culture still undergoing the process of rapid change and development. Similarly, Boyd's study suffered from the drawback of being published before the rise of white Rap superstar Eminem. In one of the most recent works on the genre British scholar Eithne Quinn's *Nuthin' but a 'g' thang* (2005) examined the origins and development of gangsta rap, concluding that the new music was born out of both the decline in black protest culture and the rise in individualist and entrepreneurial thinking that occurred in the United States from the 1970s onwards.[22]

In addition to expanding the sum of academic knowledge in the, by now, increasingly established areas of research, like film, television, music and sport, other scholars examined popular culture from previously little-explored angles. In 1994 associate professor in media studies Marilyn Kern-Foxworth analysed racial images in advertising, whilst historian Kenneth Goings and cultural scholar Patricia A. Turner focused on nineteenth and twentieth-century black collectibles, tourist memorabilia, cheap ornaments and knick-knacks that depicted African American characters. In *Stylin'* (1998) Australian scholars Shane and Graham White studied African American culture from slavery through to the 1940s, looking not just at topics like music and dance but also evolving fashions in clothes and hairstyles.[23]

With the exception of a brief but valuable analysis by J. Fred MacDonald, the role of African Americans on radio was an area largely ignored by scholars prior to the 1990s.[24] Even at the end of the decade historian Barbara Savage was still able to observe that notwithstanding 'its ubiquitous presence in American life for over half a century, radio [was] a medium whose political and cultural power and influence [were] not yet reflected in American historiography, American studies, works on American race relations, or studies of the media and popular culture'. Instead, published research focused almost exclusively on film and television.[25]

On first consideration, this parlous state of affairs might appear curious, given that commercial radio had been available to American audiences since the 1920s and network television, by comparison, was but a relative newcomer. The explanation was, however, straightforward. When cultural history first started to become fashionable as a subject for academic research in the 1960s, the golden age of radio had long since gone and the halcyon days of television only recently begun. Moreover, with every passing decade the leading scholars of the new cultural history had increasingly spent their formative childhood and adolescent years in an age where film and television were the dominant forms of popular entertainment. In a modern world that was 'literally structured by electronic media' it was hard for researchers to fully appreciate 'the sense of awe that national radio inspired in the 1930s and 1940s'.[26]

Beginning the long process of redressing the imbalance, in 1991 cultural historian Melvin Patrick Ely examined the radio show, and later television series, *Amos 'n' Andy* that entertained American audiences from the 1920s through to the 1950s. Centred on the comic experiences of two black characters, played on radio by white entertainers Charles Correll and Freeman Gosden, the production was highly popular and controversial in equal measure because of its demeaning and stereotyped portrayal of African American life. In a broader and highly acclaimed study, published at the end of the 1990s, Savage herself sought to provide a partial remedy for the malady that she had so effectively highlighted, by scrutinizing the handling of race related issues on radio during the Second World War through to the late 1940s. Adopting a still wider perspective, William Barlow looked at the relationship between African Americans and radio from the commercial introduction of the medium in the 1920s through to the late 1990s. Conversely, British historian Brian

Ward's *Radio and the Struggle for Civil Rights in the South* (2004) focused primarily on the 1950s and 1960s and one particular geographical region. In an extensively researched and ground-breaking study, Ward concluded that radio was often 'the most important mass medium' in southern black communities during these decades and that it played a key and 'occasionally decisive' role in the civil rights struggles of that era. [27]

In keeping with parallel developments in other areas of African American historiography, the 1990s also saw a growth of academic interest in the role of women and gender related issues. Communication Arts researcher Aniko Bodroghkozy looked at 'Race, Gender and Contested Meanings' in the 1960s NBC television show *Julia* as part of a series of essays, *Private Screenings: Television and the Female Consumer* (1992), edited by fellow media scholars Lynn Spigel and Denise Mann. Donald Bogle published accounts on leading black women film and musical entertainers. M. M. Manring examined the commercial represen-tation of African American femininity in *The Strange Career of Aunt Jemima* (1998) and Brian Ward examined sexist attitudes in Rhythm and Blues lyrics in a collection of essays on *Gender in the Civil Rights Movement* (1999) edited by fellow British scholars Peter J. Ling and Sharon Monteith.[28]

A less obvious development was a sudden proliferation of works examining blackface minstrelsy. In a major 1991 study, *Wages of Whiteness*, the Marxist and cultural historian David Roediger argued that nineteenth-century minstrel caricatures symbolized more than just comic racial lampoons at the expense of African Americans. Blackface characters like Zip Coon and Jim Crow were also reminders of a romanticized past that white working-class Americans were in the process of losing as a result of industrialization. More specifically, they represented a former lifestyle in which holidays were plentiful, labourers came into daily contact with nature, enjoyed unrepressed sexuality and immediate as opposed to postponed gratification. In short, minstrel stage characters were not just ridiculous racial inferiors. They also evoked for white workers images of 'their former selves', and what they in part still longed to be.[29] In subsequent studies spread across the 1990s cultural historians Eric Lott, Annemarie Bean, James V. Hatch, Brooks McNamara, Dale

Cockrell, W. T. Lhamon and William J. Mahar provided further insights on minstrelsy. Lhamon looked at racial stereotyping in minstrel acts and argued that derivations of these persisted in popular culture throughout the twentieth century through to the performances of black Hip Hop artists like M. C. Hammer.[30] Other works, however, focused predominantly on how the minstrel medium served to reinforce white working-class identity, most especially among young men, and provided a means of subverting authority and poking fun at establishment figures.[31]

Roediger's work was significant in that it was an early indication of a new dominant trend in cultural analysis in the 1990s, namely the rise of 'whiteness studies', works that examined changing perceptions and meaning of white racial identity.[32] Although the authors in question were almost invariably liberal in their outlook, this interest in the concept of whiteness can be seen as linked to the growing perception of many white Americans in the 1980s and 1990s that their interests and identity were being overlooked in favour of minority ethnic groups advantaged by affirmative action programmes. In extreme and unenlightened form this can even be viewed as being represented in the proliferation of far-right militia and white supremacy movements at this time.[33]

The minstrelsy studies of the 1990s were also an early indication of another significant historiographical development. Scholars began to move away from the approach of examining popular culture in terms of the racial stereotypes it created and sustained. Researchers started to recognize that this line of enquiry, if instructive and revealing, equally suffered from limitations. It ignored the complexity and independence of mind in the responses of audiences to the forms of popular entertainment served up for their consumption. Thus in the early 1950s many African American viewers resented the racial caricatures of the television show *Amos 'n' Andy* but at the same time were attracted to the programme because, almost unique among television productions of the day, it was set in a black community and all the lead characters were African American.[34]

Similarly, a blinkered focus on racial stereotyping emphasized race at the expense of other issues, such as class and regional identity. It also portrayed modern-day representations of race as being derived primarily from hackneyed images that could be traced back in an almost unbroken line until at least the first decades of the nineteenth century, and arguably even earlier. This perception ignored other, more modern, factors that at the very least made some contribution to the way in which the media and entertainment industries approached racial subjects. In 2003 Sasha Torres thus concluded that, in respect to television, reliance on historic stereotypes to explain the content of broadcasting was 'inadequate', because this failed 'to recognize the ways in which African American persons, collectivities, and politics have collided at crucial moments in television history with industrial self-interest, cynicism, and even, on occasion, the desire to do the right thing, to produce not only the content of television's programs, but their form and reception as well'.[35]

Typifying this new outlook in *Framing the South: Hollywood, Television, and Race during the Civil Rights Struggle* (2001), media and communications professor Allison Graham thus examined representations of the region and its inhabitants in terms of not just race but also class and gender. Similarly, in her own study on television and blacks civil rights, Torres argued that Martin Luther King and civil rights activists of the 1950s and 1960s were not just passive recipients of network coverage, but actively shaped it in a way that helped viewers to empathize with protesters against southern law enforcement agencies. Conversely, in the more conservative climate of the 1990s, programming encouraged audiences to identify with police forces in their fight against the perceived threat posed by criminals from predominantly ethnic minority backgrounds.[36] Cultural historians, if not alas television directors and producers, appeared to be entering a new era of heightened understanding, and depth and breadth of vision, in their work during the first years of the new millennium.

Notes

1 Michael T. Bertrand, *Race, Rock, and Elvis* (Urbana, Illinois, 2000), p. 8.
2 Bertrand, *Race, Rock, and Elvis*, p. 8.
3 James Baldwin, 'The Fire Next Time', *The New Yorker*, 17 November 1962; Vincent Harding, *Hope and History: Why We Must Share the Story of the Movement* (New York, 1990), pp. 126–7; Brian Ward (ed.), *Media, Culture*

and the Modern African American Freedom Struggle (Gainesville, Florida, 2001), pp. 1–2.

4 Most notably in the works of the early twentieth-century Southern white historian Ulrich B. Phillips, himself descended from a slave-owning family, for example, *American Negro Slavery* (New York, 1918); *Life and Labor in the Old South* (Boston, Massachusetts, 1929).

5 John Blassingame, *The Slave Community: Plantation Life in the Antebellum South* (New York, 1972); Eugene Genovese, *Roll, Jordan, Roll: The World the Slaves Made* (New York, 1974); Lawrence Levine, *Black Culture and Black Consciousness* (New York, 1977); Albert Raboteau, *Slave Religion: The 'Invisible Institution' in the Antebellum South* (New York, 1978); George Rawick, *From Sundown to Sunup: The Making of the Black Community* (Westport, Connecticut, 1972). A detailed consideration of the historiography on antebellum slavery is beyond the scope of this chapter. For a full discussion of the subject see the earlier publication by Hugh Tulloch in the Manchester University Press Issues in Historiography series, *The Debate on the American Civil War Era* (Manchester, 1999), pp. 33–70.

6 Herbert Gutman, *The Black Family in Slavery and Freedom, 1750–1925* (Oxford, 1976).

7 Robert M. W. Dixon and John Godrich, *Recording the Blues* (London, 1977); Dena Epstein, *Sinful Tunes and Spirituals: Black Folk Music to the Civil War* (Urbana, Illinois, 1977); Tony Russell, *Blacks, Whites and Blues* (London, 1970); Eileen Southern, *The Music of Black Americans: A History* (New York, 1971).

8 Paul Oliver, *Blues Fell This Morning: The Meaning of the Blues* (London, 1960); Paul Oliver, *Conversation With the Blues* (London, 1965); Paul Oliver, *Screening the Blues: Aspects of the Blues Tradition* (London, 1968); Paul Oliver, *The Story of the Blues* (London, 1969); Paul Oliver, *Savannah Syncopators: African Retentions in the Blues* (London, 1970).

9 Winthrop Jordan, *White Over Black: American Attitudes toward the Negro, 1550–1812* (Chapel Hill, North Carolina, 1968). A shortened version of this work was later published under the title *The White Man's Burden: Historical Origins of Racism in the United States* (New York, 1974). Gary B. Nash, 'Red, White and Black: The Origins of Racism in Colonial America', in Gary B. Nash and Richard Weiss (eds), *The Great Fear: Race in the Mind of America* (New York, 1970).

10 George M. Frederickson, *The Black Image in the White Mind: The Debate on Afro-American Character and Destiny, 1817–1914* (New York, 1972); I. A. Newby, *Jim Crow's Defense: Anti-Negro Thought in America, 1900–1930* (Baton Rouge, Louisiana, 1965).

11 Donald G. Baker, 'Black Images: The Afro-American in Popular Novels, 1900–1915', *Journal of Popular Culture* (7, 1973); Robert C. Toll, *Blacking Up: The Minstrel Show in Nineteenth-Century America* (New York, 1974), p. 274.

12 Daniel Leab, *From Sambo to Superspade: The Black Experience in Motion Pictures* (London, 1973), pp. 1, 10; Thomas Cripps, *Slow Fade to Black: The Negro in American Film, 1900–1940* (New York, 1977).

13 J. Fred MacDonald, *Blacks and White TV: Afro-Americans in Television since*

1948 (Chicago, 1983); Sam Dennison, *Scandalize My Name: Black Imagery in American Popular Music* (New York, 1982); William L. Van Deburg, *Slavery and Race in American Popular Culture* (Madison, Wisconsin, 1984); Joseph Boskin, *Sambo: The Rise and Demise of an American Jester* (New York, 1986).

14 Harry Edwards, *The Revolt of the Black Athlete* (New York, 1969); Al-Tony Gilmore, *Bad Nigger! The National Impact of Jack Johnson* (Port Washington, New York, 1975).

15 Chris Mead, *Champion: Joe Louis, Black Hero in White America* (New York, 1985); William J. Baker, *Jesse Owens: An American Life* (New York, 1986); Randy Roberts, *Papa Jack: Jack Johnson and the Era of White Hopes* (London, 1986).

16 Thomas Cripps, *Making Movies Black: The Hollywood Message Movie from World War II to the Civil Rights Era* (New York, 1993); Donald Bogle, *Toms, Coons, Mulattoes, Mammies and Bucks: An Interpretative History of Blacks in American Film*, 3rd edn (New York, 1994).

17 Sasha Torres (ed.), *Living Color: Race and Television in the United States* (Durham, North Carolina, 1998); Lynn Spigel and Michael Curtin (eds), *The Revolution Wasn't Televised: Sixties Television and Social Conflict* (New York, 1997); Sut Jhally and J. Lewis, *Enlightened Racism: The Cosby Show, Audiences and the Myth of the American Dream* (Boulder, Colorado, 1992); Krystal B. Zook, *Color By Fox: The Fox Network and the Revolution in Black Television* (New York, 1999); Donald Bogle, *Prime-Time Blues: African Americans in Network Television* (New York, 2001).

18 Thomas Hauser, with the co-operation of Muhammad Ali, *Muhammad Ali: His Life and Times* (London, 1991); Peter Heller, *Bad Intentions: The Mike Tyson Story* (New York, 1995); Richard Hoffer, *A Savage Business: The Comeback and Comedown of Mike Tyson* (New York, 1998).

19 Jules Tygiel, *Baseball's Great Experiment: Jackie Robinson and his Legacy* (New York, 1997); Bruce Adelson, *Brushing Back Jim Crow: The Integration of Minor League Baseball in the American South* (Charlottesville, Virginia, 1999); David K. Wiggins (ed.), *Glory Bound: Black Athletes in White America* (New York, 1997); Gary A. Sailes (ed.), *African Americans in Sport* (New Brunswick, New Jersey, 1998); John Hoberman, *Darwin's Athletes: How Sport Has Damaged Black America and Preserved the Myth of Race* (Boston, 1997); Darnell M. Hunt, *O. J. Simpson Fact and Fictions: News Rituals in the Construction of Reality* (Cambridge, 1999); Linda Williams, *Playing the Race Card: Melodrama of Black and White From Uncle Tom to O. J. Simpson* (Princeton, New Jersey, 2001); Thomas R. Hietala, *Fight of the Century: Jack Johnson, Joe Louis, and the Struggle for Racial Equality* (New York, 2004); Andrew M. Kaye, *The Pussycat of Prizefighting: Tiger Flowers and the Politics of Black Celebrity* (Athens, Georgia, 2004); Amy Bass, *Not the Triumph but the Struggle: The 1968 Olympics and the Making of the Black Athlete* (Minneapolis, Minnesota, 2002); Douglas Hartmann, *Race, Culture and the Revolt of the Black Athlete: The 1968 Olympic Protests and Their Aftermath* (Chicago, 2003); Patrick B. Miller and David K. Wiggins (eds), *Sport and the Color Line: Black Athletes and Race Relations in Twentieth-Century America* (New York, 2004).

20 William Barlow, 'Cashing In: 1900–1939', and Reebee Garofalo, 'Crossing Over: 1939–1992', in Jannette L. Dates and William Barlow (eds), *Split Image: African Americans in the Mass Media* (Washington DC, 1993), pp. 25–56, 57–127; Brian Ward, *Just My Soul Responding: Rhythm and Blues, Black Consciousness and Race Relations* (London, 1998).

21 Geoffrey C. Ward and Ken Burns, *Jazz: A History of America's Music* (New York, 2000); Peter Townsend, 'Free Jazz: Musical Style and Liberationist Ethic, 1956–1965', and Brian Ward, 'Jazz and Soul, Race and Class, Cultural Nationalists and Black Panthers: A Black Power Debate Revisited', in Ward (ed.), *Media, Culture and the Modern African American Freedom Struggle*; Bertrand, *Race, Rock, and Elvis*.

22 Houston A. Baker, *Black Studies: Rap and the Academy* (Chicago, 1993); Tricia Rose, *Black Noise: Rap Music and Black Culture in Contemporary America* (Hanover, New Hampshire, 1994); Todd Boyd, *Am I Black Enough For You? Popular Culture from the Hood and Beyond* (Bloomington, Indiana, 1997); Michael Eric Dyson, *Between God and Gangsta Rap: Bearing Witness to Black Culture* (New York, 1996); William E. Perkins (ed.), *Droppin' Science: Critical Essays on Rap Music and Hip Hop Culture* (Philadelphia, 1996); Nelson George, *Hip Hop America* (London, 1998); Michael Eric Dyson, *Holler If You Hear Me: Searching for Tupac Shakur* (London, 2001); Murray Forman, *The 'Hood Comes First: Race, Space and Place in Rap and Hip-Hop* (Middletown, Connecticut, 2002); Eithne Quinn, *Nuthin' but a 'g' thang: The Culture and Commerce of Gangsta Rap* (New York, 2005).

23 Marilyn Kern-Foxworth, *Aunt Jemima, Uncle Ben, and Rastus: Blacks in Advertising, Yesterday, Today, and Tomorrow* (Westport, Connecticut, 1994); Kenneth W. Goings, *Mammy and Uncle Mose: Black Collectibles and American Stereotyping* (Bloomington, Indiana, 1994); Patricia A. Turner, *Ceramic Uncles and Celluloid Mammies: Black Images and Their Influence on Culture* (New York, 1994); Shane White and Graham White, *Stylin': African American Expressive Culture from Its Beginnings to the Zoot Suit* (Ithaca, New York, 1998).

24 J. Fred MacDonald, *Don't Touch That Dial! Radio Programming in American Life, 1920–1960* (Chicago, 1979).

25 Barbara Dianne Savage, *Broadcasting Freedom: Radio, War, and the Politics of Race, 1938–1948* (Chapel Hill, North Carolina, 1999), p.5.

26 Savage, *Broadcasting Freedom*, p. 6.

27 Melvin Patrick Ely, *The Adventures of Amos 'n' Andy: A Social History of an American Phenomenon* (New York, 1991); Savage, *Broadcasting Freedom*; William Barlow, 'Commercial and Noncommercial Radio', in Dates and Barlow (eds), *Split Image*, pp. 189–264; William Barlow, *Voice Over: The Making of Black Radio* (Philadelphia, 1999); Brian Ward, *Radio and the Struggle for Civil Rights in the South* (Gainesville, Florida, 2004), p. ix.

28 Aniko Bodroghkozy, '"Is This What You Mean by Color TV?": Race, Gender, and Contested Meanings in NBC's *Julia*', in Lynn Spigel and Denise Mann (eds), *Private Screenings: Television and the Female Consumer* (Minneapolis, Minnesota, 1992), pp. 143–68; Donald Bogle, *Brown Sugar: Eighty Years of America's Black Female Superstars* (New York, 1990); Donald Bogle, *Dorothy Dandridge: A Biography* (New York, 1997); M. M. Manring,

Slave in a Box: The Strange Career of Aunt Jemima (Charlottesville, Virginia, 1998); Brian Ward, 'Sex Machines and Prisoners of Love: Male Rhythm and Blues, Sexual Politics and the Black Freedom Struggle', in Peter J. Ling and Sharon Monteith (eds), *Gender in the Civil Rights Movement* (New York, 1999).

29 David R. Roediger, *The Wages of Whiteness: Race and the Making of the American Working Class* (New York, 1991), p. 95.

30 W. T. Lhamon Jr, *Raising Cain: Blackface Performance from Jim Crow to Hip Hop* (Cambridge, Massachusetts, 1998).

31 Eric Lott, *Love and Theft: Blackface Minstrelsy and the American Working Class* (New York, 1993); Annemarie Bean, James V. Hatch and Brooks McNamara, *Inside the Minstrel Mask: Readings in Nineteenth-Century Blackface Minstrelsy* (Hanover, New Hampshire, 1996); Dale Cockrell, *Demons of Disorder: Early Blackface Minstrels and their World* (Cambridge, 1997).

32 For example, Noel Ignatiev, *How the Irish Became White* (New York, 1995); Neil Foley, *The White Scourge: Mexicans, Blacks and Poor Whites in Texas Cotton Culture* (Berkeley, California, 1997); Richard Delgado and Jean Stefancic (eds), *Critical White Studies: Looking Behind the Mirror* (Philadelphia, 1997); Grace Elizabeth Hale, *Making Whiteness: The Culture of Segregation in the South, 1890–1940* (New York, 1998); George Lipsitz, *The Possessive Investment in Whiteness: How White People Profit From Identity Politics* (Philadelphia, 1998); Michelle Brattain, *The Politics of Whiteness: Race, Workers and Culture in the Modern South* (Princeton, New Jersey, 2001).

33 Peter Kolchin, 'Whiteness Studies: The New History of Race in America', *Journal of American History* (89, 2002), p. 167.

34 Sasha Torres, *Black, White and in Color: Television and Black Civil Rights* (Princeton, New Jersey, 2003), pp. 1–2.

35 Torres, *Black, White and in Color*, p. 4.

36 Allison Graham, *Framing the South: Hollywood, Television, and Race during the Civil Rights Struggle* (Baltimore, Maryland, 2001); Torres, *Black, White and in Color*.

CONCLUSION

For almost two hundred years the issue of whether or not Thomas Jefferson, author of the 1776 Declaration of Independence and President of the United States from 1801 to 1809, fathered children by one of his slaves, Sally Hemmings, constituted a divisive and emotive controversy in American history. Scholars and admirers of Jefferson, as one of the founding fathers of the American republic, vigorously sought to protect his hallowed reputation from the claim that he had, at best, engaged in a consensual inter-racial sexual relationship, at worst, abused his power as a slave-owner to gratify his sexual desires. Conversely, successive generations of African American communities were convinced of the accuracy of the legend, despite the lack of any conclusive supporting evidence.

Writing in the 1980s, the experienced and well-respected historian Nathan Huggins concluded, not unreasonably, that the debate could never finally be resolved. The evidence was 'circumstantial' and 'we will never establish a *truth* that all will accept. Certainly, we will never get Thomas Jefferson or Sally Hemmings to testify to the facts.'[1] He was wrong. In 1998 scientific advances in DNA testing made it possible to show beyond reasonable doubt that late twentieth-century members of the Hemmings family had a shared ancestry with Jefferson. In an emotive act of reconciliation, the white descendants of the deceased President welcomed their newly recognized black relatives as long-lost family members.[2]

Unfortunately, it is unusual for historical debate to have such a clear-cut, let alone happy, ending. The Thomas Jefferson and Sally Hemmings controversy constitutes a rare exception to the rule. In the overwhelming majority of instances the nature of historiographical discussion is such that a search for any final resolution is a misconceived and unrealizable quest. In part this is because images of the past are a matter of subjective perception and can vary dramatically depending on the perspective of the various groups and individuals involved in the events. From the viewpoint of contemporary southern whites, the last decades of the nineteenth century marked a new positive era in race relations when the 'natural' order of society was restored with the re-imposition of white supremacy. For recently emancipated black slaves they were years of tragedy, as the hard-won and long-awaited freedoms achieved during the Reconstruction era, 1865–77, were systematically and ruthlessly stripped away.

Moreover, different generations of historians are also subject to changing times and values. Members of the American historical profession writing in the first three to four decades of the twentieth century were themselves the products of a society that believed in the innate inferiority of non-white races, and attributed almost all the major advances in human history to Anglo-Saxon inventiveness and western culture. Unsurprisingly, in these years mainstream scholars concentrated on researching the past experiences of white Americans, with African American history being perceived as an irrelevant and uninteresting backwater. Black history was largely perceived as a subject of interest only to scholars who were themselves African Americans, or white historians with some particular personal interest in the field. During the 1920s and 1930s the only notable exceptions to this rule were when the topic in question, such as the Great Migration, 1915–25, or lynching, attracted the attention of the wider American public.

During the 1950s and 1960s the spread of more liberal attitudes and values, reflected in the rise of Martin Luther King and the post-war Civil Rights Movement, inspired scholars to investigate the African American past. They eloquently portrayed the historical sufferings of black communities and felt moral outrage at such racial injustice in a way that would have been incomprehensible for many earlier scholars, who saw such inequalities as natural and inevitable rather than wrong or artificially imposed. Some historians, such as C. Vann Woodward, sought to examine the origins of racial segregation, the disfranchisement of black voters in the South and the careers of past black civil rights leaders like Booker T. Washington.

Many historians, such as Leon Litwack, August Meier, Mark Naison and Harvard Sitkoff, became active participants in civil rights protests. In their academic careers this commitment and idealism prompted unprecedented scholarly research into African

American history. During the 1960s and 1970s most of this work understandably focused on the Civil Rights Movement of the 1950s and 1960s and the most charismatic individuals associated with it, in particular Martin Luther King.

In the 1980s scholars began to move away from this leader-centred approach and demonstrated greater appreciation of initiatives in local communities at grassroots level. This trend also reflected the belated impact of the new social history of the 1960s and 1970s on the historiography of the African American experience. In a similar vein there was growing awareness of the fact that the post-war Civil Rights Movement was not a bolt from the blue but rather the culmination of long-term changes and developments in American society over several decades. This prompted new studies on the inter-war period and the Second World War in an attempt to identify the origins and preconditions of the protests of the 1950s and 1960s. Scholarly debate on the African American experience from the 1890s through to the early 1920s also gathered momentum with fresh studies on the spread of racial segregation, black migration to the cities and leading African American spokespersons of the period, most notably Booker T. Washington and Marcus Garvey.

By the 1990s other issues had come to the fore. The rise of feminism and growth in popularity of women's history in the closing decades of the twentieth century prompted academic researchers to pay more attention to the issue of gender in all periods of African American history. Similarly, scholarly publications highlighted important hitherto comparatively under-researched topics, such as the relationship between civil rights protests and popular culture, the international dimensions of the civil rights struggle, and the philosophy and values of the southern white opponents of integration. Whether writing about the 1890s or the 1980s historians began to recognize the importance of class divisions in African American communities and the civil rights struggle.

By the first years of the twenty-first century the African American experience was no longer the Cinderella subject of American history. More than forty years of sustained research by leading historians, both black and white, had provided rich and detailed insights into hitherto neglected aspects of the black

American past. It might seem reasonable to suppose that such prolonged and intensive activity would result in research fatigue, with each successive quarrying of the archives leaving fewer and poorer yields for later scholarly investigators. The fact that this was not the case highlights another fundamental characteristic of historiographical debate, namely that for every seeming answer provided by any line of research at least an equal, if not greater, number of new questions are raised.

The greater the richness and diversity of historical source material that is revealed, the less likely it becomes that the events under consideration can be subjected to any simple or final conclusion. On the contrary, each new finding reveals fresh issues that require investigation. The ongoing publication of the *Marcus Garvey and UNIA Papers* draws attention to the need for further research on the Garvey Movement of the 1920s. The growing number of excellent local studies on the Civil Rights Movement in the southern states during the 1950s and 1960s begs the question as to why there is not a corresponding body of work on the black freedom struggle in the North. The 2003 publication of *Freedom North: Black Freedom Struggles Outside the South, 1940–1980*, a collection of essays edited by Komozi Woodard, Jeanne Theoharis and Matthew Countryman is hopefully a recent indication that this particular need is now being addressed.[3]

The impending one-hundredth birthday celebrations of the NAACP in 2009 is a timely reminder of the desirability of more publications on the work of the Association in almost any period of its history. In this respect a welcome contribution is the recent history of the organization provided by journalist and longstanding NAACP worker Gilbert Jonas in *Freedom's Sword: The NAACP and the Struggle Against Racism in America, 1909–1969* (2005). A commendable undertaking, and more than 500 pages in length, Jonas's study is however more a broad brush survey rather than a detailed scholarly monograph. Indeed, it is probably the case that an authoritative academic history of the NAACP cannot be provided within the confines of any one-volume study, even by the most adroit and accomplished author.[4]

This unending scope for fresh exploration serves as a reminder that the notion that there can be any final resolution to the historiographical debate on black civil rights is as vain as the hope of discovering the mythical pot of gold at the end of a rainbow. The location sought recedes forever into the distance for every advance made towards it. It is the fate of all historians never to find a conclusive, definitive answer to the questions posed by their research. Their role is not to uncover any final truth, but rather to play a part in an unceasing search for a fuller and more detailed understanding of the past. In doing so, all historians, whether great or humble, take part in a shared undertaking with a clear beginning, yet no end, for, as it is observed in *The Rubaiyat of Omar Khayyam*, 'The Moving Finger writes', but 'having writ, moves on.'[5]

Notes

1 Nathan I. Huggins, 'Integrating Afro-American History into American History', in Darlene Clark Hine (ed.), *The State of Afro-American History: Past, Present, and* Future (Baton Rouge, Louisiana, 1986), p. 163.
2 Jan Ellen Lewis and Peter S. Onuf (eds), *Sally Hemmings and Thomas Jefferson: History, Memory and Civic Culture* (Charlottesville, Virginia, 1999), p. 1.
3 Komozi Woodard, Jeanne Theoharis and Matthew Countryman (eds), *Freedom North: Black Freedom Struggles Outside the South, 1940–1980* (London, 2003).
4 Gilbert Jonas, *Freedom's Sword: The NAACP and the Struggle Against Racism in America, 1909–1969* (New York, 2005). Manfred Berg's *The Ticket to Freedom: The NAACP and the Struggle for Black Political Integration* (Gainesville, Florida, 2005), is another welcome addition to the literature on the NAACP. Originally published in a German language edition in 2000, Berg's study examines the NAACP's decades-long struggle for black voting rights.
5 *The Rubaiyat of Omar Khayyam: The First Version of Edward Fitzgerald* (London, 1970), stanza 51.

SELECT BIBLIOGRAPHY

The following works provide helpful information on individual historians and the development of historiographical debates.

General

Franklin, John Hope, 'Afro-American History: State of the Art', *Journal of American History* (75, 1988).

Harris, Robert L. Jr, 'Coming of Age: The Transformation of Afro-American Historiography', *Journal of Negro History* (57, 1982).

Harris, Robert L. Jr, 'The Flowering of Afro-American History', *American Historical Review* (92, 1987).

Hine, Darlene Clark (ed.), *The State of Afro-American History: Past, Present and Future* (Baton Rouge, Louisiana, 1986).

Meier, August, *A White Scholar and the Black Community, 1945–1965: Essays and Reflections* (Amherst, Massachusetts, 1992).

Meier, August, and Elliott Rudwick, *Black History and the Historical Profession, 1915–1980* (Urbana, Illinois, 1986).

Novick, Peter, *That Noble Dream: The Objectivity Question and the American Historical Profession* (Cambridge, 1988).

Palmer, William, *Engagement With the Past: The Lives and Works of the World War II Generation of Historians* (Lexington, Kentucky, 2001).

The African American experience 1895–1945

Hawkins, Hugh (ed.), *Booker T. Washington and His Critics: The Problem of Negro Leadership* (Boston, 1974).

Kusmer, Kenneth L., 'The Black Urban Experience in American History', in Hine, Darlene Clark (ed.), *The State of Afro-American History: Past, Present, and Future* (Baton Rouge, Louisiana, 1986).

McMillen, Neil R. (ed.), *Remaking Dixie: The Impact of World War II on the American South* (Jackson, Mississippi, 1997).

Moore, Leonard J., 'Historical Interpretations of the 1920s Klan: The Traditional View and Recent Revisions', in Lay, Shawn (ed.), *The Invisible Empire in the West: Toward a New Historical Appraisal of the Ku Klux Klan of the 1920s* (Urbana, Illinois, 1992).

Smith, John David (ed.), *When Did Southern Segregation Begin?* (Boston, 2002).

Thelen, David (ed.), 'Perspectives: The Strange Career of Jim Crow', *Journal of American History* (75, 1988).

Trotter, Joe William Jr, 'Black Migration in Historical Perspective: A Review of the Literature', in Trotter, Joe William Jr, (ed.), *The Great Migration in Historical Perspective: New Dimensions of Race, Class, and Gender* (Bloomington, Indiana, 1991).

Verney, Kevern, 'Booker T. Washington and African-American History: A Historiographical Perspective', in Verney, Kevern, *The Art of the Possible: Booker T. Washington and Black Leadership in the United States, 1881–1925* (New York, 2001).

Whayne, Jeannie M., 'Oil and Water: The Historiography of the Elaine Riots', *Arkansas Review* (32, 2001).

Williamson, Joel, 'Wounds Not Scars: Lynching, the National Conscience and the American Historian', *Journal of American History* (83, 1997).

Williamson, Joel (ed.), *The Origins of Segregation* (Boston, 1968).

The African American experience since 1945

Dyson, Michael Eric, 'X Marks the Plots: A Critical Reading of Malcolm's Readers', in Dyson, Michael Eric, *Making Malcolm: The Myth and Meaning of Malcolm X* (New York, 1995).

Eagles, Charles W., 'Toward New Histories of the Civil Rights Era', *Journal of Southern History* (66, 2000).

Fairclough, Adam, 'State of the Art: Historians and the Civil Rights Movement', *Journal of American Studies* (24, 1990).

Kirk, John A., 'State of the Art: Martin Luther King, Jr.', *Journal of American Studies* (38, 2004).

Lawson, Steven F., 'Review Essay: Martin Luther King, Jr., and the Civil Rights Movement', *Georgia Historical Quarterly* (71, 1987).

Lawson, Steven F., 'Freedom Then, Freedom Now: The Historiography of the Civil Rights Movement', *American Historical Review* (96, 1991).

Rehin, George, 'Of Marshalls, Myrdals and Kings: Some Recent Books about the Second Reconstruction', *Journal of American Studies* (22, 1988).

Rogers, Kim Lacy, 'Oral History and the History of the Civil Rights Movement', *Journal of American History* (75, 1988).

Labour, class and ethnicity

Arnesen, Eric, 'Up From Exclusion: Black and White Workers, Race, and the State of Labor History', *Reviews in American History* (26, 1998).

Hill, Herbert, 'The Problem of Race in American Labor History', *Reviews in American History* (24, 1996).

Kolchin, Peter, 'Whiteness Studies: The New History of Race in America', *Journal of American History* (89, 2002).

Trotter, Joe William Jr, 'African-American Workers: New Directions in U.S. Labor Historiography', *Labor History* (35, 1994).

Individual historians

Franklin, John Hope, 'Their War and Mine', *Journal of American History* (77, 1990).

Hackney, Sheldon et al., 'C. Vann Woodward, 1908–1999: In Memoriam',

Journal of Southern History (66, 2000).

Harlan, Louis R., *All at Sea: Coming of Age in World War II* (Urbana, Illinois, 1996).

Meier, August, 'Introduction: A Liberal and Proud of It', in Meier, August, *A White Scholar and the Black Community, 1945–1965: Essays and Reflections* (Amherst, Massachusetts, 1992).

Moses, Wilson J., 'Emma Lou Thornbrough's Place in American Historiography', *Indiana Magazine of History* (91, 1995).

Murrell, Gary, 'On Herbert Aptheker and His Side of History: An Interview with Eric Foner', *Radical History Review* (78, 2000).

Naison, Mark D., *White Boy: A Memoir* (Philadelphia, 2002).

Selective bibliographies for individual chapters

1 Segregation and accommodation, 1895–1915

Anderson, James, *The Education of Blacks in the South, 1860–1935* (Chapel Hill, North Carolina, 1988).

Ayers, Edward L., *The Promise of the New South: Life after Reconstruction* (New York, 1992).

Bernstein, Barton, '*Plessy v. Ferguson*: Conservative Sociological Jurisprudence', *Journal of Negro History* (48, 1963).

Brundage, William Fitzhugh, *Lynching in the New South: Georgia and Virginia, 1880–1930* (Urbana, Illinois, 1993).

Brundage, William Fitzhugh (ed.), *Under Sentence of Death: Lynching in the South* (Chapel Hill, North Carolina, 1997).

Brundage, William Fitzhugh (ed.), *Booker T. Washington and Black Progress: Up From Slavery 100 Years Later* (Gainesville, Florida, 2003).

Cell, John, *The Highest Stages of White Supremacy: The Origins of Segregation in South Africa and the American South* (Cambridge, 1982).

Daniel, Peter, *The Shadow of Slavery: Peonage in the South, 1901–1969* (Urbana, Illinois, 1990).

Denton, Virginia Lantz, *Booker T. Washington and the Adult Education Movement* (Gainesville, Florida, 1993).

Dray, Philip, *At the Hands of Persons Unknown: The Lynching of Black America* (New York, 2002).

Dyer, Thomas, *Theodore Roosevelt and the Idea of Race* (Baton Rouge, Louisiana, 1980).

Fairclough, Adam, *Better Day Coming: Blacks and Equality, 1890–2000* (New York, 2001).

Fox, Stephen, *The Guardian of Boston: William Monroe Trotter* (New York, 1970).

Franklin, John Hope, and Meier, August (eds), *Black Leaders of the Twentieth Century* (Urbana, Illinois, 1982).

Frederickson, George M., *White Supremacy: A Comparative Study in American and South African History* (New York, 1981).

Frederickson, George M., *Black Liberation: A Comparative History of Black Ideologies in the United States and South Africa* (New York, 1995).

Gilmore, Glenda Elizabeth, *Gender and Jim Crow: Women and the Politics of*

White Supremacy in North Carolina, 1896–1920 (Chapel Hill, North Carolina, 1996).

Graves, John William, 'Jim Crow in Arkansas: A Reconsideration of Urban Race Relations in the Post-Reconstruction South', *Journal of Southern History* (55, 1989).

Graves, John William, *Town and Country: Race Relations in an Urban-Rural Context, Arkansas, 1865–1905* (Fayetteville, Arkansas, 1990).

Hale, Grace Elizabeth, *Making Whiteness: The Culture of Segregation in the South, 1890–1940* (New York, 1998).

Hall, Jacquelyn Dowd, *Revolt Against Chivalry: Jessie Daniel Ames and the Women's Campaign Against Lynching* (New York, 1979).

Harlan, Louis R., *Booker T. Washington: The Making of a Black Leader, 1856–1901* (New York, 1972).

Harlan, Louis R., *Booker T. Washington: The Wizard of Tuskegee, 1901–1915* (New York, 1983).

Harlan, Louis R. et al. (eds), *The Booker T. Washington Papers,* 14 vols (Urbana, Illinois, 1972–89).

Hawkins, Hugh (ed.), *Booker T. Washington and His Critics: The Problem of Negro Leadership* (Boston, 1974).

Kousser, J. Morgan, *The Shaping of Southern Politics: Suffrage Restriction and the Establishment of the One-Party South, 1880–1910* (New Haven, 1974).

Litwack, Leon, *Trouble in Mind: Black Southerners in the Age of Jim Crow* (New York, 1998).

Lofgren, Charles A., *The Plessy Case: A Legal-Historical Interpretation* (New York, 1987).

McMillen, Neil, *Dark Journey: Black Mississippians in the Age of Jim Crow* (Urbana, Illinois, 1989).

McMurray, Linda O., *To Keep the Waters Troubled: The Life of Ida B. Wells* (New York, 1998).

Mancini, Matthew J., *One Dies, Get Another: Convict Leasing in the American South, 1866–1928* (Columbia, South Carolina, 1996).

Mandle, Jay R., *The Roots of Black Poverty: The Southern Plantation Economy After the Civil War* (Durham, North Carolina, 1978).

Meier, August, *Negro Thought in America, 1880–1915* (Ann Arbor, Michigan, 1963).

Meier, August, and Rudwick, Elliott, *Along the Color Line: Explorations in the Black Experience* (Urbana, Illinois, 1976).

Newby, I. A., *Jim Crow's Defense: Anti-Negro Thought in America, 1900–1930* (Baton Rouge, Louisiana, 1965).

Novak, Daniel A., *The Wheel of Servitude: Black Forced Labor After Slavery* (Lexington, Kentucky, 1978).

Patler, Nicholas, *Jim Crow and the Wilson Administration: Protesting Federal Segregation in the Early Twentieth Century* (Boulder, Colorado, 2004).

Perman, Michael, *Struggle for Mastery: Disfranchisement in the South, 1888–1908* (Chapel Hill, North Carolina, 2001).

Rabinowitz, Howard N., *Race Relations in the Urban South, 1865–1890* (New York, 1978).

Smith, John David (ed.), *When Did Southern Segregation Begin?* (Boston, 2002).

Smock, Raymond (ed.), *Booker T. Washington in Perspective: Essays of Louis R. Harlan* (Jackson, Mississippi, 1988).

Thelen, David (ed.), 'Perspectives: The Strange Career of Jim Crow', *Journal of American History* (75, 1988).

Thornbrough, Emma Lou, *T. Thomas Fortune: Militant Journalist* (Chicago, 1972).

Verney, Kevern, *The Art of the Possible: Booker T. Washington and Black Leadership in the United States, 1881–1925* (New York, 2001).

Washington, Booker T., *Up From Slavery* (New York, 1901).

Williamson, Joel, *The Crucible of Race: Black-White Relations in the American South Since Emancipation* (New York, 1984).

Woodward, C. Vann, *The Strange Career of Jim Crow*, revised 3rd edn (New York, 1974).

2   The Great Migration and the 'New Negro', 1915–1930

Aptheker, Herbert (ed.), *The Correspondence of W. E. B. Du Bois*, 3 vols (Amherst, Massachusetts, 1973–78).

Avery, Sheldon, *Up From Washington: William Pickens and the Negro Struggle For Equality, 1900–1954* (Newark, Delaware, 1989).

Baker, Houston, *Modernism and the Harlem Renaissance* (New York, 1987).

Blee, Kathleen M., *Women of the Klan: Racism and Gender in the 1920s* (Berkeley, California, 1991).

Clarke, John H. (ed.), *Marcus Garvey and the Vision of Africa* (New York, 1974).

Cronon, E. David, *Black Moses: The Story of Marcus Garvey and the Universal Negro Improvement Association* (Madison, Wisconsin, 1955).

Du Bois, W. E. B., *Dusk of Dawn: An Essay Toward an Autobiography of a Race Concept* (New York, 1940).

Du Bois, W. E. B., *The Autobiography of W. E. B. Du Bois: A Soliloquy on Viewing My Life from the Last Decade of its First Century* (New York, 1968).

Ellis, Mark, '"Closing Ranks" and "Seeking Honors": W. E. B. Du Bois in World War I', *Journal of American History* (79, 1992).

Essien-Udom, E. U., and Garvey, Amy Jacques (eds), *More Philosophy and Opinions of Marcus Garvey* (New York, 1977).

Feldman, Glen, *Politics, Society and the Klan in Alabama, 1915–1949* (Tuscaloosa, Alabama, 1999).

Franklin, John Hope, and Meier, August, *Black Leaders of the Twentieth Century* (Urbana, Illinois, 1982).

Goings, Kenneth W., *The NAACP Comes of Age: The Defeat of Judge John J. Parker* (Bloomington, Indiana, 1990).

Gottlieb, Peter, *Making Their Own Way: Southern Blacks' Migration to Pittsburgh, 1916–1930* (Urbana, Illinois, 1987).

Grossman, James R., *Land of Hope: Chicago, Black Southerners, and the Great Migration* (Urbana, Illinois, 1989).

Harrison, Alferteen (ed.), *Black Exodus: The Great Migration from the American South* (Jackson, Mississippi, 1991).

Helbling, Mark, *The Harlem Renaissance: The One and the Many* (Westport, Connecticut, 1999).

Hellwig, David J., 'Black Meets Black: Afro-American Reactions to West Indian

Immigrants in the 1920s', *South Atlantic Quarterly* (77, 1978).

Henri, Florette, *Black Migration, Movement North, 1900–1920: The Road From Myth to Man* (New York, 1976).

Higgs, Robert, 'The Boll Weevil, the Cotton Economy, and Black Migration, 1910–1930', *Agricultural History* (1976).

Hill, Robert et al. (eds), *The Marcus Garvey and Universal Negro Improvement Association Papers*, Vols I–IX (Berkeley, California, 1983–95).

Huggins, Nathan Irvin, *Harlem Renaissance* (New York, 1971).

Jackson, Kenneth T., *The Ku Klux Klan in the City, 1915–1930* (New York, 1967).

James, Winston, *Holding Aloft the Banner of Ethiopia: Caribbean Radicalism in Early Twentieth-Century America* (London, 1998).

Janken, Kenneth Robert, *White: The Biography of Walter White, Mr. NAACP* (New York, 2003).

Jenkins, William D., *Steel Valley Klan: The Ku Klux Klan in Ohio's Mahoning Valley* (Kent, Ohio, 1996).

Johnson, James Weldon, *Along This Way: The Autobiography of James Weldon Johnson* (New York, 1933).

Jordan, William, '"The Damnable Dilemma": African American Accommodation and Protest During World War I', *Journal of American History* (81, 1995).

Kellogg, Charles Flint, *NAACP: A History of the National Association for the Advancement of Colored People, Volume I, 1909–1920* (Baltimore, Maryland, 1967).

Kornweibel, Theodore, 'Apathy and Dissent: Black America's Negative Responses to World War I', *South Atlantic Quarterly* (80, 1981).

Kusmer, Kenneth, *A Ghetto Takes Shape: Black Cleveland, 1870–1930* (Urbana, Illinois, 1976).

Lay, Shawn, *Hooded Knights of the Niagara: The Ku Klux Klan in Buffalo, New York* (New York, 1995).

Lay, Shawn (ed.), *The Invisible Empire in the West: Toward a New Historical Appraisal of the Ku Klux Klan of the 1920s* (Urbana, Illinois, 1992).

Levy, Eugene, *James Weldon Johnson: Black Leader, Black Voice* (Chicago, 1973).

Lewis, David Levering, *When Harlem Was in Vogue* (New York, 1981).

Lewis, David Levering, *W. E. B. Du Bois: Biography of a Race, 1868–1919* (New York, 1993).

Lewis, David Levering, *W. E. B. Du Bois: The Fight For Equality and the American Century, 1919–1963* (New York, 2000).

Lewis, David Levering (ed.), *W. E. B. Du Bois: A Reader* (New York, 1995).

MacLean, Nancy, *Behind the Mask of Chivalry: The Making of the Second Ku Klux Klan* (New York, 1994).

Marable, Manning, *W. E. B. Du Bois: Black Radical Democrat* (Boston, 1986).

Marks, Carole, *Farewell – We're Good and Gone: The Great Black Migration* (Bloomington, Indiana, 1989).

Martin, Tony, *Race First: The Ideological and Organizational Struggles of Marcus Garvey and the Universal Negro Improvement Association* (Westport, Connecticut, 1976).

Meier, August, and Bracey, John H., 'The NAACP as a Reform Movement, 1909–1965: "To Reach the Conscience of America"', *Journal of Southern*

History (59, 1993).

Meier, August, and Rudwick, Elliott, *Along the Color Line: Explorations in the Black Experience* (Urbana, Illinois, 1976).

Moore, Leonard J., *Citizen Klansman: The Ku Klux Klan in Indiana, 1921–1928* (Chapel Hill, North Carolina, 1991).

Osofsky, Gilbert, *Harlem: The Making of a Ghetto, Negro New York, 1890–1930* (New York, 1966).

Ovington, Mary White, *The Walls Came Tumbling Down* (New York, 1947).

Renshaw, Patrick, 'The Black Ghetto, 1890–1940', *Journal of American Studies* (8, 1974).

Ross, B. Joyce, *J. E. Spingarn and the Rise of the NAACP, 1911–1939* (New York, 1972).

Schneider, Mark Robert, *'We Return Fighting': The Civil Rights Movement in the Jazz Age* (Boston, 2002).

Stein, Judith, *The World of Marcus Garvey: Race and Class in Modern Society* (Baton Rouge, Louisiana, 1986).

Taylor, Ula Yvette, *The Veiled Garvey: The Life and Times of Amy Jacques Garvey* (Chapel Hill, North Carolina, 2002).

Thomas, Richard, *Life For Us Is What We Make It: Building Black Community in Detroit, 1915–1945* (Bloomington, Indiana, 1992).

Trotter, Joe William Jr (ed.), *The Great Migration in Historical Perspective: New Dimensions of Race, Class, and Gender* (Bloomington, Indiana, 1991).

Vincent, Theodore, *Black Power and the Garvey Movement* (Berkeley, California, 1971).

Wedin, Carolyn, *Inheritors of the Spirit: Mary White Ovington and the Founding of the NAACP* (New York, 1998).

White, Walter, *A Man Called White: The Autobiography of Walter White* (New York, 1949).

Wintz, Cary D., *Black Culture and the Harlem Renaissance* (Houston, Texas, 1988).

Wolters, Raymond, *Du Bois and His Rivals* (Columbia, Missouri, 2002).

Zangrando, Robert L., *The NAACP Crusade Against Lynching, 1909–1950* (Philadelphia, 1980).

3   The Great Depression and the Second World War, 1930–1945

Arneson, Eric, *Brotherhoods of Color: Black Railroad Workers and the Struggle for Equality* (Cambridge, Massachusetts, 2001).

Bates, Beth Tompkins, *Pullman Porters and the Rise of Protest Politics in Black America, 1925–1945* (Chapel Hill, North Carolina, 2001).

Carter, Dan, *Scottsboro: A Tragedy of the American South* (1969: reprint, New York, 1971).

Chateauvert, Melinda, *Marching Together: Women of the Brotherhood of Sleeping Car Porters* (Urbana, Illinois, 1998).

Cole, Olen, *The African-American Experience in the Civilian Conservation Corps* (Gainesville, Florida, 1999).

Dalfiume, Richard M., 'The Forgotten Years of the Negro Revolution', *Journal of American History* (55, 1968).

Dalfiume, Richard M., *Fighting on Two Fronts: Desegregation of the U.S. Armed*

Forces, 1939–1953 (Columbia, Missouri, 1969).

Eagles, Charles W., 'Two "Double Vs": Jonathan Daniels, FDR, and Race Relations During World War II', *North Carolina Historical Review* (Summer, 1982).

Eagles, Charles W., *Jonathan Daniels and Race Relations: The Evolution of a Southern Liberal* (Knoxville, Tennessee, 1982).

Fairclough, Adam, *Race and Democracy: The Civil Rights Struggle in Louisiana, 1915–1972* (Athens, Georgia, 1995).

Fairclough, Adam, *Better Day Coming: Blacks and Equality, 1890–2000* (New York, 2001).

Finkle, Lee, 'The Conservative Aims of Militant Rhetoric: Black Protest During World War II', *Journal of American History* (60, 1973).

Finkle, Lee, *Forum For Protest: The Black Press During World War II* (London, 1975).

Franklin, John Hope, 'Their War and Mine', *Journal of American History* (77, 1990).

Gavins, Raymond, *The Perils and Prospects of Southern Black Leadership: Gordon Blaine Hancock, 1884–1970* (Durham, North Carolina, 1993).

Grant, Nancy L., *TVA and Black Americans: Planning for the Status Quo* (Philadelphia, 1990).

Harris, William H., *Keeping the Faith: A. Philip Randolph, Milton P. Webster, and the Brotherhood of Sleeping Car Porters, 1925–37* (Urbana, Illinois, 1977).

Harris, William H., *The Harder We Run: Black Workers Since the Civil War* (New York, 1982).

Honey, Maureen (ed.), *Bitter Fruit: African American Women in World War II* (Columbia, Missouri, 1999).

Hutchinson, Earl Ofari, *Blacks and Reds: Race and Class in Conflict, 1919–1990* (East Lansing, Michigan, 1995).

Jackson, Walter A., *Gunnar Myrdal and America's Conscience* (Chapel Hill, North Carolina, 1994).

Janken, Kenneth Robert, *White: The Biography of Walter White, Mr. NAACP* (New York, 2003).

Kirby, John B., *Black Americans in the Roosevelt Era: Liberalism and Race* (Knoxville, Tennessee, 1980).

Kryder, Daniel, *Divided Arsenal: Race and the American State During World War II* (Cambridge, 2000).

Lewis, David Levering, *W. E. B. Du Bois: The Fight For Equality and the American Century, 1919–1963* (New York, 2000).

McGuire, Philip, *Taps For a Jim Crow Army: Letters from Black Soldiers in World War II* (Oxford, 1983).

McMahon, Kevin J., *Reconsidering Roosevelt on Race: How the Presidency Paved the Road to Brown* (Chicago, 2003).

McMillen, Neil R. (ed.), *Remaking Dixie: The Impact of World War II on the American South* (Jackson, Mississippi, 1997).

McNeil, Genna Rae, *Groundwork: Charles Hamilton Houston and the Struggle for Civil Rights* (Philadelphia, 1983).

Mershon, Sherie, and Schlossman, Steven, *Foxholes and Color Lines: Desegregating the U.S. Armed Forces* (Baltimore, Maryland, 1998).

Modell, John, Goulden, Mark, and Magnusson, Sigurder, 'World War II in the

Lives of Black Americans: Some Findings and Interpretation', *Journal of American History* (76, 1989).

Myrdal, Gunnar, *An American Dilemma: The Negro Problem and Modern Democracy*, 2 vols (New York, 1944).

Naison, Mark, *Communists in Harlem During the Depression* (Urbana, Illinois, 1983).

Natanson, Nicholas, *The Black Image in the New Deal: The Politics of FSA Photography* (Knoxville, Tennessee, 1992).

Nelson, Bruce, *Divided We Stand: American Workers and the Struggle for Black Equality* (Princeton, New Jersey, 2001).

Pfeffer, Paula F., *A. Philip Randolph: Pioneer of the Civil Rights Movement* (Baton Rouge, Louisiana, 1990).

Reed, Merl E., *Seedtime for the Modern Civil Rights Movement: The President's Committee on Fair Employment Practice, 1941–1946* (Baton Rouge, Louisiana, 1991).

Salmond, John A., 'The Civilian Conservation Corps and the Negro', in Sternsher, Bernard (ed.), *The Negro in Depression and War: Prelude to Revolution, 1930–1945* (Chicago, 1969).

Sitkoff, Harvard, 'Racial Militancy and Interracial Violence in the Second World War', *Journal of American History* (58, 1971).

Sitkoff, Harvard, *A New Deal for Blacks: The Emergence of Civil Rights as a National Issue. Volume I: The Depression Decade* (New York, 1978).

Solomon, Mark, *The Cry Was Unity: Communists and African Americans, 1917–1936* (Jackson, Mississippi, 1998).

Southern, David W., *Gunnar Mrydal and Black-White Relations: The Use and Abuse of an American Dilemma, 1944–1969* (Baton Rouge, Louisiana, 1987).

Sullivan, Patricia, *Days of Hope: Race and Democracy in the New Deal Era* (Chapel Hill, North Carolina, 1996).

Tushnet, Mark V., *The NAACP's Legal Strategy Against Segregated Education, 1925–1950* (Chapel Hill, North Carolina, 1987).

Washburn, Patrick S., *A Question of Sedition: The Federal Government's Investigation of the Black Press During World War II* (New York, 1986).

Watts, Jill, *God, Harlem, USA: The Father Divine Story* (Berkeley, California, 1992).

Weisbrot, Robert, *Father Divine and the Struggle for Racial Equality* (Urbana, Illinois, 1983).

Weiss, Nancy J., *The National Urban League, 1910–40* (New York, 1974).

Weiss, Nancy J., *Farewell to the Party of Lincoln: Black Politics in the Age of FDR* (Princeton, New Jersey, 1983).

White, Walter, *A Rising Wind* (1945: reprint, Westport, Connecticut, 1971).

White, Walter, *A Man Called White: The Autobiography of Walter White* (1948; reprint; Athens, Georgia, 1995).

Wilkins Roy, with Mathews, Tom, *Standing Fast: The Autobiography of Roy Wilkins* (New York, 1982).

Wolters, Raymond, *Negroes and the Great Depression: The Problem of Economic Recovery* (Westport, Connecticut, 1970).

Wynn, Neil A., *The Afro-American and the Second World War* (London, 1993).

4   The post-war Civil Rights Movement, 1945–1968

Baldwin, Lewis V., *Toward the Beloved Community: Martin Luther King Jr. and South Africa* (Cleveland, Ohio, 1995).

Bartley, Numan V., *The Rise of Massive Resistance: Race and Politics in the South During the 1950s* (Baton Rouge, Louisiana, 1997).

Borstelmann, Thomas, *The Cold War and the Color Line: American Race Relations in the Global Arena* (Cambridge, Massachusetts, 2001).

Branch, Taylor, *Parting the Waters: Martin Luther King and the Civil Rights Movement, 1954–63* (London, 1991).

Branch, Taylor, *Pillar of Fire: America in the King Years, 1963–65* (New York, 1998).

Brauer, Carl M., *John F. Kennedy and the Second Reconstruction* (New York, 1977).

Burk, Robert F., *The Eisenhower Administration and Black Civil Rights* (Knoxville, Tennessee, 1984).

Burner, Eric R., *And Gently He Shall Lead Them: Robert Parrish Moses and Civil Rights in Mississippi* (New York, 1994).

Burns, Stewart (ed.), *Daybreak of Freedom: The Montgomery Bus Boycott* (Chapel Hill, North Carolina, 1997).

Carson, Clayborne, *In Struggle: SNCC and the Black Awakening of the 1960s* (Cambridge, Massachusetts, 1981).

Carson, Clayborne (ed.), *The Eyes on the Prize Civil Rights Reader, 1954–90* (London, 1991).

Carson, Clayborne et al. (eds), *The Papers of Martin Luther King, Jr.,* 5 vols to date (Berkeley, California, 1992–).

Carter, Dan T., *The Politics of Rage: George Wallace, the Origins of the New Conservatism, and the Transformation of American Politics* (New York, 1995).

Chappell, David L., 'Religious Ideas of the Segregationists', *Journal of American Studies* (32, 1998).

Collier-Thomas, Bettye, and Franklin, V. P. (eds), *Sisters in the Struggle: African-American Women in the Civil Rights and Black Power Movements* (New York, 2001).

Crawford, V. L., Rouse, J. A., and Woods, B. (eds), *Women in the Civil Rights Movement: Trailblazers and Torchbearers, 1941–1965* (Bloomington, Indiana, 1993).

Dickerson, Dennis C., *Militant Mediator: Whitney M. Young Jr.* (Lexington, Kentucky, 1998).

Dudziak, Mary L., *Cold War, Civil Rights: Race and the Image of American Democracy* (Princeton, New Jersey, 2000).

Eagles, Charles W., 'Toward New Histories of the Civil Rights Era', *Journal of Southern History* (66, 2000).

Evans, Sara, *Personal Politics: The Roots of Women's Liberation in the Civil Rights Movement and the New Left* (New York, 1980).

Fairclough, Adam, *To Redeem the Soul of America: The Southern Christian Leadership Conference and Martin Luther King, Jr.* (Athens, Georgia, 1987).

Fairclough, Adam, 'State of the Art: Historians and the Civil Rights Movement', *Journal of American Studies* (24, 1990).

Fairclough, Adam, *Martin Luther King, Jr.* (Athens, Georgia, 1995).

Fairclough, Adam, *Race and Democracy: The Civil Rights Struggle in Louisiana, 1915–1972* (Athens, Georgia, 1995).

Gardner, Michael R., *Harry Truman and Civil Rights: Moral Courage and Political Risks* (Carbondale, Illinois, 2002).

Garrow, David J., *Bearing the Cross: Martin Luther King, Jr., and the Southern Christian Leadership Conference* (New York, 1986).

Garrow, David J. (ed.), *The Montgomery Bus Boycott and the Women Who Started It: The Memoir of Jo Ann Gibson Robinson* (Knoxville, Tennessee, 1987).

Garrow, David J. et al., 'A Round Table: Martin Luther King, Jr.', *Journal of American History* (74, 1987).

Hall, Simon, *Peace and Freedom: The Civil Rights and Antiwar Movements of the 1960s* (Philadelphia, 2004).

Horowitz, David A., 'White Southerners' Alienation and Civil Rights: The Response to Corporate Liberalism, 1956–1965', *Journal of Southern History* (54, 1988).

Jacoway, Elizabeth, and Colburn, David R. (eds), *Southern Businessmen and Desegregation* (Baton Rouge, Louisiana, 1982).

Kirk, John A., 'State of the Art: Martin Luther King, Jr.', *Journal of American Studies* (38, 2004).

Kirk, John A., *Martin Luther King* (London, 2004).

Klarman, Michael J., 'How Brown Changed Race Relations: The Backlash Thesis', *Journal of American History* (81, 1994).

Kluger, Richard, *Simple Justice: The History of Brown versus the Board of Education and Black America's Struggle for Equality* (New York, 1975).

Korstad Robert, and Lichtenstein, Nelson, 'Opportunities Found and Lost: Labor, Radicals, and the Early Civil Rights Movement', *Journal of American History* (75, 1988).

Lawson, Steven F., *Black Ballots: Voting Rights in the South, 1944–1969* (New York, 1976).

Lawson, Steven F., 'Review Essay: Martin Luther King, Jr., and the Civil Rights Movement', *Georgia Historical Quarterly* (71, 1987).

Lawson, Steven F., 'Freedom Then, Freedom Now: The Historiography of the Civil Rights Movement', *American Historical Review* (96, 1991).

Layton, Azza Salama, *International Politics and Civil Rights Policies in the United States, 1941–1960* (Cambridge, 2000).

Levine, Daniel, *Bayard Rustin and the Civil Rights Movement* (New Brunswick, New Jersey, 2000).

Lewis, George, *The White South and the Red Menace: Segregationists, Anticommunism, and Massive Resistance, 1945–1965* (Gainesville, Florida, 2004).

Ling, Peter, *Martin Luther King, Jr.* (London, 2002).

Ling Peter J., and Monteith, Sharon (eds), *Gender in the Civil Rights Movement* (New York, 1999).

McKnight, Gerald B., *The Last Crusade: Martin Luther King, Jr., the FBI, and the Poor People's Campaign* (Oxford, 1998).

McMillen, Neil R., *The Citizens' Council: Organized Resistance to the Second Reconstruction, 1954–64* (Urbana, Illinois, 1971).

Manis, Andrew M., *A Fire You Can't Put Out: The Civil Rights Life of Birmingham's Reverend Fred Shuttlesworth* (Tuscaloosa, Alabama, 1999).

Marable, Manning, *Race, Reform and Rebellion: The Second Reconstruction in Black America, 1945–1990*, revised 2nd edn (London, 1991).

Meier, August, 'On the Role of Martin Luther King', in Meier, August, *A White Scholar and the Black Community, 1945–1965: Essays and Reflections* (Amherst, Massachusetts, 1992).

Meier, August, and Rudwick, Elliott, *CORE: A Study in the Civil Rights Movement, 1942–1968* (Urbana, Illinois, 1973).

Meriwether, James H., *Proudly We Can Be Africans: Black Americans and Africa, 1935–1961* (Chapel Hill, North Carolina, 2002).

Miller, Keith D., *Voice of Deliverance: The Language of Martin Luther King, Jr. and Its Sources* (New York, 1992).

Morris, Aldon, *The Origins of the Civil Rights Movement: Black Communities Organising for Change* (London, 1984).

Newman, Mark, *Getting Right With God: Southern Baptists and Desegregation, 1945–1995* (Tuscaloosa, Alabama, 2001).

Niven, David, *The Politics of Injustice: The Kennedys, the Freedom Rides, and the Electoral Consequences of a Moral Compromise* (Knoxville, Tennessee, 2003).

Patterson, James T., *Brown v. Board of Education: A Civil Rights Milestone and Its Troubled Legacy* (New York, 2001).

Ralph, James R., *Northern Protest: Martin Luther King, Jr., Chicago, and the Civil Rights Movement* (Cambridge, Massachusetts, 1993).

Ransby, Barbara, *Ella Baker and the Black Freedom Movement: A Radical Democratic Vision* (Chapel Hill, North Carolina, 2002).

Reed, Roy, *Faubus: The Life and Times of an American Prodigal* (Fayetteville, Arkansas, 1997).

Rehin, George, 'Of Marshalls, Myrdals and Kings: Some Recent Books about the Second Reconstruction', *Journal of American Studies* (22, 1988).

Robnett, Belinda, *How Long? How Long? African-American Women in the Struggle for Civil Rights* (New York, 1997).

Rogers, Kim Lacy, 'Oral History and the History of the Civil Rights Movement', *Journal of American History* (75, 1988).

Sarat, Austin (ed.), *Race, Law and Culture: Reflections on Brown v. Board of Education* (New York, 1997).

Thelen, David (ed.), 'Becoming Martin Luther King, Jr. – Plagiarism and Originality: A Round Table', *Journal of American History* (78, 1991).

Thornton, J. Mills III, *Dividing Lines: Municipal Politics and the Struggle for Civil Rights in Montgomery, Birmingham, and Selma* (Tuscaloosa, Alabama, 2002).

Ward, Brian, and Badger, Tony (eds), *The Making of Martin Luther King and the Civil Rights Movement* (London, 1996).

Webb, Clive, *Fight Against Fear: Southern Jews and Black Civil Rights* (Athens, Georgia, 2001).

Westheider, James, E., *Fighting on Two Fronts: African Americans and the Vietnam War* (New York, 1997).

Woods, Jeff, *Black Struggle, Red Scare: Segregation and Anti-Communism in the South, 1948–1968* (Baton Rouge, Louisiana, 2004).

5   Malcolm X and Black Power, 1960–1980

Breitman, George, *The Last Year of Malcolm X: The Evolution of a Revolutionary* (New York, 1967).

Breitman, George (ed.), *By Any Means Necessary: Speeches, Interviews and a Letter by Malcolm X* (New York, 1970).

Breitman, George, Porter, Herman, and Smith, Baxter (eds), *The Assassination of Malcolm X* (New York, 1976).

Brown, Elaine, *A Taste of Power: A Black Woman's Story* (New York, 1992).

Brown, Scot, *Fighting for US: Maulenga Karenga, the US Organization, and Black Cultural Nationalism* (New York, 2003).

Carmichael, Stokely, and Hamilton, Charles, *Black Power: The Politics of Liberation in America* (London, 1967).

Carson, Clayborne, *In Struggle: SNCC and the Black Awakening of the 1960s* (Cambridge, Massachusetts, 1981).

Carson, Clayborne (ed.), *Malcolm X: The FBI File* (New York, 1991).

Clarke, John Henrik (ed.), *Malcolm X: The Man and His Times* (New York, 1969).

Cleaver, Eldridge, *Soul on Ice* (New York, 1968).

Cleaver, Kathleen, and Katsiaficas, George (eds), *Liberation, Imagination, and the Black Panther Party: A New Look at the Panthers and Their Legacy* (New York, 2001).

Clegg, Claude Andrew III, *An Original Man: The Life and Times of Elijah Muhammad* (New York, 1997).

Cone, James H., *Martin and Malcolm and America: A Dream or a Nightmare* (New York, 1996).

Curtis, Edward E., *Islam in Black American Identity: Liberation and Difference in African American Islamic Thought* (Albany, New York, 2002).

DeCaro, Louis A., *On the Side of My People: A Religious Life of Malcolm X* (New York, 1996).

DeCaro, Louis A., *Malcolm and the Cross: The Nation of Islam, Malcolm X, and Christianity* (New York, 1998).

Draper, Theodore, *The Rediscovery of Black Nationalism* (London, 1970).

Dyson, Michael Eric, *Making Malcolm: The Myth and Meaning of Malcolm X* (New York, 1995).

Essien-Udom, E. U., *Black Nationalism: The Rise of the Black Muslims in the U.S.A.* (Urbana, Illinois, 1962).

Fairclough, Adam, *To Redeem the Soul of America: The Southern Christian Leadership Conference and Martin Luther King, Jr.* (Athens, Georgia, 1987).

Fanon, Frantz, *The Wretched of the Earth* (New York, 1961).

Foner, Philip S. (ed.), *The Black Panthers Speak* (New York, 1970).

Forman, James, *The Making of Black Revolutionaries* (New York, 1972).

Forman, James, *High Tide of Black Resistance and Other Political and Literary Writings* (Seattle, 1994).

Goldman, Peter, *The Death and Life of Malcolm X* (New York, 1973).

Haley, Alex, and X, Malcolm, *The Autobiography of Malcolm X* (New York, 1965).

Hill, Lance, *The Deacons for Defense: Armed Resistance and the Civil Rights Movement* (Chapel Hill, North Carolina, 2004).

Hilliard, David, and Cole, Lewis, *This Side of Glory: The Autobiography of David*

Hilliard and the Story of the Black Panther Party (Boston, 1993).

Hilliard, David, and Wise, Donald (eds), *The Huey P. Newton Reader* (New York, 2002).

Horne, Gerald, *Fire This Time: The Watts Uprising and the 1960s* (Charlottesville, Virginia, 1995).

Jackson, George, *Soledad Brother: The Prison Letters of George Jackson* (New York, 1970).

Jackson, George, *Blood in My Eye* (New York, 1972).

Jeffries, Judson L., *Huey P. Newton: The Radical Theorist* (Jackson, Mississippi, 2002).

Jones, Charles E. (ed.), *The Black Panther Party Reconsidered* (Baltimore, Maryland, 1998).

Karim, Benjamin, *Remembering Malcolm* (New York, 1996).

Kotlowski, Dean J., *Nixon's Civil Rights: Politics, Principle and Policy* (Cambridge, Massachusetts, 2001).

Marine, Gene, *The Black Panthers* (New York, 1969).

Meier, August, and Rudwick, Elliott, *CORE: A Study in the Civil Rights Movement, 1942–1968* (Urbana, Illinois, 1973).

Morrison, Toni (ed.), *To Die For The People: The Writings of Huey P. Newton* (New York, 1972).

Newton, Huey P., *Revolutionary Suicide* (New York, 1973).

Newton, Huey P., *War Against the Panthers: A Study of Repression in America* (New York, 1996).

O'Reilly, Kenneth, 'The FBI and the Politics of the Riots, 1964–1968', *Journal of American History* (75, 1988).

O'Reilly, Kenneth, *'Racial Matters': The FBI's Secret File on Black America, 1960–1972* (New York, 1989).

O'Reilly, Kenneth, *Nixon's Piano: Presidents and Racial Politics from Washington to Clinton* (New York, 1995).

Pearson, Hugh, *The Shadow of the Panther: Huey P. Newton and the Price of Black Power in America* (Reading, Massachusetts, 1994).

Perry, Bruce, *Malcolm: The Life of a Man Who Changed Black America* (New York, 1991).

Pinckney, Alphonse, *Red, Black and Green: Black Nationalism in the United States* (Cambridge, 1976).

Sailes, William W., *From Civil Rights to Black Liberation: Malcolm X and the Organization of Afro-American Unity* (1994).

Seale, Bobby, *Seize the Time: The Story of the Black Panther Party and Huey P. Newton* (London, 1970).

Seale, Bobby, *A Lonely Rage: The Autobiography of Bobby Seale* (New York, 1978).

Rabb, William K., *The Political Economy of the Black Ghetto* (New York, 1970).

Tyson, Timothy B., *Radio Free Dixie: Robert F. Williams and the Roots of Black Power* (Chapel Hill, North Carolina, 1999).

Van Deburg, William L. *New Day in Babylon: The Black Power Movement and American Culture, 1965–75* (Chicago, 1992).

Williams, Robert F., *Negroes With Guns* (New York, 1962).

Wolfenstein, Eugene Victor, *The Victims of Democracy: Malcolm X and the Black*

Revolution (Berkeley, California, 1981).

Woodard, Komozi, *A Nation Within a Nation: Amiri Baraka (Le Roi Jones) and Black Power Politics* (Chapel Hill, North Carolina, 1999).

6   The new conservatism: black civil rights since 1980

Alexander, Amy (ed.), *The Farrakhan Factor: African-American Writers on Leadership, Nationhood, and Minister Louis Farrakhan* (New York, 1998).

Atkin, S. Beth, *Voices From the Streets: Young Former Gang Members Tell Their Stories* (Boston, 1996).

Barkun, Michael, *Religion and the Racist Right: The Origins of the Christian Identity Movement* (Chapel Hill, North Carolina, 1997).

Bing, Leon, *Do Or Die* (New York, 1991).

Broh, C. Anthony, *A Horse of a Different Color: Television's Treatment of Jesse Jackson's 1984 Presidential Campaign* (Washington DC, 1987).

Bushart, H. L., Craig, J. R., and Barnes, M., *Soldiers of God: White Supremacists and Their Holy War for America* (New York, 1998).

Clemente, Frank, and Watkins, Frank (eds), *Keep Hope Alive: Jesse Jackson's 1988 Presidential Campaign* (Boston, 1989).

Colburn, David R., and Adler, Jeffrey S. (eds), *African-American Mayors: Race, Politics and the American City* (Urbana, Illinois, 2001).

Collins, Sheila D., *The Rainbow Challenge: The Jackson Campaign and the Future of U.S. Politics* (New York, 1986).

Coppola, Vincent, *Dragons of God: A Journey Through Far-Right America* (Atlanta, Georgia, 1996).

Daniels, Jesse, *White Lies: Race, Class, Gender and Sexuality in White Supremacist Discourse* (New York, 1997).

Dawson, Michael C., *Behind the Mule: Race and Class in African-American Politics* (Princeton, New Jersey, 1994).

Dees, Morris, with James Concoron, *Gathering Storm: America's Militia Threat* (New York, 1996).

Dobratz, Betty A., and Shanks-Miele, Stephanie A., *'White Power, White Pride!': The White Supremacist Movement in the United States* (New York, 1997).

Ezekiel, Raphael S., *The Racist Mind: Portrayals of American Neo-Nazis and Klansmen* (New York, 1995).

Frady, Marshall, *Jesse: The Life and Pilgrimage of Jesse Jackson* (New York, 1996).

Gardel, Matthias, *Countdown to Armageddon: Louis Farrakhan and the Nation of Islam* (London, 1996).

George, John, and Wilcox, Laird, *American Extremists: Militias, Supremacists, Klansmen, Communists and Others* (New York, 1996).

Gibbons, Arnold, *Race, Politics and the White Media: The Jesse Jackson Campaigns* (Lanham, Maryland, 1993).

Gooding-Williams, Robert (ed.), *Reading Rodney King: Reading Urban Uprising* (New York, 1993).

Hill, Dilys M., and Herrnson, Paul S. (eds), *The Clinton Presidency: The First Term, 1992–1996* (London, 1999).

Horne, Gerald, *Reversing Discrimination: The Case for Affirmative Action* (New York, 1992).

Jah, Yusuf, and Shah' Keyah, Sister, *Uprising: Cripps and Bloods Tell the Story of*

America's Youth in the Crossfire (New York, 1995).

Laham, Nicholas, *The Reagan Presidency and the Politics of Race: In Pursuit of Colorblind Justice and Limited Government* (Westport, Connecticut, 1998).

Magida, Arthur J., *Prophet of Rage: A Life of Louis Farrakhan and his Nation* (New York, 1996).

Marable, Manning, *Beyond Black and White: Transforming African-American Politics* (London, 1995).

Marable, Manning, *Black Liberation in Conservative America* (Boston, 1997).

O'Reilly, Kenneth, *Nixon's Piano: Presidents and Racial Politics from Washington to Clinton* (New York, 1995).

Parenti, Christian, *Lockdown America* (London, 1999).

Reed, Adolph L., *The Jesse Jackson Phenomenon: The Crisis of Purpose in Afro-American Politics* (New Haven, Connecticut, 1986).

Ridgeway, James, *Blood in the Face: The Ku Klux Klan, Aryan Nations, Nazi Skinheads and the Rise of a New White Culture* (New York, 1995).

Rodriguez, Luis J., *Always Running: LA Vida Loca, Gang Days in LA* (n.p., 1994).

Rose, Douglas (ed.), *The Emergence of David Duke and the Politics of Race* (Chapel Hill, North Carolina, 1992).

Rueter, Theodore (ed.), *The Politics of Race: African Americans and the Political System* (New York, 1995).

Shakur, S., *Monster: The Autobiography of an LA Gang Member* (New York, 1993).

Shull, Steven, *A Kinder, Gentler Racism? The Reagan-Bush Civil Rights Legacy* (New York, 1993).

Sikes, Gina, *8 Ball Chicks: A Year in the Violent World of Girl Gangs* (New York, 1997).

Singh, Robert, *The Farrakhan Phenomenon: Race, Reaction and the Paranoid Style in American Politics* (Washington DC, 1997).

Smith, Robert C., *We Have No Leaders: African Americans in the Post-Civil Rights Era* (Albany, New York, 1996).

Stanford, Karin L., *Beyond the Boundaries: Reverend Jesse Jackson in International Affairs* (Albany, New York, 1997).

Stern, Kenneth S., *A Force Upon the Plain: The American Militia Movement and the Politics of Hate* (Norman, Oklahoma, 1997).

Walker, Lucius J., and Walters, Ronald W., *Jesse Jackson's 1984 Presidential Campaign: Challenge and Change in American Politics* (Chicago, 1989).

Wilson, William J., *The Declining Significance of Race* (Urbana, Illinois, 1978).

Wilson, William J., *The Truly Disadvantaged: The Inner City, the Underclass, and Public Policy* (Chicago, 1987).

Wolters, Raymond, *Right Turn: William Bradford Reynolds, the Reagan Administration, and Black Civil Rights* (New Brunswick, New Jersey, 1996).

Zatarain, Michael, *David Duke: Evolution of a Klansman* (Gretna, Louisiana, 1990).

7   African Americans and US popular culture since 1895

Baker, William J., *Jesse Owens: An American Life* (New York, 1986).

Barlow, William, *Voice Over: The Making of Black Radio* (Philadelphia, 1999).

Bean, A., Hatch, J. V., and McNamara, B. (eds), *Inside the Minstrel Mask:*

SELECT BIBLIOGRAPHY

Readings in Nineteenth-Century Blackface Minstrelsy (Hanover, New Hampshire, 1996).

Bertrand, Michael T., *Race, Rock, and Elvis* (Urbana, Illinois, 2000).

Bogle, Donald, *Toms, Coons, Mulattoes, Mammies and Bucks: An Interpretative History of Blacks in American Film*, 3rd edn (New York, 1994).

Bogle, Donald, *Prime-Time Blues: African Americans in Network Television* (New York, 2001).

Boskin, Joseph, *Sambo: The Rise and Demise of an American Jester* (New York, 1986).

Boyd, Todd, *Am I Black Enough For You? Popular Culture From the Hood and Beyond* (Bloomington, Indiana, 1997).

Cockrell, Dale, *Demons of Disorder: Early Blackface Minstrels and Their World* (Cambridge, 1997).

Dates, Janet L., and Barlow, William (eds), *Split Image: African Americans in the Mass Media*, 2nd edn (Washington DC, 1993).

Dennison, Sam, *Scandalize My Name: Black Imagery in American Popular Music* (New York, 1982).

Dyson, Michael Eric, *Between God and Gangsta Rap: Bearing Witness to Black Culture* (New York, 1996).

Dyson, Michael Eric, *Holler If You Hear Me: Searching for Tupac Shakur* (London, 2001).

Edwards, Harry, *The Revolt of the Black Athlete* (New York, 1969).

Eisen Gary, and Wiggins, Daniel K., *Ethnicity and Sport in North American History and Culture* (Westport, Connecticut, 1994).

Ely, Melvin Patrick, *The Adventures of Amos 'n' Andy: A Social History of an American Phenomenon* (New York, 1991).

Frederickson, George M., *The Black Image in the White Mind: The Debate on Afro-American Character and Destiny, 1817–1914* (New York, 1972).

Goings, Kenneth W., *Mammy and Uncle Mose: Black Collectibles and American Stereotyping* (Bloomington, Indiana, 1994).

Graham, Alison, *Framing the South: Hollywood, Television and Race During the Civil Rights Struggle* (Baltimore, Maryland, 2001).

Gray, Herman, *Watching Race: Television and the Struggle for Blackness* (Minneapolis, Minnesota, 1995).

Hauser, Thomas, *Muhammad Ali: His Life and Times* (London, 1991).

Heller, Peter, *Bad Intentions: The Mike Tyson Story* (New York, 1995).

Hietala, Thomas R., *Fight of the Century: Jack Johnson, Joe Louis, and the Struggle for Racial Equality* (New York, 2004).

Hoberman, John, *Darwin's Athletes: How Sport Has Damaged Black America and Preserved the Myth of Race* (Boston, 1997).

Hoffer, Richard, *A Savage Business: The Comeback and Comedown of Mike Tyson* (New York, 1998).

Jhally, S., and Lewis, J., *Enlightened Racism: The Cosby Show, Audiences and the Myth of the American Dream* (Boulder, Colorado, 1992).

Kaye, Andrew M., *The Pussycat of Prizefighting: Tiger Flowers and the Politics of Black Celebrity* (Athens, Georgia, 2004).

Kern-Foxworth, Marilyn, *Aunt Jemima, Uncle Ben, and Rastus: Blacks in Advertising, Yesterday, Today, and Tomorrow* (Westport, Connecticut, 1994).

Kolchin, Peter, 'Whiteness Studies: The New History of Race in America', *Journal of American History* (89, 2002).

Leab, Daniel, *From Sambo to Superspade: The Black Experience in Motion Pictures* (London, 1973).

Levine, Lawrence, *Black Culture and Black Consciousness* (New York, 1977).

Lhamon, W. T., *Raising Cain: Blackface Performance from Jim Crow to Hip Hop* (Cambridge, Massachusetts, 1998).

Ling, Peter J., and Monteith, Sharon (eds), *Gender in the Civil Rights Movement* (New York, 1999).

Lott, Eric, *Love and Theft: Blackface Minstrelsy and the American Working Class* (New York, 1993).

MacDonald, J. Fred, *Blacks and White TV: Afro-Americans in Television since 1948* (Chicago, 1983).

Mahar, William J., *Behind the Burnt Cork Mask: Early Blackface Minstrelsy and Ante-bellum American Popular Culture* (Urbana, Illinois, 1999).

Mandell, R. D., *The Nazi Olympics* (New York, 1971).

Manring, M. M., *Slave in a Box: The Strange Career of Aunt Jemima* (Charlottesville, Virginia, 1998).

Mead, Chris, *Champion: Joe Louis, Black Hero in White America* (New York, 1985).

Miller, Patrick B., and Wiggins, David K. (eds), *Sport and the Color Line: Black Athletes and Race Relations in Twentieth-Century America* (New York, 2004).

Oliver, Paul, *Blues Fell This Morning: Meaning in the Blues* (Cambridge, 1990).

Perkins, William E., *Droppin' Science: Critical Essays on Rap Music and Hip Hop Culture* (Philadelphia, 1996).

Quinn, Eithne, *Nuthin' but a 'g' thang: The Culture and Commerce of Gangsta Rap* (New York, 2005).

Roberts, Randy, *Papa Jack: Jack Johnson and the Era of White Hopes* (London, 1986).

Roediger, David R., *The Wages of Whiteness: Race and the Making of the American Working Class* (New York, 1991).

Rose, Tricia, *Black Noise: Rap Music and Black Culture in Contemporary America* (Hanover, New Hampshire, 1994).

Sailes, Gary A. (ed.), *African Americans in Sport* (New Brunswick, New Jersey, 1998).

Savage, Barbara Dianne, *Broadcasting Freedom: Radio, War, and the Politics of Race, 1938–1948* (Chapel Hill, North Carolina, 1999).

Southern, Eileen, *The Music of Black Americans: A History* ([New York, 1971], 3rd edn, New York, 1997).

Spigel, Lynn, and Curtin, Michael, *The Revolution Wasn't Televised: Sixties Television and Social Conflict* (New York, 1997).

Suster, Gerald, *Champions of the Ring: The Lives and Times of Boxing's Heavyweight Heroes* (London, 1992).

Toll, Robert C., *Blacking Up: The Minstrel Show in Nineteenth-Century America* (New York, 1974).

Torres, Sasha, *Black, White and in Color: Television and Black Civil Rights* (Princeton, New Jersey, 2003).

Torres, Sasha (ed.), *Living Color: Race and Television in the United States* (Durham, North Carolina, 1998).

Turner, Patricia A., *Ceramic Uncles and Celluloid Mammies: Black Images and Their Influence on Culture* (New York, 1994).

Tygiel, Jules, *Baseball's Great Experiment: Jackie Robinson and his Legacy* (New York, 1997).

Van Deburg, William L., *New Day in Babylon: The Black Power Movement and American Culture, 1965–1975* (Chicago, 1992).

Van Deburg, William L., *Black Camelot: African-American Culture Heroes in Their Times, 1960–1980* (Chicago, 1997).

Verney, Kevern J., *African Americans and U.S. Popular Culture* (London, 2003).

Ward, Brian, *Just My Soul Responding: Rhythm and Blues, Black Consciousness and Race Relations* (London, 1998).

Ward, Brian, *Radio and the Struggle for Civil Rights in the South* (Gainesville, Florida, 2004).

Ward, Brian (ed.), *Media, Culture, and the Modern African American Freedom Struggle* (Gainesville, Florida, 2001).

Ward, Geoffrey C., and Burns, Ken, *Jazz: A History of America's Music* (London, 2001).

White, Shane, and White, Graham, *Stylin': African American Expressive Culture from its Beginnings to the Zoot Suit* (Ithaca, New York, 1998).

Wiggins, David K. (ed.), *Glory Bound: Black Athletes in White America* (New York, 1997).

Willis, Sharon, *High Contrast: Race and Gender in Contemporary Hollywood Film* (Durham, North Carolina, 1997).

Woodard, Komozi, *A Nation Within a Nation: Amiri Baraka (Le Roi Jones) and Black Power Politics* (Chapel Hill, North Carolina, 1999).

Zook, Kristal B., *Color By Fox: The Fox Network and the Revolution in Black Television* (New York, 1999).

INDEX